Dennis Mc

THE FINAL BATTLE

and
the return of the Lord

ERNEST J. MILLER
Ph.D., M.Sc., D.I.C., F.R.I.C.

A Scientist's Study of Bible History and Prophecy
with Special Reference to Coming Events

Revised Edition

New Wine Press

New Wine Press,
P.O. Box 17,
Chichester,
West Sussex PO20 6RY

Revised Edition 1987

Scripture quotations are from the King James Bible.

Printed and bound in Great Britain by
Anchor Brendon Ltd, Tiptree, Essex.

ISBN 0 947852 27 1

FOREWORD

When God first created man, He gave him authority over every living thing on earth (*Genesis 1*:28) — he was superior to every other creature and virtually governor of the planet, but another claimed that sovereignty and, in direct challenge to the Almighty, sought to frustrate His purposes by effecting the ruin of this new creature. From Eden until now, the battle for supremacy has raged, with the human race little more than pawns in the game, and the conflict is destined to continue until the powers of evil are for ever crushed.

The story is a fascinating — even if somewhat frightening — one. Its details and implications are disclosed only in the Word of God, but the revelation given in Holy Writ is one demanding attention. An appreciation of the significance of this revelation will inevitably lead to an understanding of the relevance of the eschatological picture painted by the Bible, for the final defeat of the hosts of darkness cannot take place until "the times of the end".

Dr. Miller is a scientist and, in this remarkable survey of the past and of its relationship to the future, he brings a logical mind to bear upon the progressive disclosure of the Divine purpose. God's plans are irrevocably linked with man's ultimate blessing, and the author shows how those plans are gradually being put into effect, precisely as predicted. The second half of this book is appropriately concerned almost entirely with the prophetic programme and the author shows the inevitability of the final overthrow of evil and the victory of good.

This careful study of history and prophecy in relation to the age-long struggle is one which will hold the reader enthralled and he will be unable to put down the book until he has finished reading it. Dr. Miller has made a valuable contribution to the subject and has presented his material in a very readable fashion which will appeal to all.

FREDERICK A. TATFORD

INTRODUCTION

With the present condition of the world in mind one wonders why, if there is a beneficent God, it should be in such a state as it is and how it will all end. This book is presented to the public with a view to answering these questions authoritatively from the Bible and, in doing so, at the same time to show how one can face the future with assurance *if the right choice is made.*

Of course, only God knows the future and He has seen fit to reveal it to man in His Word, the Bible. The difficulty is that the predictions are mainly in symbol or picture forms, and in the past these have been interpreted in a hundred and one different ways. For the first time, I believe, a reasonable and *consistent* interpretation of *all* the relevant prophecies has been put forward. In other words, if the interpretation of any one prophecy has been found to conflict with that of any other prophecy on a related subject, it has been rejected in favour of one in agreement with all others on the subject.

Today, more than ever before, there is an urgent need for a right understanding of what Scripture tells us about coming events. A study of Bible chronology, detailed in Appendix III, suggests that the end of the age will occur *before* the close of the present century, and this is confirmed by other scriptures, considered in Appendix V, and by the signs of the times. It is important that the public should be warned of the probable nearness of this culminating event which will be heralded by disturbances in the heavens and distress on earth leading to the battle of Armageddon and the coming of Christ to judge the world and reign over it. Hitherto, for nearly six thousand years, God has given man almost a free hand to run the world as he wishes, to go his own way independent of his Creator. God has long borne with man's incompetence and must shortly come down, in the person of His Son, to take the kingdom of this world into His own hands. Yet first He will allow the arch-enemy Satan, hitherto working behind the scenes to help man to his ruin, a short period in which to manifest himself in the person of a superman and be worshipped by the world at large — a time of unprecedented trouble for mankind! Fortunately, however,

God has provided a way of escape from this 'great tribulation', as Scripture terms it, for all those prepared to avail themselves of it on His conditions, explained in chapter 7. Very simply put, it is a case of 'repentance towards God and faith in our Lord Jesus Christ'. These faithful ones will take part in a secret but world-shaking event which will occur suddenly, just before the onset of the great tribulation. At a summons from the Lord in the clouds, the 'dead in Christ' will be resurrected and the living will be immortally changed, and together they will be caught up to meet Him and be taken to Heaven. The rest of the living — those who have neglected or rejected Christ — will have to endure the rigours of the tribulation. The rest of the *dead* will not be raised until the final judgment after Christ's millennial reign, a judgment leading only to their condemnation and doom.

It is tragic that these things, which must shortly begin to come to pass, are rarely if ever spoken of in our churches and chapels today. Indeed it is doubtful if anything is known except that, in the words of the old Prayer Book, Christ 'shall come to judge the quick and the dead'. Of course books on prophecy have been written but most of them have been little or no help because they have tried to prove that nearly all scriptural predictions have already been fulfilled. This 'historicist' system of interpretation, as it has been called, has had to resort to fanciful, even farcical, attempts to allegorise prophecies and correlate them with past events. Rather surprisingly, the Protestant Truth Society and the Banner of Truth Trust both appear to foster this system of interpretation, to judge by some of their publications: for example, "The War with Satan" (1940) by Basil B.C. Atkinson; also "The Puritan Hope" (1971) by Iain H. Murray. This view of prophecy breaks down because, if for no other reason, the interpretations are not scripturally consistent — a principle, as already mentioned, I have endeavoured to observe in the present studies. The system is therefore untenable.

The only logical alternative to the historicist system of interpretation (especially of the book of the Revelation) is the 'futurist' view, which takes all the predictions literally unless they are clearly symbolical. Since most of them cannot be shown to have been literally fulfilled in the past, they must apply to the future.

This futurist view was held by the churches, following the apostles up to about the fourth century. They believed, at least, that Christ would come again in person to the earth and reign with His saints for a thousand years — taking the prophecy (Rev 20.4) literally, of course. From the fourth century onwards belief in a literal Millennium began to decline, mainly through the influence of Constantine the Great in A.D. 324, and the alternative view, virtually the historicist one, held sway without serious opposition until the nineteenth century. In 1825, Edward Irving started to revive the futurist view — the pre-millennial one, as it is sometimes termed, i.e. that Christ will return to earth *before* the Millennium. Following Irving, J.N. Darby, an outstanding leader of the Brethren movement (founded in 1825), elaborated the view that Christ's appearing before the Millennium would be in two stages: the first, a secret 'rapture' removing the Church before a great tribulation smites the earth; the second, His coming with all His saints to set up His millennial kingdom. Darby, in his turn, influenced two notable Americans, D.L. Moody and C.I. Scofield. The famous Bible college was named after the former; the notes in the latter's Bible (published 1909) were based on Darby's teaching. Within fifty years, about three million copies of the Scofield Reference Bible were printed in America and a proportionate number in Britain, making Darby's futurist views the norm for many evangelicals in the English-speaking world. Since then (about 1950) interest in coming events has declined lamentably and today, as already indicated, Christendom as a whole is content just to believe that the Lord is coming again some time, the later the better. One of the aims of the present volume is to revive that interest.

CONTENTS

CONTENTS (continued)

TABLES, etc.

PAST EVENTS

PART I

SATAN'S INITIAL TRIUMPH

CHAPTER 1

THE AGENCIES INVOLVED

GOD

God is an Almighty Power, a Trinity (Father, son and Holy Spirit), who is from everlasting to everlasting. Not only is He Almighty but He knows everything and sees and hears everything, past, present and future. In fact with Him there is no past or future but an everlasting present; thus He calls Himself "I AM", and to Him one day is as a thousand years and a thousand years as one day. He remembers everything with recording precision but can exercise His will to forget what He chooses.

The Trinity of His being cannot be understood by the finite mind, but may be likened to a perfectly harmonious family. Each Member of the Triune Godhead has a special office and function: the Father is the Originator; the Son the Operator; the Spirit, the Energising Agent — All working as One. The Son carries out the plans of the Father through the power of the Holy Spirit. When the Son visited this earth in human form, He was called Jesus, which means God the Saviour.

Fortunately for us, God is a power for GOOD. He is Himself perfect Goodness and absolute Truth: the unerringly just, the undeviatingly right. Yet at the same time He is merciful, compassionate and long-suffering — God is Love. He is grieved and righteously angry at anything that is not in accord with His will: at wickedness, wrongdoing and wrong thinking; untruthfulness, injustice and cruelty — at Sin, in a word; and He will not allow it to come into His immediate presence. For, although He is omnipresent, He has a special dwelling-place, a secret abode where no shade of evil can enter or even approach. As the Bible (see Appendix 1) puts it, He dwells in 'the light which no man can approach unto' (1 *Timothy* 6:16).

ANGELS

These attendants of God are spiritual beings created by Him, the Source and Sustainer of all life. They are invisible to the human eye but occasionally, when He so wills, He gives special (spiritual) sight to selected people so that they can see these divine messengers. When revealed, the angel appears in a form resembling man but with a shining face and dazzling snow-white clothing, such as to strike fear and prostrating awe into the human heart. An attested angelic appearance was at the battle of Mons in World War I, which safeguarded the retreat of the British forces, doubtless in answer to national prayer. A much earlier instance of angelic intervention was the sudden destruction of the Assyrian army of 185,000 men under Sennacherib at the siege of Jerusalem, in answer to the prayer of Hezekiah, king of Judah (2 *Kings 19*:35). One of the chief angels, Michael, acts particularly on behalf of the people of Israel (*Daniel 12*:1). Another notable one, Gabriel, was sent to reveal the future to Daniel, Jewish prime minister to King Darius the Mede in 538 B.C. This angel also appeared to the virgin Mary in 4 B.C., to tell her that she was chosen to be the mother, by miraculous conception through the power of the Holy Spirit, of Jesus Christ (*Luke 1*:26—35). His birth took place in due time and was heralded by an angelic host, seen by shepherds. Later, after His crucifixion and burial, two angels at His tomb announced that He had risen from the dead (*Luke 24*:4). A further angelic declaration was made forty days after when Jesus ascended up to Heaven in a cloud, saying that He would come again in like manner to His going (*Acts 1*:9—11). Since that time there has been little manifestation of angels except for a few appearances to the early apostles, but these beings are still very active in human affairs, although unseen by the human eye; for example, in guarding the faithful from harm and danger.

SATAN

Before he rebelled against his Creator, this anointed cherub was perhaps the highest of the angels. His fulness of wisdom and perfection of beauty (as the king of Tyrus) is revealed to us in *Ezekiel 28*:12—15. As 'Lucifer, son of the morning' (Isaiah 14:12—14) he said in his pride: 'I will exalt my throne above the stars of God .... I will be like the most High'. Thus he fell from his high estate and many angels joined him in his impiety. Sin had begun in the spiritual realm and, in effect, the conflict between evil and good, between Satan and God, had also begun and was to develop into *the battle of the ages*. Since man's creation, Satan has sought to attack the Godhead through man and we shall see how far he has succeeded. During this present age he is the unseen prince of this world and today, especially, he has numerous devotees. In the near future, his person and power will become more manifest, as we shall show later in these studies.

MAN — AND HIS ENVIRONMENT

Subsequent to the creation of the angels, God planned a lower order of beings, mankind. God is love (1 *John 4*:16) and love is always sharing and giving. Man would provide Him with a special object for His love; people with whom He could have fellowship and who would be capable of reciprocating His affection. In the beginning God created the heavens and the earth (*Genesis 1*:1), the latter for man's habitation. Everything was provided for his every possible need; only God could and would cater for him so lavishly. A brief look at the earth as we know it should be sufficient to convince even the sceptic that it is the work of a God of all knowledge and power, on a scale to be expected only from One so beneficent and majestic. Its position in space, its atmosphere, its climate, its seas, its mountains, its clouds; its trees, its grass, its flowers in manifold variety and colour; its creatures of all shapes and sizes, and ways of life — animals, birds, fishes, and hosts of microscopic forms of life — all these things declare the glory of God! Many of them are interdependent: for example, atmospheric nitrogen is converted by soil microbes into nitrates and ammonium salts, which are necessary for the growth of plants which, in turn, support animal life — a precise balance being preserved. In fact, the more closely we look at earthly things the more wonderful they appear in all their intricacy and beauty, and the more they reveal the Master mind of their Creator. Moreover, they provide an inexhaustible study; the world libraries today are full of books about them, and there is still unlimited scope for research into them. What would there be to discover if there had been no Designer and Maker? Look where you will and you will see the wisdom of His mind and the work of His hand, Truly 'the fool hath said in his heart, There is no God' (*Psalm 53*:1), and the believer in evolution (see Appendix II), who virtually asserts that all things came by chance, is worthy of no better appellation.

Thus God prepared the earth, and from its constituent elements He made man, giving him dominion over the lower forms of creation (*Genesis 1*:26). Whereas they, by God-given instinct, unwittingly lived their individual ways of life, he was a thinking and God-knowing being — in fact, man was a tripartite person of spirit, soul and body. The spiritual part of his nature enabled him to know and commune with God Who is a Spirit. When man was tempted and fell, his link with his Maker was broken and his spiritual part virtually died (*Ephesians* 2:1), leaving him then, as now, with only soul and body. His soul is his ego (individuality) and includes the mind which thinks, reasons, wills, feels and remembers. His body is the vehicle of the soul, the means by which the soul can appreciate, and express itself in, the material world around. In the garden of Eden (delight), with its rivers, trees, flowers, animals, birds etc., God provided the first man, Adam, with everything necessary for his body and pleasing to his soul, and his spirit found satisfaction in daily talks with God (Genesis 3:8). As a helpmate for Adam, a woman (Eve) was created — formed from a 'rib which the Lord had taken from man' during 'a deep sleep' (*Genesis* 2:21—22), so that she would have a natural desire to be with him.

CHAPTER 2

SATAN'S ATTACK

MAN'S FALL

Our first parents were innocent when they were created (the year of Adam's creation is estimated to be 4126 B.C. — see Appendix III), with no knowledge of good and evil. They were naturally good and did those things which pleased God; they had not yet tasted evil. They had been given a free will to do as they chose, with one exception: they had been commanded not to eat of the fruit of one particular tree, standing conspicuously in the middle of the garden. Of this tree 'of the knowledge of good and evil' the Lord had said: 'In the day that thou eatest thereof thou shalt surely die' (*Genesis 2*:16—17). In this way God tested man's loyalty and obedience to Himself, and Adam and Eve were quite willing and content to obey the command, until the tempter came along in the person of Satan (see *Genesis 3*). Like the deceiver he was, and is, he approached the two in the guise of another — that most subtle of creatures, the serpent — and spoke to them through it.

"Hath God said, Ye shall not eat of every tree of the garden?" came the words, cunningly addressed to the woman as the 'weaker vessel'.

"We may eat of the fruit of the trees in the garden", she replied, "but of the fruit of the tree which is in the midst of the garden, God hath said, Ye shall not eat of it, lest ye die".

"Ye shall not surely die", said the serpent, "for God doth know that in the day ye eat thereof, then your eyes shall be opened, and ye shall be as gods, knowing good and evil".

In fact the Devil, liar as he is, was telling only part of the truth; but Eve was beguiled by him and, wishing to be wise, partook of the fruit of the forbidden tree and persuaded Adam to do the same. It was true that their eyes were opened to good and evil — evil at least, as evidenced by the sudden awareness of their nakedness; but this miserable feeling of shame, guilt and fear was a new and decidedly unpleasant experience for them. Their first reaction was to make themselves aprons of fig leaves, and the next was to seek to hide themselves from the presence of God when the time came for their daily communion with Him. Such has been the nature of man ever since: he tries to cover his sin rather than confess it, and to keep away from his Maker.

Adam and Eve could not of course hide themselves from omnipresent God — He put the question 'Where art thou?', to Adam in order to evoke his confession of guilt. It is good for us likewise to apply the same question to ourselves, to see where we stand in our relationship to God. Adam's reply, 'I heard thy voice in the garden, and I was afraid, because I was naked; and I hid myself' so far admitted no culpability on his part. Even when asked whether he had eaten from the forbidden tree he put the blame on Eve: 'The woman whom thou gavest to be with me, she gave me of the tree, and I did eat', insinuating indeed that it was really God's fault in the first place for giving him Eve. How quick are we, too, in blaming others and even God for our troubles! The woman also, when asked what she had done, transferred the responsibility to the serpent: 'The serpent beguiled me, and I did eat'. Not until the last book of the Bible is the identity of 'the serpent' directly revealed (*Revelation 12*:9), as 'the great dragon .... that *old serpent,* called the Devil, and Satan, which deceiveth the whole world'. Evidently Satan had the power to control the serpent and speak through it. This is not surprising in a potent person of the spirit world such as is the Devil; his demonic underlings are capable of possessing even human beings — there are instances of this not only in the Bible (e.g. *Luke 8*:26—39) but also in our own times.

THE PENALTY

The serpent having been blamed by Eve, God said to it:

"Because thou hast done this, thou art cursed above all cattle, and above every beast of the field; upon thy belly shalt thou go, and dust shalt thou eat all the days of thy life".

Evidently the serpent was not the creeping reptile it now is but was the most intelligent of the beasts of the field. As such it would cause the least surprise to Eve when it spoke to her, and thus it was a fitting medium for Satan to use. Although innocent itself it suffered degradation possibly to prevent its being used in the same way again. Along with other animals it was the object of God's curse, brought upon them by man's fall, and henceforward he would no longer have their natural subjection as was originally granted to him. God had said (*Genesis 1*:28): 'Have dominion over the fish of the sea, and over the fowl of the air, and over everything that moveth upon the earth'. A more obvious effect of the curse had been the disturbance of the peaceful relationship between creature and creature, as doubtless existed at their creation. They became imbued with an urge to harm and destroy one another, and even to attack man — as is largely the case today throughout the animal kingdom, from the lion to the humblest pathogenic microbe. Of course this evil element is less marked in domesticated creatures but can still be discerned, for example, even in the sheep with its well-known tendency to go astray.

The Lord God has more to say to the serpent but since this further statement was evidently addressed to Satan himself it will be considered under the next heading. The woman then receives her sentence: 'I will greatly multiply thy sorrow and thy conception; in sorrow shalt thou bring forth children; and thy desire shall be to thy husband, and he shall rule over thee'. Apparently, but for the fall, conception would have been a naturally painless process without any danger to mother or child. As the situation is, however, there is a promise for the faithful: 'Notwithstanding she shall be saved in childbearing, if they (she and her husband) continue in faith and charity and holiness with sobriety' (*Timothy 2*:15). The previous verses (11—14) of the chapter give the reason for the second part of Eve's punishment (that she would henceforth have an inherent sense of submission to Adam). The reason given is that he had a right to this, even before the fall, by virtue of his prior creation, and further, he had not been deceived by the tempter as Eve had been, thereby showing her poorer judgment and her unfitness to take the lead. In the penalty God was, so to speak, implanting in Eve a *consciousness* of subordinacy to Adam, the only position which Eve had already in practice, proved herself capable of taking. Woman, in the natural way, has had this consciousness of subordinacy to man ever since. The fact that many woman have stifled this inward voice does not alter the truth of her place in the divine order: 'But I would have you know, that the head of every man is Christ; and *the head of the woman is man;* and the head of Christ is God' (1 *Corinthians 11*:3). In every sphere of life today woman is increasingly usurping man's God-given authority; little wonder that there is disorder everywhere as a result of her frequent ill-judged and faulty directions. Man himself is partly to blame in not exercising his authority and in submitting to woman's rule.

To Adam, God said: "Because thou has hearkened to the voice of thy wife, and hast eaten of the tree, of which I commanded thee, saying, Thou shalt not eat of it, cursed is the ground for thy sake; in sorrow shalt thou eat of it all the days of thy life; thorns also and thistles shall it bring forth to thee; and thou shalt eat the herb of the field; in the sweat of thy face shalt thou eat bread, till thou return unto the ground; for out of it wast thou taken: for dust thou art, and unto dust shalt thou return".

Adam's previous occupation had been merely to 'dress and to keep' the garden of Eden (*Genesis 2*:15), evidently involving no laborious toil, and the numerous fruit-trees of the garden provided adequate sustenance. Henceforward it was to be very different for him. He and his wife were to be expelled from the garden of delight, a garden in fact 'planted' by the Lord God Himself. Outside this earthly paradise it would be a hard struggle for existence. The ground was now cursed and would prove hostile to man's efforts to support himself. The plant kingdom, like the animal kingdom, had come under the curse and was infected with evil elements which could hinder and even (as the thorns) harm man.

The second part of Adam's punishment — that he would eventually die — confirmed what God had forewarned him of. Actually God's original words implied that the couple would die immediately after eating the forbidden fruit, and this was true in a spiritual sense. They were dead to God; they had cut themselves off from Him Who is the source of all life — sin had separated them from Him by a great gulf. Indeed this *spiritual death* was far more terrible than the physical death which ultimately and inevitably followed it. This can best be explained by reference to Adam's descendants — mankind in general, you and I in particular. As a result of the fall humanity is tainted; we are all born with a sinful nature, which is present throughout our earthly lives and causes us all to be sinners to a greater or less degree. As such we are separated from a holy God, as were our first parents when they disobeyed Him, and are in a state of spiritual death, 'dead in trespasses and sins' (*Ephesians 2*:1). This may mean little or nothing to us during our human span of life; we may in fact be quite unconscious of it, as a dead man does not know that he is dead, physically. Yet the death of the body does not end the personality: the soul, our real self, continues to exist endlessly (e.g. see *Luke 16*:19—31). The tragedy is to spend this eternity still in a condition of spiritual death — in hell, banished from God's presence for ever. This doom, however, may not necessarily be ours, as we shall see in the next section.

THE PROMISE

Of course, man's fall from innocence came as no surprise to an omniscient God, as is evident in His announcement to Satan (through the serpent), in the very hour of his victory and in the presence of his victims: 'I will put enmity between thee and the woman, and between thy seed and her seed; IT shall bruise thy head, and thou shalt bruise his heel' (*Genesis 3*:15). The 'woman' here is used in a larger sense, as the mother of humanity, and thus as humanity itself, of which the Devil is now made the avowed enemy. At first his motive in attacking the first pair was his antagonism to *God; they* were merely tools in his hands to thwart the Almighty, but in fact Satan *acted* as their enemy and God made him such. Yet he really wanted their allegiance and this he procured when they believed him rather than their Maker, and, since then, every one has been born not only in sin (Psalm 51:5) but also in Satan's power (2 *Timothy 2*:26). Thus by nature we are all his 'seed' and we remain such throughout our lives unless we turn in faith to God and become His 'seed'. Satan's 'children' have always been, consciously or unconsciously, at enmity with God's 'children' — the 'enmity' .... between thy seed and her seed'. It is true that, initially, 'her seed' refers not to God's children generally but to His Son in particular: 'IT shall bruise thy head, and thou shalt bruise his heel'. Here was a wonderful promise for our first parents, announced even before their penalty, that in due time among their descendants One should be born to be a Champion of their lost cause. This early promise was not to be fulfilled, as history has since shown, until some 4,000 years later, when Jesus Christ was to come into the world (see Part III). 'IT shall bruise thy head' signified that Christ would deal a crushing blow at Satan, not so much at his person as at his *power* over humanity. 'Thou shall bruise his heel' indicated that, in the encounter, the Devil would inflict Christ with a crippling injury. We know that this injury, slight as it appears, would mean for Him a sacrificial death; but when we consider His eternal pre-existence, His death (only three days in the grave) — important though it would be for mankind — was essentially only a short cutting off, so to speak, of His earthly walk.

The long interval that was to be between the giving of the promise and its fulfilment was necessary, in the purposes of God, to prepare humanity for their coming Deliverer — Who would provide by His death and resurrection a just way for man to get his sins forgiven, to be reconciled to an offended God and to be liberated from Satan's dominion. Yet, until this way of salvation had been made possible for man — involving the age-long period from Adam to Christ — man would still be separated from God unless He devised a temporary way of approach to Himself. How God did in fact accomplish this and what His further dealings with man were, until the coming of Christ, form the contents of the Old Testament, and the more important features that concern us here are described in Part II.

PAST EVENTS

PART II

THE INTERVAL

CHAPTER 3

SOME SIGNIFICANT INCIDENTS

The Old Testament is a chronicle of events from the creation of the world to the first coming of Christ. Yet it is not concerned directly with the *secular* history of man during this period, but rather with his relationship to God — in this respect it contains everything that man needs to know, both for his spiritual and for his physical well-being. The Old Testament, like all the Bible, is inspired by God, and its words are therefore pre-eminently full of truth and meaning. Moreover the subjects spoken of, whether things or people or even incidents, are not only real in themselves but frequently also have a deeper significance, as types and shadows of more important entities to come. A few of these incidents will now be described.

THE COATS OF SKINS

Very soon after their fall from grace Adam and Eve were provided by God with clothing of skins (*Genesis 3*:21), evidently obtained from animals after they had been killed. This was to teach them that they could no longer come into His presence except by way of *sacrifice.* Their sin merited death, and although they already carried the sentence of death in themselves and must ultimately die, a more immediate sacrifice was necessary to appease a holy God. The 'coats of skins', procured at the cost of life, thus afforded a temporary covering and atonement for their sin. No more than this could of course be expected in the sacrifice of an animal, itself under the curse; and such a sacrifice could only be accepted by God in anticipation of the promised Deliverer's perfect and sinless self-sacrifice which would make a full and final expiation for sin.

CAIN AND ABEL

These first two children of Adam and Eve were doubtless told by their parents of the need for sacrifice when approaching God; and the responses of the two brothers to this teaching illustrate the exercise of the human will today — either for or against God, in belief or unbelief. When each of the brothers brought an offering to the Lord (see *Genesis 4*), Cain, evidently disbelieving or disregarding what his parents had said to him, gave the products of the ground (which was under the curse) and was rejected by God; whereas Abel, obeying parental instruction, in *faith*,(see *Hebrews 11*:4) sacrificed his best lambs to the Lord and was accepted. Thenceforth all the world in God's sight has consisted of Cains or Abels, those unwilling and those willing to put their faith in Him; and the Bible says (v.6), 'without faith it is impossible to please him'. When Cain's offering was not accepted he was angry with his brother and killed him, because 'his own works were evil, and his brother's righteous' (1 *John 3*:12). Since then, the people of the Cain type (Satan's seed), as already noted, have always had, at heart, enmity against the Abel type (the children of God) and would do them to death in sufficiently provoking circumstances. In fact, since Abel's martyrdom, countless others have suffered persecution and death simply because, as God's children, they have incurred the enmity of Satan and his human instruments — we have a record (see *Hebrews 11*:35—38) of a few of these victims in Old Testament (B.C.) times. The enmity reached a climax against the Son of God Himself; right from infancy He was the object of a bitter atack by the Devil and his followers, who finally hounded Him to a felon's death. Yet for this very purpose had He come into the world in human form (see Part III), that 'through death he might destroy him that had the power of death, that is, the devil' (*Hebrews 2*:14).

JUDGMENT BY FLOOD

The sinful nature inherited from Adam and Eve, already shown in Cain, continued to manifest itself in their later descendants. A tempter was no longer necessary to induce man to sin; the inclination was inborn. Only a small minority made any effort to follow in the way of Abel. Corruption and violence ultimately became so widespread that a long-suffering God was forced to intervene in judgment but as always, He gave adequate warning and made provision for escape. Faithful Noah (see *Genesis 7* and *8*) was told of the Lord's intention to destroy the earth by a flood; and in preparation for it he was to build an ark, three-storied and of given dimensions, to hold himself and his family (eight souls) and two (male and female) of every living thing. During the long period (probably one hundred and twenty years) of the ark's construction there was abundant time in the mercy of God, for Noah to warn the world of his day that disaster was coming. Yet nobody outside Noah's family believed him until the deluge was upon the earth — and then it was too late for any one to seek safety in the ark; its door was fast closed.

"The rain was upon the earth forty days and forty nights .... and all flesh died that moved upon the earth .... all in whose nostrils was the breath of life, and of all that was in the dry land died .... and Noah only remained alive, and those that were with him in the ark" (*Genesis* 7:12, 21—23).

The flood waters rose to some twenty feet (6m.) above all the mountains and 'prevailed upon the earth an hundred and fifty days'. Since the ark rested on the mountains of Ararat (probably the highest point of the range, Mount Ararat itself, 16,946 feet — 5,182 m.) at the expiry of this period, the level of the water must have begun to fall at some time before — the 'prevailing' of the waters being reckoned to the time of the resting of the ark on Ararat. It took another seventy three days for 'the tops of the mountains' to be seen, confirming the probability that the ark had rested at the higher point, of Mount Ararat itself. Remains of marine creatures found on the mountain prove that it has once been flooded, but there is a popular misconception that the ark remained lodged on the mountain. In fact, from time to time, there have been 'scientific' expeditions there in attempts to find pieces of the ark still on the mountain! A brief study of the scriptural account in *Genesis 8* would have convinced the investigators that their search would be in vain — as indeed all expeditions have been. The reasons for believing that the ark did not remain fixed on Ararat but continued (after a momentary rest thereon) to float down to earth on the subsiding waters, are as follows:

1. The evacuation of the ark on Ararat would have involved a long and probably dangerous descent for Noah and his family, not to mention the animals. In any case we know that no one left the ark for a further one hundred and twenty days, so the

evacuation could not begin until the close of this long period — not a very pleasant or comfortable situation for Noah and his family, confined in the ark on the mountain top. Moreover, the ark may not have come to rest on an even keel but in a tilted and possibly unstable position, making its evacuation difficult or even impracticable.

2. Even assuming all the occupants were able to leave the ark and descend the mountain without casualty, they would doubtless find themselves in an inhospitable mountain region, almost certainly devoid of sustenance, especially after being so long under water. Doubtless there would be food remaining in the ark but it would certainly take several journeys to it, from time to time, to bring sufficient down to provide for the occupants for a limited period — such journeys would tax the strength of Noah and his family to the utmost.

3. When Noah sent the dove from the ark one hundred and thirteen days after it had rested on Ararat, it 'found no rest for the sole of her foot' and was forced to return to the ark. If the ark had remained fixed on Ararat, the dove would certainly have found rest on the surface of the mountain all around. *This circumstance alone conclusively disproves the idea that the ark was fixed on the mountain.* Evidently at this point the ark, again floating on the subsiding waters, had drifted well away from the mountains and was surrounded by water to a considerable distance on every side, compelling the dove to return to the ark.

4. When Noah built the Ark he probably lived in the plain not too far from the site of the garden of Eden, assumed to be near the mouth of the Euphrates — about 600 miles (960 km.) from Ararat. Thus, when the ark rested on the mountain it would have drifted at least this distance on the flood waters. It seems likely that, under God's hand, the ark, after floating away from Ararat, would drift back to the region where Noah had lived and to which he had become accustomed. Regarding food for the occupants of the ark after leaving it, there would doubtless be sufficient still in the ark for them as long as they needed it, and it would be quite accessible for them — as it certainly would not have been if the ark had remained on Ararat.

For our present purpose there is no need to go into further details of the incident of the flood, except to mention that it lasted 370 days in all — a luni-solar year of 360 days plus 10 days — from the time it started to the time it dried up and the ark was evacuated.

The importance of the flood for us today is that it is typical of judgment to come (see *Luke 17*:26—27). The people of Noah's day were certainly no more wicked than the present generation, and only those who take refuge in Christ will be saved — like the people in the ark who believed God's warning of the coming flood and availed themselves of the way of escape, taking refuge in the ark.

JUDGMENT BY FIRE

Although Noah and his family, because of their faith, had been spared to re-people the earth, it soon became evident that sin was still present in the human heart. God was again long-suffering and it was not until the tenth generation from Noah, when immorality had become so rife (especially in Sodom and Gomorrah — see *Genesis 19*:1—26), that God had to make an example of these cities by destroying them by fire — only Lot and his two daughters were saved. The destruction occurred in 2019 B.C. but in order to understand the situation we must go back some twenty years when Lot parted from his uncle Abram (afterwards called Abraham) and came to live in Sodom. Both of them believers in God, they had been travelling in Canaan (later Palestine), dwelling in tents. Both men were rich in cattle, which became so numerous that strife broke out between the respective herdsmen, and Abram suggested that he and Lot should separate and go their own ways (*Genesis 13*:8—13). Lot, given the preference, chose the well-watered plain of Jordon and journeyed east towards Sodom. He had less strength of character than his uncle and was probably tired of tent-life in the country, especially among the hills which Abram favoured. Doubtless too, Lot yearned for the amenities of the city of Ur (then, at or near the mouth of the Euphrates) in which he and Abram had previously lived. Abram had responded to a call from God to leave his home country and go to a land (Canaan) where he would eventually become a great nation (*Genesis 12*:1—2). Lot had decided to go with his uncle but by the time they had journeyed through Canaan he probably thought the prospects were not so good as he had anticipated. Thus, as mentioned, he separated from Abram and settled in Sodom, although he had doubtless heard of its bad name. Little by little he became established in the city, married a woman of the city, set up his own house and eventually became a leading citizen. All the time he had been vexed with the filthy behaviour of the Sodomites (2 *Peter* 2:7), but he had endeavoured to shut his eyes to it. Earlier he may have made up his mind to leave the city but had not done so for one reason or another, and now he was older he felt he could not bear to be uprooted.

Meanwhile Abram, still a tent-dweller, had settled in the vicinity of Hebron in the hill country and, on the eve of the destruction of Sodom and Gomorroh, had received a visit from what appeared to be three men (*Genesis 18*). Abram showed them the customary courtesy of the east, washed their feet and got Sarah, his wife, to provide a succulent meal for them. Although they accepted these attentions it was soon evident that they were no ordinary mortals; in fact one of them was the Lord Himself and the others were two angels, about to visit Sodom. Indeed, the Lord had visited Abram partly to inform him of the impending destruction of that city, knowing how he would be concerned about the fate of his nephew Lot. Actually Abram, when he heard the news, was so affected that he pleaded long with the Lord to spare Sodom for the sake of the righteous there, and at last was assured that the city would not be destroyed if only *ten* righteous were found there. Abram hoped that Lot, by his godly living, might perhaps have induced nine others to turn to God. Yet it is clear that Abram feared the worst because, early the next morning, he scanned the horizon towards Sodom (possibly distant some 30 miles — 48km.) and, sure enough, over there 'the smoke of the country went up as the smoke of a furnace'. Plainly, there were not even ten godly people in the city and its destruction was in progress.

However, God had not forgotten His servant Abram! The previous evening, the two angels, after visiting him, had proceeded to Sodom where they were able to see for themselves — if they were not already aware of it — its open immorality. At first, however, they were received with every courtesy by Lot who 'sat in the gate' of the city. He persuaded them, with some difficulty, to come into his house and stay the night with him, his wife and their two unmarried daughters; but there was little sleep for any of them that night because of the despicable behaviour of the men of the city (*Genesis 19*:4—9) — sodomites, indeed. Yet their wicked intentions were defeated by the angels, who then told Lot of their mission to destroy the city and they ordered him to go out and warn any relatives of his to come back with him without delay, to escape from Sodom before its destruction. Lot hastened to his two sons-in-law, probably having to rouse them from sleep, and told them of the coming catastrophe. It is not perhaps very surprising that their father-in-law seemed to them 'as one that mocked'. He had been content to live in Sodom all those years, to marry there and see his daughters grow up and two of them married, with his consent, to men of the city. Apparently he had made no serious attempt to expose the wickedness of Sodom — if he had done so, it is unlikely that he would have been appointed to an official position which in fact he occupied. If he had thought that the city deserved God's judgment, why had he not quitted it before? By some such reasoning the sons-in-law failed to be convinced by Lot and he returned to his house alone. Possibly indeed they had influenced him instead to think that the threatened disaster might not occur after all. Certainly he was reluctant to leave Sodom when, at morning light, he was urged to do so by the angels. In fact, they had to take by the hand himself and his wife and their two daughters, and lead them out of the city, with the command: 'Escape for thy life; look not behind thee, neither stay thou in all the plain; escape to the mountains lest thou be consumed' (*Genesis 19*:17). Even at this point Lot, unwilling if not unable to face the harder life of the hills, begged to be allowed to dwell in the little city of Zoar, itself in the plain and marked out for destruction. The angels granted his plea and promised to spare Zoar from the general conflagration — which began no sooner than Lot and his family had reached this city.

"The sun was risen upon the earth when Lot entered into Zoar. Then the Lord rained upon Sodom and upon Gomorrah brimstone and fire from the Lord out of heaven; and he overthrew those cities, and all the plain and all the inhabitants of the cities, and that which grew upon the ground. But his wife looked back from behind him, and she became a pillar of salt" (vv.23—26).

There is a moral for Christians here. Abraham dwelt among the hills, typical of heavenly things; but Lot preferred the cities of the plain, symbolic of earthly things. The former was a life of self-denial; the latter, one of self-indulgence — characteristic, respectively, of spiritual and worldly Christians. Abraham was called the friend of God whereas Lot proved himself a friend of the world. Of course, all true believers in Christ, whether spiritual or worldly, will be saved; but 'every one of us shall give account of himself to God' (*Romans 14*:12), and it is possible, in an extreme case (like Lot's), to be saved 'yet so as by fire' (1 *Corinthians 3*:15) — see later, 'The Judgment Seat of Christ'.

The incident concerning Sodom, like that of the Flood, was recorded not only as an historical fact but also, again, as a warning of coming judgment. Although God promised Noah, by the token of the rainbow, that He would never *drown* the world again, He has forewarned us by the apostles (e.g. 2 *Peter 3*:7) that He will one day destroy it by *fire*. The history of Sodom will be repeated on a world-wide scale:

"As it was in the days of Lot; they did eat, they drank, they bought, they sold, they planted, they builded; but the same day that Lot went out of Sodom it rained fire and brimstone from heaven, and destroyed them all. Even thus shall it be when the Son of man is revealed" (*Luke 17*:28—30).

The last sentence cited has referred to Christ's second coming to this earth, which is felt to be fast approaching, but before that event all believers in Him will have been removed from the world and will escape the judgment (see later, 'The Translation of the Saints'). Reader, if you are not such a believer, hasten to become one — 'Remember Lot's wife' (*Luke 17*:32).

THE PEOPLE AND THE PLAGUES

In furtherance of God's purpose to send in due time a Saviour (Jesus Christ) into the world, born of Adam's line, He first selected a man of faith, Abraham (first called Abram), to be the progenitor of a tribe of people through whom He would reveal Himself and from whom the Saviour would spring. First, however, Abraham's faith had to be severely tested, when he was commanded by God to take his only son, the child of his old age, to Mount Moriah (now the temple area of Jerusalem) and offer him up as a burnt sacrifice (*Genesis 22*:1—4). Just as he was about to kill Isaac, however, God intervened and provided a ram as a substitute offering. This ordeal was imposed on Abraham not only for his own sake but also that it might prefigure, in a limited way, the infinite cost to God Himself of offering *His* Son to be the Saviour of the world.

Isaac had two sons, Esau and Jacob, Esau was a man of the world but Jacob was a man of faith and through his twelve sons came the twelve tribes of Israel (the name God gave Jacob), chosen by God to be His own special people and nation. While still a small community of seventy kinsfolk they were forced by a famine to leave their promised land and settle in Egypt, being cordially received by the Pharaoh of that time. His successor, however, fearing that the fast-growing tribe would soon become a menace to his country, treated the Israelites cruelly and made them slaves, to build treasure cities (see *Exodus 1*).

For more than a century the plight of these people of Israel was wretched in the extreme, but God was not unmindful of their distress. As a first step to their liberation he singled out *Moses* from among them to be their leader; a man who, by providential circumstances, had been brought up in the court of Pharaoh himself (*Exodus 2*:1—10) and was 'learned in all the wisdom of the Egyptians' (*Acts 7*:22). Although he was eligible for the highest positions in the land, he willingly refused all its honours and sought out his own kindred of Israel. His active support on their behalf came to the ears of the Egyptian king and Moses was compelled to flee for his life to the land of Midian (now southern Sinai). He was now forty years old and he spent another forty years in that country, mainly as a shepherd. Different as this life was from what he had been used to in Egypt, it too played its part in training him for what was yet to be his chief work — strong and active as he still was at eighty — for the last forty years of his life.

It was at the start of this last forty-year period that God appeared to Moses out of a burning bush (see *Exodus 3*) to call him to his life's special work. He was told of God's intention to deliver His people from the hand of the Egyptians and to bring them into their promised land; and he, Moses, was to be the instrument for his purpose. He must first return to Egypt and tell Pharaoh, the successor to the one he had previously known, that he was commanded by God to let Israel go free. In fact, such was the king's disbelief in God and consequent hardness of heart that he, on being approached by Moses and warned of the penalty of his refusal to let the people go, made their burdens heavier. Retribution came on Egypt in the form of a series of judgments known as the Ten Plagues (*Exodus 7—12*). In the first plague, all the waters of rivers, streams and ponds (even water stored in vessels) were turned into blood for a period of seven days — all the fish died and polluted the water. This plague has special significance in that it will be re-enacted on a much larger scale (affecting even the seas) in two of seven plagues which will come on the whole world towards the close of this present age. Pharaoh's continued obduracy brought on his country the second visitation, the plague of frogs — which became so severe that he promised to let the Israelites go, if Moses would only entreat the Lord to remove the creatures. When the plea was granted, the king hardened his heart and broke his promise, as of course God knew that he would. There followed successively a further seven plagues: lice, flies, murrain (cattle disease), boils (on man and beast), freak lightning and hail storms (killing man and beast, and destroying crops), locusts, and intense darkness for three days. The land of Goshen (in the Nile delta), where the Israelites dwelt, was immune from the plagues, even that of the darkness which was perhaps the most terrible of them thus far to the Egyptians. It was a darkness that 'could be felt', and 'they saw not one another, neither rose any from his place for three days'. This plague, like some of the previous ones, forced Pharaoh to temporise but when the plague was withdrawn he was still unyielding.

The tenth and last visitation, which finally broke down his resistance, is so significant that it must be described in some detail. Briefly, at midnight on a specified day, the 14th day of the month of Abib (April, roughly) in the year 1613 B.C., the Lord declared that He would pass through the land of Egypt and kill the first-born of man and beast. The people of Israel were not automatically exempt from this 'plague', as they had been from the previous ones; their escape depended on their individual obedience to God's command, which was as follows. On the 10th of Abib, each household was to take a lamb, 'a male of the first year', and keep it until the 14th Abib, when they were to kill it in the evening. A bunch of hyssop, the common wall-plant, was to be dipped into a basin of the blood and struck on the lintel and two side-posts of the door of the house. The lamb was to be roasted and the flesh eaten the same evening with bitter herbs and unleavened bread, and what was left of the carcase was to be burnt. All this had to be done without undue delay, and every one must stay indoors and be in instant readiness for a journey. The above instructions were faithfully observed by the Israelites when the specified time arrived, and at midnight on the fateful day the destroying angel began his deady mission. Every dwelling without the blood on the door was entered and the first-born struck, throughout the land. There was not a house belonging to the Egyptians where there was not one dead, from the first-born of Pharaoh in his palace to the first-born in the dungeon, and the first-born of cattle. Only the people of God, in their blood-marked dwellings, were safe that night; for He had said, 'When I see the blood, I will *pass over* you, and the plague shall not be upon you to destroy you' (*Exodus 12*:13) — hence the Feast of the Passover, thereafter annually commemorated on the 14th Abib by the Israelites. Yet for the Egyptians it was a night of terror and lamentation for their dead. Pharaoh himself rose up in the night in haste to summon Moses and Aaron (his brother) and to urge them to be gone with all their people. Thus the whole host of Israel, over a million strong, were released from their long captivity, and they set out for the land promised to their forefather Abraham four hundred and thirty years before.

The above event (the tenth plague), like most of those recorded in the Old Testament, was both actual and typical of later events in New Testament times, including the present era (A.D.) and beyond. 'All these things happened unto them for ensamples (types): and they were written for our admonition, upon whom the ends of the world are come' (1 *Corinthians 10*:11). Clearly the Bible is no ordinary book but is, as it claims to be, the inspired Word of God.

Thus, Israel in bondage to Pharaoh is a miniature figure of the world taken captive by the Devil (2 *Timothy 2*:26), as a result of man's fall in Eden. Just as the Israelites were safe from the avenging hand of God by a personal application of the lamb's blood upon the entrance of each house, so you and I can only be saved from the wrath to come by our individual faith in the blood of God's Lamb, the Lord Jesus Christ — as will be explained later.

Israel oppressed by Pharaoh is also a type of a yet future event when she will suffer a more intense, if shorter persecution at the hands of a much more powerful tyrant, and he and his subjects will be punished, in their turn, by the seven last plagues. Scripture has much to say, as we shall see, about this evil world-potentate, whom it aptly terms 'the Beast' and who will, we believe, shortly appear on the scene in the present generation. Suffice it to say here that he will be a manifestation of Satan himself — a superman worshipped by the world at large but a blasphemer of God and a persecutor of His saints.

DAVID AND GOLIATH

In little more than a year after their release from Egypt the Israelites had almost reached the borders of their promised land, but such was their disbelief in God and their fear of the occupying inhabitants that they would not go in to conquer it (see *Numbers 13* and *14*). As a punishment for their lack of faith, they were forced to wander in the wilderness for nearly forty years before they entered Canaan. Under the leadership of Joshua, Moses' successor, they subdued the various nations of the land, which was then partitioned among the twelve tribes of Israel. For a period of four hundred and fifty years the country was ruled by judges and thereafter by kings, of whom the second, David, was perhaps the most famous. At that time the Philistines were still a rebellious element in the land, in the region recently known as the 'Gaza strip' — a trouble spot, too, for modern Israel after her six-day war in 1967. Against God's ancient people under their first king, Saul, the Philistines had mustered their forces, and had a notable champion in Goliath of Gath. Every morning and evening for forty days, he approached the armies of Israel and challenged it to provide a man to meet him in single combat (see 1 *Samuel 17*). So far there had been no one brave enough to fight the giant, who stood some ten feet (3 m.) high, was helmeted and armour-clad (his coat of mail weighed 200 lb. — 89 kg.), carried a sword at his side and wielded a spear (its head weighed 25 lb. — 11 kg.). Saul himself, standing head and shoulders above his fellows, might have been something of a match for Goliath but he also was loath to engage the formidable Philistine. At this point David, then but a humble youth who tended the sheep of his father Jesse, heard the challenge for the first time and volunteered to fight the giant. At first Saul tried to dissuade David from the seemingly unequal encounter but David, in his zeal for God and confident of His help, assured the king of his ability to kill the Philistine. Thus, armed only with his sling, the young shepherd hurried down the hill to the valley which separated the two armies and collected five smooth stones from the brook there.

By this time Goliath, on the opposite bank with his shield-bearer before him, was aware of David's approach and shouted disdainfully at him: "Am I a dog that thou comest to me with staves (a reference to David's staff, which he carried as well as his sling) .... Come to me, and I will give thy flesh unto the fowls of the air, and to the beasts of the field"; and he cursed David by his gods.

David answered: "Thou comest to me with a sword, and with a spear, and with a shield: but I come to thee in the name of the Lord of hosts, the God of the armies of Israel, whom thou hast defied. This day will the Lord deliver thee into mine hand; and I will smite thee, and take thine head from thee; and I will give the carcases of the host of the Philistines this day unto the fowls of the air .... for the battle is the Lord's, and he will give you into our hands".

So saying, he ran towards the now advancing giant, and putting into his sling a stone he slung it at Goliath with such force and accuracy that it penetrated his forehead. The Philistine fell on his face to the ground and David, having no sword, took that of his fallen foe and cut off his head. Their champion slain, the Philistines fled and were pursued with great slaughter by the Israelites, who won a great victory that day.

This incident is a picture of mankind (typified by Israel) in danger from Satan (Goliath) and his demon forces (the Philistines) until Christ (typified by David) should come to meet, so to speak, the Devil's challenge and overcome him (see later, 'Christ Conquers at Calvary'). Jesus was indeed, in His humanity, a descendant of David and was the Good Shepherd Who gave His life for the sheep, i.e. the people who follow Him (see *John 10*) — generally called His saints.

Goliath typifies not only Satan but also the superman in whom he will shortly manifest himself — the Beast who, like the giant, will probably be outstanding in stature, a man of war and even more arrogant and blasphemous than Goliath (see also Appendix IV).

CHAPTER 4

SOME PROPHETIC DREAMS AND VISIONS

The Old Testament records not only historical events, themselves frequently prophetical as we have already shown, but God-given dreams and visions to reveal the future. Those described in the book of Daniel give us perhaps the clearest and most comprehensive picture of coming events. We shall therefore confine our study here mainly to the writings of this prophet. For the sake of connection we shall outline the history of his people the Jews until his time.

The *kingdom of Israel* attained its greatest power in the reign of Solomon (1023—983 B.C.), David's son, who was the wisest man that has ever lived, because he sought and received wisdom from God. Yet such is the human heart that even he fell into grievous sin by having many foreign wives and worshipping their gods. As a punishment for his disobedience to God's commands in this respect, his kingdom, at his death, was divided and thereafter became a dual monarchy: Judah (two tribes) passing to his son, and Israel (ten tribes) to his servant (see 1 *Kings 11* and *12*). Their subsequent history was a sad one because most of the kings were idolaters, especially those of the ten-tribed kingdom which God therefore brought to an end first — it was overthrown by Assyria in 720 B.C. The turn of the two-tribed kingdom came when Nebuchadnezzar, king of Babylon, destroyed Jerusalem by fire in 587 B.C. From this year Israel (all twelve tribes) ceased from being a nation and her land has been under foreign yoke until recent times.

Among the captive Jews (the name given to the two-tribed kingdom of Judah, including Benjamin — the other ten tribes of Israel intermingled with their Assyrian captors and ultimately lost their identity) taken by Nebuchadnezzar to Babylon was a young man of royal birth named Daniel (see *Daniel 1*). Highly educated as well as naturally intelligent, discreet and good looking, he was chosen along with three other well-favoured youths for special training in Nebuchadnezzar's court. It was not long before these four exiles made a stand for God against the idolatrous practices of the heathen country in which they found themselves. In fact God had chosen them to witness for Him in Babylon, and had endowed them with exceptional moral and mental powers for the purpose. Daniel in particular had special understanding of dreams and visions, through which God was to reveal His future plans for man, from that day to the future millennial reign of Christ. Of course, some of the events foretold are now a matter of history, because more than 2,500 years have elapsed since Daniel's time, but frequently even these events which have been fulfilled are themselves prophetical forerunners of the still future happenings. In any case, the fulfilled and unfulfilled portions of the prophecies are so closely connected in the various dreams and visions that it will be necessary to described them both in their entirety.

Incidentally, in what follows, we have observed the scriptural distinction between dreams and visions. Although both were equally prophetic, the former were given to a heathen king whereas the latter, a more direct communication from God, were revealed to the inspired prophet.

THE GREAT IMAGE

This dream (*Daniel 2*) God gave to Nebuchadnezzar because, in its first application, it intimately concerned the king himself. The dream so troubled him that it woke him up and he quickly summoned his wise men to explain it — or forfeit their lives! In spite of this severe threat to them they were unable to interpret the dream — which was not surprising, because Nebuchadnezzar could not even remember the dream itself. Fortunately for them, at this point Daniel comes on the scene. Apparently he and his three friends, although they had been appointed (after training) to the king's council of wise men, were not among those who had been called to interpret the forgotten dream. When Daniel was told that he and his friends were condemned to death along with the others for their failure to satisfy the king in the matter, he approached Nebuchadnezzar and promised, if given time, to show him the interpretation. The respite granted, Daniel and his three fellow-exiles, Shadrach, Meshach and Abednego (to give them their Chaldean names) went into his house to pray for God's help. That night the secret was revealed to Daniel, who, thrilled to be so honoured, praised the God of heaven in grateful appreciation of the disclosure. Obtaining audience of the king he thereupon made known to him both the dream and its interpretation, humbly disclaiming all personal credit and giving God all the glory.

The *dream* had been of an image, awe-inspiring in its magnitude and its dazzling brightness, with its head of fine gold, its breast and arms of silver, its belly and thighs of brass, its legs of iron, and its feet part of iron and part of clay. Presently a stone, 'cut out without hands', struck the image on its feet and caused its collapse and disintegration into dust, the stone becoming a great mountain which filled the whole earth.

The *interpretation:* The image, in four component parts, depicted four successive world empires which would arise after the downfall of Israel. The head of gold represented *Babylon* and in particular the king, Nebuchadnezzar, who, by God's hand, had raised the kingdom to imperial status. 'Babylon', the capital city, is used conveniently here and hereafter to denote also the empire, more strictly Babylonia. Concerning Nebuchadnezzar, Daniel could say, '*Thou* art the head of gold' — in God's sight the man stood for the empire. The breast and arms of silver prefigured the next empire of *Medo-Persia* with Darius (the Mede) as its first king. The belly and thighs of brass typified the *Grecian* empire, startling with Alexander the Great. The iron legs and iron-clay feet were a symbol of the *Roman* empire, rising to power under Augustus Caesar. There is a progressive decrease in both the quality and weight of the metals, but a corresponding increase in strength. So too would the empires be successively inferior in godliness and true greatness but superior in brute force. The breakdown of the image by the stone striking its feet signified the future overthrow of all the kingdoms of this world by Christ at His second coming (in the days of the last form of the Roman empire) when He will reign over the whole earth. Further comment on this dream and its interpretation will be reserved till we come to consider the parallel vision of the Four Great Beasts, later revealed to Daniel himself; but we must first study Nebuchadnezzar's second dream, as follows.

THE GREAT TREE

In this dream (*Daniel 4*) the king saw a tree which 'grew and was strong, and the height thereof reached unto heaven, and the sight thereof to the end of all the earth: the leaves thereof were fair, and

the fruit thereof much' (vv.11,12). It gave shelter and shade to bird and beast, and food for 'all flesh'. There came down from heaven 'a watcher and an holy one' who cried in a loud voice:
"Hew down the tree .... nevertheless leave the stump of his roots in the earth, even with a band of iron and brass, in the tender grass of the field; and let it be wet with the dew of heaven .... Let his heart be changed from a man's, and let a beast's heart be given unto him, and let seven times pass over him" (vv.14—16). Again Daniel was the only one who could interpret the dream. The *interpretation,* as revealed to the prophet was as follows.

The tree typified Nebuchadnezzar himself whose power and greatness had grown 'unto heaven' (v.22 — certainly his was a God-given kingdom) and his dominion 'to the end of the earth' — wide indeed were his conquests. The threatened cutting down of the tree signified a warning from Heaven (through the angelic 'watcher') that the king's conduct was being observed and that if he did not improve his ways — he had become self-exalting (see *Daniel 3*) and tyrannical — he would be struck down with a form of insanity. His character would be changed so that he would act like a 'beast of the field', eating grass and living outdoors 'till his hairs were grown like eagles' feathers, and his nails like birds' claws' (*Daniel 4*:33).

Daniel urged the king to reform so that he might escape this visitation from God (v.27), but in twelve months he had still not humbled himself. In fact his pride had reached a pinnacle, as is evident from his words, as he surveyed the capital from the roof of his palace: 'Is not this great Babylon that I have built .... by the might of my power, and for the honour of my majesty?' (v.30). While 'the word was in the king's mouth, there fell a voice from heaven' saying,

"O king Nebuchadnezzar, to thee it is spoken; The kingdom is departed from thee. And they shall drive thee from men, and thy dwelling shall be with the beasts of the field: they shall make thee to eat grass as oxen, and seven times shall pass over thee, until thou know that the most High ruleth in the kingdom of men, and giveth it to whomsoever he will" (vv.31—32). Immediately the king was struck with the threatened madness; it persisted for the specified *'seven times'*.

The measure of this mystic period was not revealed, probably for two reasons: in the first instance, mercifully for the king's sake, that he might not know beforehand for how long he would have to endure the calamity that was to come to him. Yet we believe that there was a much more significant reason, namely that the period applied more especially to the more distant future, which God did not then purpose to disclose. In fact it was only when the New Testament came to be written long after, that the secret of the 'times' was revealed by a comparison of vv.6 and 14 in *Revelation 12*. There we learn that 3½ times = 1,260 days and therefore 1 time = 360 days, the length of a luni-solar year, as originally used in Noah's time (cf. *Genesis 7*:11 and *8*:3,4 assuming twelve months to the year). Thus we know, as a matter of academic interest, that Nebuchadnezzar's madness lasted seven luni-solar years, the year used in Babylon; but clearly the 'seven times' would apply to something more informative for us than that long past event. We believe in fact that, as seven years, the mystic expression gives us the *duration of the Beast's rule,* closing with the end of the age. The very incident of Nebuchadnezzar's behaviour as a *beast* for the period strikingly foreshadows the coming kingdom of the Beast. Also, just as the ancient monarch was the first Gentile ruler (after Israel's downfall), so the Beast will be the last: his empire too, like Nebuchadnezzar's, is referred to as Babylon, as we shall see.

The seven times not only stand for seven years but also constitute, as will be shown, an accurate measure of a much longer period, *the Times of the Gentiles* (*Luke 21*:24) when Jerusalem would be 'trodden down' and Israel be without national status as a punishment for her continued idolatry. The period of her punishment had been predicted centuries before her actual downfall; it was to be 'seven times' (see *Leviticus 26*:28—33), the very term used in connection with Nebuchadnezzar's insanity which, however, lasted only seven years. Clearly then, the seven times specified for the long period of Israel's rejection by God, coincident with the Times of the Gentiles, must be on a different scale. We need not leave the book of Daniel to discover what the new scale is. In the Seventy Weeks prophecy (*Daniel 9*), described later, it is revealed to us: 1 day = 1 year. Thus seven times, or 2,520 (7 × 360) days, would denote *2,520 years,* the exact period that elapsed between 604 B.C. (the date of Nebuchadnezzar's accession — the start of Israel's downfall) and A.D. 1917, when Jerusalem was liberated from the Turk; and Palestine, after its age-long thraldom to Gentile powers, was offered to the Jews as their national home. Although this was a memorable year for Israel it did not see the final end of her troubles and tribulations, or of the final overthrow of the Gentile powers themselves; but it is pin-pointed as the *beginning* of the end, just as 604 B.C. was the *initial* starting-point of Israel's debasement, her final subjugation was in 587 B.C. Bible prophecy lays special emphasis on this beginning of the end, in 1917, even to giving us the very day of the month in that year (see Appendix V). It seems that God, in His mercy, wished to give mankind adequate and *precise* warning of the outset of 'time of the end' (1917 to the end of the age) because He knew that the period would involve two world wars and, in the last seven years a time of unparalleled affliction for humanity, but from which He has provided a way of escape (see ch.7).

Referring back to the 'seven times', we intimated that this mystic period would represent not only the seven years of Nebuchadnezzar's madness but also the long period of the Times of the Gentiles which idea is confirmed by the details of the incident itself. Thus, the monarch, as the first of the line of predicted Gentile rulers, might well represent the *whole* line, from himself to the Beast. Also, his behaviour like a beast is typical of all four empires, which are depicted as four *beasts,* described in the section that follows.

THE FOUR GREAT BEASTS

This vision of Daniel revealed to him in the first year of Belshazzar, king of Babylon (541—538 B.C.), had essentially the same scope as Nebuchadnezzar's image dream, given sixty two years before. The empire of Babylon was now nearing its end; thus Daniel's vision of it as the first wild beast, portrays only its final collapse and its future revival in another form, as we shall show. The second and third beasts symbolise the same empires as do the ram and he-goat of Daniel's second vision and will therefore be considered when we come to it. Here we shall deal briefly with the first beast and then, mainly, with the fourth beast. The general significance of the whole vision and of the parallel dream (the great image, already partly described) is shown in the accompanying table.

THE PARALLEL SIGNIFICANCE OF THE IMAGE DREAM AND THE BEAST'S VISION

The Image Dream of Nebuchadnezzar	The Four Beasts of Daniel's Vision	Interpretation	Time of Empire
The Head of Gold	The 1st beast, like a LION with eagle's wings... wings are 'plucked'....	Empire of Babylon	604-538 B.C. Ist. king, Nebuchadnezzar)
	...and it stands on its feet 'as a man'	Last world empire 'Babylon' revived	Future (Ruler the Beast)
The Breast & Arms of Silver	The 2nd. beast, like a BEAR, raised up on one side (dual character?)	Empire of Medo-Persia	538-336 B.C. (Ist. king, Darius and Cyrus)
The Belly & Thighs of Brass	The 3rd. beast, like a LEOPARD... ...having four heads	Grecian Empire	336-27 B.C. (Ist. king, Alexander the Great - empire then split into four parts)
The Legs of Iron...	The 4th beast - an unspecified monster with iron teeth...	Roman Empire	27 B.C.-A.D. 476 (Ist. king, Augustus Caesar)
...with feet & ten toes of Iron & Clay	... and ten horns From these comes...	A coming ten-kingdom confederacy, based on Rome	Future
	... a little horn		(Ruler, the Beast)

It can be seen that the vision goes further than the dream in that it reveals, in the case of the fourth beast especially, the coming of the Beast (typified in the little horn), the head of the final world empire which will be in character a revival of that of Babylon, as a study of the first beast shows (see the table). We shall now consider the visions of the first and fourth beasts in detail, passing over those of the second and third beasts until the next section ('The Ram and the He-Goat').

The First Beast. The vision is recorded thus (*Daniel* 7:2—4): "I saw in my vision by night, and, behold, the four winds of the heaven strove upon the great sea (the Mediterranean). And four great beasts came upon from the sea, diverse from one another. The first was like a lion, and had eagle's wings: I beheld till the wings thereof were plucked, and it was lifted up from the earth, and made stand upon the feet as a man, and a man's heart was given to it".

This first beast initially represents, like the dream image's 'head of gold', the ancient empire of Babylon. Yet the vision is concerned only with the end of that empire (in 538 B.C.) — depicted by the expression 'the eagle's wings .... were plucked (torn off)' — and also, more important to us today, with the appearance of the Beast in the closing years of this present age, symbolised by the first beast's being 'made to stand upon the feet as a *man,* and a man's heart .... given it'. It is as though the last world empire of this age, itself regarded by God as a 'beast', becomes concentrated in a man, a superman, the Beast — just as, in Nebuchadnezzar's dream, the image's 'head of gold' typified not only the empire (of Babylon) but also the monarch himself. Thus, as ancient Babylon under him was virtually the first world empire to a limited extent, so the last world empire under the Beast will be a revived form of Babylon on a truly world-wide scale, dominated by a much more powerful ruler.

The Fourth Beast. This vision opens as follows (*Daniel* 7:7): "After this I saw in the night visions, and behold a fourth beast, dreadful and terrible, and strong exceedingly; and it had great iron teeth .... and ten horns".

In the first instance, the beast — like the iron legs of the image — depicts the old Roman empire, but the reference to the ten horns (comparable to the ten toes of the image) leaps over the centuries to the time, in our near future, when a ten-kingdom union will be formed. That it will be based on Rome, occupying much of the territory that was formerly part of her ancient empire, follows from the circumstance that the fourth beast and the lowest part of the image (i.e. the legs and the feet), from which the ten horns and ten toes respectively spring, plainly symbolise that empire (as the table shows). It was thought that the European Economic Community, at least when it consisted of ten member-states, might itself be the predicted ten-kingdom union from which the Beast would arise. Yet the entry of Spain and Portugal into the E.E.C. in 1985 has brought its member-states up to twelve. Even so, it seems certain that the predicted union must ultimately develop from the E.E.C. because its component states will also be mainly European.

The vision continues as follows: "I considered the (ten) horns, and, behold, there came up among them another little horn, before whom there were three of the first horns plucked up by the roots: and, behold, in this horn were eyes like the eyes of a *man*, and a mouth speaking great things" (*Daniel* 7:8).

We shall pause here to give the interpretation of the vision thus far, as revealed to Daniel by 'one of them that stood by' (an angel, doubtless): "The fourth beast shall be the fourth kingdom upon earth .... and the ten horns out of this kingdom are ten kings that shall arise: and another shall arise after them .... and he shall subdue three kings. And he shall speak great words against the most High" (vv.23—25).'

The Beast's rise to power among the ten kingdoms will be achieved by the subjugation of three of them. If he first appears in Italy, as seems likely from this and other prophecies, he may well conquer the *smaller* neighbouring states of Belgium, Luxembourg and the Netherlands, assuming these states will be in the predicted ten-kingdom combine as they are in fact in the present E.E.C. Later prophetic visions, which we shall consider in due course, indicate that the Beast quickly dominates the ten kingdoms and in a few years the whole world. His speaking 'great words against the most High', or (as we might say) his loud-voiced and arrogant utterances against God, remind us of the lion-like characteristics of the first beast, itself a type of the Beast.

The vision continues (*Daniel* 7:21—22): "I beheld, and the same horn made war with the saints, and prevailed against them; until the Ancient of days came, and judgment was given to the saints of the most High; and the time came that the saints possessed the kingdom".

As the Beast is against God, so will he be against His saints and make war with them and, as the interpretation (latter part of v.25) adds, 'they shall be given into his (the Beast's) hands until a time and times and the dividing of time', i.e. for a period of 3½ 'times' (3½ luni-solar years, as previously explained). The 'saints' here, as the context proves, are not members of the Church of God now on earth because, as we shall show later, they will be translated to Heaven before the Beast appears on earth at the outset of the last seven years of the age. The 'saints' who will be the object of his persecution will thus be those who, although they will not have trusted in Christ for salvation during this day of grace and will therefore not take part in the translation, will remain faithful to God.

Another thing, not in the vision but disclosed in the interpretation, is that the Beast will seek to change 'times and laws' (*Daniel* 7:25). These may well include the annual religious festivals — Christmas, Easter, Whitsuntide — which he would doubtless resolve to eliminate because they commemorate God's Son and the Holy Spirit. These holy days could perhaps be replaced by licentious and demonic orgies for the worship of the Beast and his master Satan.

The vision next portrays a divine court of justice presided over by the 'Ancient of days' (God the Father), in which the fourth beast — here denoting the Roman empire in its last phase, the final world kingdom of the Beast — is condemned to destruction by fire (vv. 9—11), evidently at the close of the age. Incidentally, the phrase 'the close of the age' is not a scriptural one in the Authorised Version, which gives instead 'the end of the *world*' (*Matthew* 24:3). Although 'age' is the more accurate translation of the original Greek word, the translators were doubtless led to render it 'world' because, in many ways and for many people, the world, as we know it, will come to an end when the present age comes to a close, as will be explained in due course. Also 'the end (or close) of the age' is almost meaningless to the man in the street, whereas he is quite familiar with 'the end of the world' and expects that it will bring judgment and disaster as in fact it will. Reverting to the destruction of the Beast's kingdom, further details will be given when we come to later visions on the subject.

The present vision closes as follows (*Daniel* 7:12—13, 27): "I saw .,... one like the Son of man (Christ) came with the clouds of heaven, and came to the Ancient of days (God, His Father) .... and there was given him dominion, and glory, and a kingdom, that all people, nations, and languages, should serve him: his dominion which shall not pass away, and his kingdom that which shall not be destroyed .... And the kingdom .... shall be given to the people of the saints of the most High .... and all dominions shall serve and obey him''.

We shall explain all this in due course; it will suffice here to indicate that, at the end of the age, Christ will come again to this earth with all His saints to reign over the world for a thousand years.

In reviewing the vision concerning the fourth beast with ten horns, it is evident that the Roman empire, typified by the beast, is regarded as existing from the time of its rise right on to the end of this present age. No notice is taken of its actual fall in A.D. 476 or of its subsequent history to the time of its reappearance in the form of a ten-kingdom union and its development into a world empire under the Beast, there is, in fact, a chronological gap in the prophecy which the vision ignores. No information is provided at this stage of our studies as to when the break started. We know of course, that it has not closed yet, but we do not know when it opened *until* we refer to a later revelation to Daniel, the Seventy Weeks prophecy (*Daniel* 9:24—27), in which a similar chronological break is discernible (see ch.5 for a full explanation of the prophecy). The break lies between the 69th and 70th 'week' and, since it can be shown that the 69th week closed with Christ's crucifixion in A.D.32, it follows that that was the year when the break started, and it will end when the 70th 'week' (i.e. the last 7-year period of the age) begins, which it may do shortly. The break (or gap), therefore, has extended to date (1987) for 1,955 years. There is no reason to doubt that the same gap occurs in the vision (of the four beasts) we have been studying as well as in the parallel dream of the great image — in that which typifies, in both vision and dream, the Roman empire. In the vision, the break is in the fourth beast; in the dream, it is in the lower part (the legs and feet) of the image; this will become clearer as we examine the table again. Of course, there is no actual break in the image itself; it is seen as an intact and integral structure. Nor, by analogy, is there any break (so to speak) in the existence of the fourth beast. It is that, in God's sight, the break just does not exist. His purpose in disregarding it from A.D.32 onwards is that Israel, because of her crucifixion of Christ (her Messiah) on that date, was *set aside* in favour of a people (the Church) whom He would then choose among the Gentiles, and only when the Church is complete (as we expect it shortly will be) will He resume His dealings with His ancient people. This fast-approaching point of time will close the present era of grace (but not the *age*) and open 'the day of vengeance of our God' (as explained later) — a 'day' occupying the last seven years of the age, in which the Beast will be in power. Evidently then, in God's reckoning, the Beast's kingdom is a continuation without interruption of the Roman empire as from A.D.32, when Rome was at the height of her imperial power. Thus, the prophetic scriptures recognise only FOUR world empires (of man), beginning with the downfall of Israel as a nation and ending at the close of the age: the empires of Babylon, Medo-Persia, Greece and Rome. The FIFTH KINGDOM will be that of Christ (the 'Son of man' in the vision; the 'Stone' in the image dream) Who will reign with His saints for a thousand years.

THE RAM AND THE HE-GOAT

In the original text of the Old Testament, the section from *Daniel* 2:4 to *Daniel* 7:28 was in Aramaic ('Syriac') the *lingua franca* of the world in which Daniel lived, and this is understandable when it is realised that the dreams and the vision recorded in this portion of Daniel's book are concerned more especially with the Gentile nations. Of course, as a whole, the Old Testament was originally written in Hebrew because it was intended initially for the Jew. In the vision of The Ram and He-Goat, therefore, the language reverts to Hebrew, since this and later visions of Daniel have mainly a Jewish application.

The vision (see *Daniel 8*) was given to the prophet in Elam (a Persian province) in the third year of Belshazzar, 538 B.C.; the year in which the king was to be slain, Babylon was to fall, and its empire to be superseded by that of Medo-Persia, followed in turn by Grecia. These two empires are seen in the vision as the ram and he-goat, whereas in Daniel's previous vision they appeared as the bear and leopard respectively. Babylon is not referred to at all — understandably, as it was about to pass away; nor, however, is Rome, because this vision is not concerned with the Beast, whom we may regard as the *western* 'little horn' arising out of her empire. Rather is it leading up to another little horn, originating in this case from the goat, symbolic of the Grecian empire: this *eastern* 'little horn', as we shall thus term it for distinction, clearly dominates the vision. Indeed the ram was perhaps included in the vision just to confirm what the bear of Daniel's first vision had indicated, that the empire succeeding that of Babylon would be Medo-Persia — the dual nature of the empire being shown respectively by the two horns of the ram and by the bear which 'raised up itself on one side', suggesting that one of the joint empires would be greater than the other. History has demonstrated that, in fact, Persia became the dominating one. Medo-Persia, however, has little or no relevance for us today, and little further is said about the ram in the vision except by way of introducing us to the he-goat, with which it is mainly concerned. We shall thus need to study this part of the vision in detail, as it has much to tell us of coming events.

Actually it is the interpretation of the vision, as revealed to the prophet by the angel Gabriel in the latter part of the chapter (*Daniel 8*:23—27), that directly concerns us today. Yet it will first be necessary to consider the vision itself, in order fully to understand its application. The vision, as already indicated, has the 'little horn' mainly in view, and we shall deal with it in the sub-section under the following heading; the ultimate interpretation will be considered under the heading after that.

The Little Horn — Antiochus Epiphanes. The rise of this infamous king, symbolised by the 'little horn', is thus described in the vision (*Daniel 8*:5—9): "And as I was considering, behold an he goat came from the west on the face of the whole earth, and touched not the ground: and the goat had a notable horn between its eyes. And he came to the ram .... in the fury of his power .... And he cast him down to the ground .... Therefore the he goat waxed very great: and when he was strong, the great horn was broken; and for it came up four notable ones towards the four winds of heaven. And out of one of them came forth a *little horn,* which waxed exceeding great, toward the south, and toward the east, and toward the pleasant land".

The 'great horn' on the goat stands for the first king of the Grecian empire (v.21), i.e. Alexander the Great, whose meteoric rise to power is vividly portrayed (vv.5—7). After his sudden death in 323 B.C.) at the height of his career, his empire was ultimately divided among his four generals (v.22). History tells us that they were:

1. Cassander — he took Greece with Thessaly and Macedonia.

2. Lysimachus — he had Thrace, Cappadocia and northern Asia Minor.

3. Ptolemy — he took Egypt and Cyprus.

4. Seleucus — he seized Babylonia, Media and *Syria.*

Out of Syria, ultimately rose the king whom the vision depicts as the little horn. History demonstrates that he was Antiochus IV (called Epiphanes), who became king of Syria in 176 B.C. Relatively unimportant at first, he eventually became extremely powerful ('waxed exceeding great') towards Egypt ('the south') and *Palestine* ('the pleasant land'). The vision mainly deals, as we might expect, with his treatment of the Jews in the latter country, as recorded in the verses following those quoted above:

"And it (the little horn, Antiochus) waxed great, even to the host of heaven (God's people, the Jews); and it cast down some of the host, and of the stars (outstanding Jewish leaders) to the ground, and stamped upon them. Yea, he (Antiochus, in person) magnified himself even to (or against) the *prince* of the host (the Lord Jesus Christ, see *Daniel 9*:25), and from Him the daily sacrifice was taken away, and the place of His sanctuary was cast down" (*Daniel 8*:10—11).

It was the custoim of the Jews, in their temple ritual (initiated by Moses at God's command; see *Exodus 29*:38—42), to sacrifice every day (morning and evening) of the year a lamb as a burnt offering to the Lord. These offerings were abolished by the order of Antiochus, and the Jews were forced to sacrifice swine instead. He even desecrated their sanctuary (or temple) by setting up a statue of Jupiter in the Holy of Holies (the inner temple, or sanctuary proper). This infamous act is doubtless that designated as 'the transgression of desolation in *Daniel 8*:13, and as 'the abomination that maketh desolate' in *Daniel 11*:31 of a parallel passage concerning Antiochus (*Daniel 11*:21—35).

Reverting to *Daniel 8*:12: "And an host was given him (Antiochus) against the daily sacrifice by reason of transgression, and it (the transgression) cast the truth to the ground; and it practised, and prospered".

At first sight this statement scarcely makes sense and some of the modern versions have had to make wild guesses to try to make it understandable, as indeed have most commentators hitherto. Probably, too, the translators who gave us the Authorised Version were puzzled by the verse but recorded what they thought was the true rendering, whether they understood it or not. In fact, although the verse is rather cryptic — as one might expect in a book of prophecy — its words, here given in the Authorised Version, convey the basic truth and the meaning can be discerned with a little study of the text and the context! Essentially the verse indicates that a large number of Jews (the 'host', as in vv.10 and 11, refers to God's ancient people), evidently those disloyal to their faith, supported Antiochus in his action against their daily sacrifices — an historical fact, see Apocrypha, 1 Maccedonians 1:11—15, 43—61. The Jews were indeed, as the verse indicates, 'given' into his hand by God as a punishment for their 'transgression', doubtless their apostasy, which 'cast down the truth', and 'practised and prospered' as wrongdoing frequently does, for a time!

The vision closes thus (*Daniel 8*:13—14): "Then I heard one saint speaking, and another saint said unto that certain saint which spake, How long shall be the vision, concerning the transgression of desolation, to give both the sanctuary and the host to be trodden under foot? And he said unto me, Unto two thousand and three hundred days; then shall the sanctuary be cleansed".

These 'days' are evidently not prophetic days which represent years (as in the Seventy Weeks prophecy, already mentioned and later explained), but ordinary 24-hour days, because the original Hebrew word here used for days means, literally, 'evenings-mornings'. The period is given with precision in *days* (it amounts to six years and about three months) because God, in His justice and mercy, does not punish for a day longer than is necessary for correction and, doubtless, many days fewer than are deserved. In a yet future punishment of Israel (the Great Tribulation, see ch.10) also involving the abolition of her sacrifices and the setting up of the ultimate 'abomination of desolation' the period is similarly given with exactness: 1,260 days.

With regard to the 2,300 days in the time of Antiochus, history tells us (1 *Maccedonians 4*:52; *Josephus,* Antiquities, Book XII, ch.VII) that the cleansing of the temple, which ended the period, occurred on the 25th day of the ninth month (Chisleu — December) in 165 B.C. According to the vision, the period started 2,300 days before this date, that is during the year 171 B.C. (in the 6th month, Elul — September). In that year Menelaus, an apostate Jew, bribed Antiochus to appoint him high priest, so this may have been the incident that started the period, but we cannot be certain of this because the exact date of the incident is apparently not known. Moreover, the question, 'How long' etc. quoted above, applies mainly to the 'transgression of desolation' (the placing of the statue of Jupiter in the sanctuary) and one might suppose, therefore, that this incident marked the start of the period. Yet according to *Josephus* and 1 *Maccedonians*, the incident occurred at about the middle of the period.

The King of Fierce Countenance. We have shown that the 'little horn' of the vision in *Daniel 8* typified, *initially,* Antiochus Epiphanes, but the interpreter of the vision makes it quite clear that the *ultimate* fulfilment has nothing to do with that ancient king but with the 'king of fierce countenance' who appears at *'the time of the end'* (v.17). Frequent reference is made in the book of Daniel to this momentous period, especially to the last seven years of it, which close at the end of the age, but we must go to the New Testament for light as to the start of the period. In answer to His disciples' query concerning the end of the world (*Matthew 24*:3), the Lord indicated that the end must not be expected before the outbreak of a world war (vv.6—7): 'For nation shall rise against nation, and kingdom against kingdom' .... He then added: 'All these are the *beginning* of sorrows', suggesting that a world war would mark the beginning of the end period. Evidently the reference was to the first world war (1914—1918) during which we may conclude that the end period, or the time of the end, started; the period will end with the coming of the Son of man, when 'the times of the Gentiles shall be fulfilled' (*Luke 21*:24, 27). We have already shown (ch.4) that the beginning of the end of the times of the Gentiles occurred in 1917, which is thus marked as the *year* in which the time of the end began. In that year the Gentile nations were virtually receiving notice from God that their end, along with that of all Gentile authority, was in sight. It is to this final end that the *fulfilment* of the 'times of the Gentiles' refers: the end of the age.

We have established that 'the time of the end' commenced in 1917 and therefore it is from this year onwards that we are to expect, according to Daniel, the rise of 'the king of fierce countenance'. Before attempting to identify him we shall study what the prophecy reveals about him (*Daniel 8*:23—25), this: 'A king of fierce countenance' (i.e. brazen-faced), he is quite unmoved by feelings of shame or qualms of conscience; 'and understanding dark sentences', he is a master of dissimulation and deceit. 'His power shall be mighty'; a world power? .... 'but not by his own power': raised up and inspired by Satan? .... 'and he shall destroy wonderfully': he brings about the downfall of peoples and nations in an extraordinary way, not by force of arms? .... 'and shall prosper and practise': prospers in all he does; 'and shall destroy the mighty and the holy people': he shall vanquish great powers and particularly, as did his forerunner Antiochus, the Jews. 'And through his policy also he shall cause craft to prosper in his hand': he will achieve success by cunning and fraud, as already indicated; .... 'he shall magnify himself in his heart': he will impiosly exalt himself; .... 'and by peace shall destroy many': his conquests will not be attained by open warfare but by intrigue; .... 'he shall stand up against the Prince of princes; but he shall be broken without hand', i.e. he will finally seek to attack Christ Himself (at His coming to earth?) but will be destroyed not by human agency, but by a stroke from the Lord.

There is more recorded of this end-time king (or power-'king' in Scripture is often used for kingdom) but under a different title: 'The king of the north' (*Daniel 11*:40—45) and 'Gog and Magog' (*Ezekiel 38*and *39*). We shall show evidence as we proceed for the belief that all three kings or kingdoms are one and the same, and represent Communist Russia at various stages of her existence; from her beginning in 1917, to the end of the age. It is indeed significant that she was born with the Russian Revolution of November 1917, the very year marking the outset of the time of the end when the king of fierce countenance appears. Moreover, his character and deeds, as sketched for us in *Daniel 8* and quoted above, strikingly tally with what we have known of Communist Russia. Her self-deification, her dethronement of God, her subjugation of many nations by 'cold war' (subversive propaganda, espionage, etc.) rather than by military might and her hostility to Israel are all indicated in the prophecy. Yet the king of fierce countenance, we believe, stands not only for the State (the U.S.S.R.) but also for its future ruling head just as the head of gold of the image in Nebuchadnezzar's dream stood both for his empire and for the monarch himself, and as the Beast depicts both the coming world empire and its ruler as well.

In the case of Communist Russia, the present republic and its future head are separately referred to, we believe, in the titles Gog and Magog (*Ezekiel 38*:2), the ruler (Gog) being there mentioned before his people (Magog). As we study the verse (2) in more detail we find that it strikingly depicts Russia and especially its revolution in 1917. Thus, Gog is described as 'the chief prince of Meshech (Moscow?) and Tubal (Tobolsk?); or 'the chief prince' could be rendered 'the prince of Rosh (Russia?)'; the similarity in structure of the ancient names and their modern equivalents is too striking to be a coincidence. Doubtless, in Ezekiel's day (600 B.C.) there were, south of the Black Sea, districts bearing the actual names of Meshech and Tubal but these, like the tribes Moschoi and Tibarenoi derived from them, have long since disappeared. Moreover, the two Bible names occur here in a prophetic vision which has yet to be finally fulfilled and would thus be quite irrelevant unless applicable to our own time. *Moscow,* the present capital of the U.S.S.R., is sufficiently important to make it worthy of mention in the prophecy; it is pertinent that the city became the capital in 1918, only a year after the formation of the Republic at the start of the end-time. It is significant also that Tobolsk, a town in western Siberia, was where the ex-tzar Nicholas II was imprisoned after the Russian Revolution 1917, the year of the downfall of the old order and the rise of Communism, again at the beginning of the time of the end. Support is thus afforded for the belief that the Tubal of *Ezekiel 38* represents the present Tobolsk and that Meshech is Moscow; also that Rosh indicates Russia, by analogy as well as by similarity of name. All this together provides strong evidence that Gog and Magog depict the Soviet Union, at least in its last phase as Israel's northern aggressor in the attack on her described in *Ezekiel 38.* It is plain that the chapter applies to the present generation because the Jews are stated (v.8) to be back in their own country, as they are today. Also, the destruction of the northern host by the Lord (vv.22, 23) shows that it is the last battle of the age that is in question. The details of the battle will be left for later consideration under the heading 'The Battle of Armageddon'.

We have adduced scriptural and historical evidence to show that 'the king of fierce countenance' and 'Gog and Magog' both symbolise Communist Russia. Another character has been alluded to also as a symbol of that republic (and its future last ruler?), namely 'the king of the north' (see *Daniel 11*:40—45). A few facts from this passage, studied in detail later, support this view. Thus, the king (or kingdom) is from 'the north'; that is, the north of Palestine because that country is regarded as the centre of God's dealings on earth and all other countries or powers are viewed in relation to that promised land of His ancient people Israel. A consideration of the historic portion of the chapter (vv.5—25, for example) confirms this, the kings of the south and north there referring to Egypt and Syria. In the prophetic part (vv.36—45), however, the last king of the north is clearly a great power (v.40) and Russia is the only country to the north of Palestine that could be so symbolised. Further, the account of the northern invasion of Palestine, both in this passage (vv.40—45) and in that concerned with Gog and Magog (*Ezekiel 38* and *39*), suggests a major assault on Israel at the end of the age. In both passages also, the northern aggressor suffers a crushing defeat. There could be only *one* such invasion by such a power from the north at such a time and coming to such an end (making a second invasion impossible), namely the invasion of Israel by Russia at the close of the age. Finally, in both accounts, Ethiopia and Libya are mentioned as supporters of the northern aggressor, confirming the aforesaid conclusion.

We have considered three scriptural titles for the future northern invader of Israel: 'the king of fierce countenance', 'Gog and Magog' and 'the king of the north'. There is yet another title for the same person (or power); it is 'the Assyrian' — see *Isaiah 10*:5,12,24; *14*:1,25; *30*:30—31; *Micah 5*:5. The contexts of these verses make it clear that it is the *last-day* 'Assyrian' to whom they refer. The term aptly applies to Russia, which lies even more to the north of Israel than did ancient Assyria and whose fierce onslaught on Israel at the last day will be the antitype, on a much larger scale and with modern weapons, of Sennacherib's rapid march on Jerusalem in 712 B.C., described so vividly in Byron's famous lines:

"The Assyrian came down like a wolf on the fold,
And his cohorts were gleaming in purple and gold;
And the sheen of their spears was like stars on the sea
When the blue waves roll nightly on deep Galilee."

Another verse portrays the destruction of Sennacherib's large army by divine intervention:

"For the Angel of Death spread his wings on the blast,
And breathed on the face of the foe as he passed:
And the eyes of the sleepers waxed deadly and still,
And their hearts but once heaved, and for ever grew still!"

It will be similarly by the Lord's hand that the last 'Assyrian' and his forces will be cut off, in this case with 'devouring fire .... and hailstones' (*Isaiah 30*:30—31).

CHAPTER 5

SOME PROPHETIC REVELATIONS

In the Old Testament, as we have shown, significant events, dreams and visions were used by God to make known His future dealings with mankind, for those with eyes to see. What we might term direct revelation, however, was also given by God for this purpose. The Old Testament prophets, with their 'Thus saith the Lord', clearly had his mind revealed in some way to them, more often in relation to the present than to the future. We shall refer to a few where they do predict coming events in this manner, presumably by inspiration. we shall, however, mainly have recourse again to the book of Daniel, who, unlike most of the other prophets, received revelations of the future by *angelic* communication, when they did not come to him by dream or vision.

THE SEVENTY WEEKS

This prophecy (*Daniel* 9:24—27), communicated to Daniel by the angel Gabriel in the first year of Darius the Mede (538 B.C.), is probably one of the most remarkable in Scripture. Daniel, now about nintey years old, had been studying the 'books' (the inspired writings which then existed) and discovered that the seventy years of his people's servitude in Babylon were nearly at an end. This period of their punishment, which Jeremiah had prophesied (*Jeremiah* 25:12) would come upon the Jews because of their idolatry, started in 606 B.C. when Nebuchadnezzar first besieged Jerusalem and was due to end in 536 B.C. Daniel had just seen the downfall of the Babylonian empire (538 B.C.) and its supersession by Medo-Persia under Darius, but there was no sign as yet that this change of overrule would have any favourable effect on the still captive people. So the downcast prophet besought the Lord on behalf of the Jews, and though he received an answer through Gabriel it was not what he expected. Nothing was told him about the anticipated near end of the seventy years' servitude, because God expected him to believe what He had already revealed about it through Jeremiah; the Lord always keeps his word. Instead, the much more far-reaching 'seventy weeks' prophecy concerning Israel was communicated to Daniel, predicting when her Messiah would come and her own ultimate blessing at the close of the age. The seventy weeks were to begin from 'the going forth of the commandment to restore and to build Jerusalem' and were to be divided into three parts: 7 + 62 + 2 = 70 weeks. It is clear from the context that these 'weeks' are not weeks of days; it will be demonstrated later that they are, in fact, weeks of years, i.e. 7-year periods. Thus 70 'weeks' stood for 490 years, divided as follows: 49 + 434 + 7. At this point it will be more understandable to quote the angel's words (*Daniel 9*:25):

"Know therefore and understand, that from the going forth of the commandment to restore and to build Jerusalem unto the Messiah the Prince (Christ) shall be seven weeks (equivalent to 49 years), and threescore and two weeks (434 years): the street shall be built again, and the wall, even in troublous times".

From the specified starting-point to the time of Christ there would be thus 69 weeks, representing 483 years on the day/year scale. Sir Robert Anderson ('Daniel in the Critics' Den', 1926) has, in fact, proved that there was exactly this period in luni-solar years *to the very day, from* 1st Nisan (14th March) 445 B.C., when the edict to rebuild Jerusalem was issued by Artaxerxes in his 20th year (see *Nehemiah 2*:1—8) *to* 10th Nisan (6th April) A.D. 32, when Christ made His only public entry into Jerusalem and was acclaimed as King (see *Matthew 21*:1—11, *Zechariah 9*:9 and *Luke 19*:38). Yet, less than a week later, the same people (the Jews who had thus acclaimed Him sided with their rulers in bringing about His crucifixion, foretold in the next verse of the prophecy (*Daniel 9*:26) as follows: 'And after threescore and two weeks shall Messiah be cut off, but not for himself'. It was indeed ;'not for Himself' but *for our sakes* He was 'cut off'. What a striking testimony to the inspiration of Scripture is the above-detailed fulfilment of the 69 weeks of the prophecy. Before going any further we shall seek to explain why the period is divided up in the way it is, in the passage (v.25): 7 + 62 weeks.

At first sight it might be reasoned that it took the first 7 weeks (49 years) to rebuild Jerusalem but there is no evidence for this:

we know only that the *wall* round the city was finished in a mere 52 days (*Nehemiah 6*:15). A more probable answer would be that the point of division of the period was so fixed as to coincide with the year when the original Old Testament was concluded. This point of time, which marked the close of God's old covenant with His people dependent on their obedience to the law and the prophets, was certainly worthy of notice in a prophecy which promised them without any stated condition, ultimate blessings (*Daniel 9*:24). Forty-nine years from 445 B.C. brings us to 396 B.C. which is sufficiently near to 397B.C., the postulated date of Malachi's prophecy.

The 70th Week and the Roman Prince. We come now to the 70th week, for us the most relevant part of the Seventy Weeks prophecy. This last 'week' (7 years) is described for us in v.27, but in order to get the connection we shall also quote v.26 from where we previously left off.

"And the people of *the prince that shall come,* shall destroy the city and the sanctuary; and the end thereof shall be with a flood, and unto the end of the war desolations are determined. And he shall confirm the covenant with many for *one week:* and in the *midst* of the week he shall cause the sacrifice and the oblation to cease, and for the overspreading of abominations he shall make it desolate, even until the consummation, and that determined shall be poured upon the desolate".

Although this passage, especially the latter verse (27), is not easy to understand (designedly so, we believe, like many of God's secrets), it yields its message to the spiritually minded. It is clear, to begin with, that an interval must occur between the end of the 69th week, when Messiah is 'cut off', and the 70th week, because several events are recounted as taking place between. In particular it is predicted that the people of a future prince will destroy Jerusalem and its temple, and continual desolations, extending through the interval right on to the close of the 70th week, are appointed for the Jews and their land. The destruction of their city and temple, as we know from history, was carried out in A.D. 70 by the Romans — nearly 40 years after the crucifixion of Christ at the end of the 69th week; which proves that there is a gap at least this long between the two weeks. In fact a consideration of the final verse 27, quoted above, makes it plain that the gap has not even yet been bridged and *the 70th week is still future.* The predictions of this verse have never yet been fulfilled, as will be appreciated when its meaning is elucidated, as follows.

'And he shall confirm the covenant with many for one week'. The 'he' clearly refers back to the last person mentioned, that is 'the prince that shall come' whose 'people .... shall destroy the city and the sanctuary'. The destruction of Jerusalem and its temple, as history tells us, was carried out by the Romans in A.D. 70 but their leader, the emperor Titus, was certainly not 'the prince that shall come'. The latter will be a Roman ruler *in the closing years of this age*, of which the final end is denoted in the latter part of the verse as 'the consummation, as we shall show. The 'many' with whom he will make a 7-year pact ('the covenant .... for one week') refer to the 'people' mentioned in v.24, that is the Jews, of whom the *majority* will be apostate and thus ready to link up with a Roman ruler. This 'prince that shall come' must in fact be the Beast who will rise, as we have seen, among the ten kingdoms based on Rome. According to all prophecies only *one* potentate will spring from such territory, so the two titles — the Roman prince ('the prince that shall come') and the Beast — must apply to the same individual.

Verse 27 continues, 'and in the midst of the week he shall cause the sacrifice and the oblation to cease'. In other words, half-way through the last septennium of this present age (the 70th 'week'), the Beast (to give him his more usual title) will break his seven-year covenant with Israel by ordering the abolition of her temple sacrifices and offerings. At this predicted time, the Jews are evidently back in their own land and have regained their national status as at present. Also, *they will have rebuilt their temple in Jerusalem and re-established their daily offerings:* the sacrifice of a lamb, morning and evening continually (*Exodus 29*:38—42). The performance of these religious ceremonies, however, will not imply that the people of Israel have at last turned to God and accepted the Lord Jesus as their Messiah. On the contrary, as we shall show under the next heading, they will — except for a minority who are true to God — have acknowledged the Antichrist as their king in Israel and have entered into the 7-year covenant with the Beast of Rome. Probably, under the terms of the covenant, he permitted them to rebuild their temple and re-establish their offerings, although such services, at least nominally offered to God, would naturally be anathema to him. In exchange for this concession he will require, as described later, much of Israel's wealth and 'strong holds' in her land, which will assist him in rising to full power as world dictator. We believe that he will attain this pinnacle of his authority at the mid-point of his seven-year pact with Israel, when he would be sufficiently powerful to be independent of her help and to break the pact and order the cessation of her daily sacrifices. At the same time he will be permitted (by God), 'for the overspreading of abominations', to 'desolate' her sanctuary ('it referring back to this). This 'desolation' of the Jewish temple is presumably the act termed in other prophecies 'the abomination of desolation', initially perpetrated by Antiochus Epiphanes but ultimately by the Beast, as indicated here and fully described later under that heading. The act will evidently be a punishment for Israel's acceptance of Antichrist as their Messiah and king, which will surely reach the 'overspreading' or pinnacle (as the cited word could be rendered) of her idolatry or 'abominations'. The period of 'desolation' will extend, as divinely predetermined with judicial accuracy, through the final three and a half years of the last septennium to the 'consummation', that is the end of the age.

Having shown that the 70th week of the Seventy Weeks prophecy constitutes the last seven years of this present age, it follows that the chronological gap between the 69th and 70th weeks must be the period *from* Christ's crucifixion in A.D. 32 — the year shown to be at the close of the 69th week — *to* the beginning of that last 7-year period to come. The purpose of this time-gap has already been explained in our study of the Four Great Beasts vision (Ch.4).

Israel's Ultimate Blessing under her Messiah. The close of the 70th week and of the present age, when Christ sets up His millennial kingdom, will usher in a time of special blessing for the people of Israel, which indeed was the main purpose of the Seventy Weeks prophecy to predict. Its opening verse (*Daniel 9*:24) makes this clear, thus:

"Seventy weeks are determined upon thy people (Daniel was a Jew) and upon thy holy city (Jerusalem), to finish the transgression (in particular, perhaps, their acceptance of Antichrist), and to make an end of sins, and to make reconciliation for iniquity, and to bring in *everlasting righteousness,* and to seal up the vision and the prophecy (these will be needed no more when the Millennium dawns) and to anoint the most Holy".

The promised blessing is not of course to Israel as a whole, because the major part (the 'many' of v;27) of the present nation will be in league with the Beast and Antichrist when they make their appearance. These apostate Jews will perish; only the faithful remnant (see *Isaiah 10*:20—23) will benefit.

The 'most Holy' has been thought by some commentators to mean the most Holy *place*; suggesting that the Holy of Holies of Israel's future temple will be 'anointed' with the presence of the Shekinah glory at the outset of the Millennium. Although it is true that the 'glory of the Lord' will then come into the temple by the 'east gate' (*Ezekiel 43*:4), it is fanciful to believe that the term 'anointing' signifies that glory. Also, although the tabernacle and holy vessels were anointed in the time of the Aaronic priesthood (*Exodus 29*:36; *30*:26—28), a precedent put forward to support the above-mentioned theory, there is no record of the Holy of Holies itself being anointed. It is indeed rather surprising that such a complicated theory has been held at all, the alternative view that the most Holy refers to Christ is much simpler and has scriptural support, as we shall show. One of the reasons for not accepting the latter interpretation has been the belief that Christ, having once been anointed for His past work on earth (e.g. *Isaiah 61*:1), can have no fresh anointing for His millennial reign; but, again, there is nothing in Scripture to justify this idea.

The 'most Holy', literally 'a holy one of holy ones', is carefully connected by the words 'know therefore' to the verse which follows and which contains 'Messiah the Prince', suggesting that the 'most Holy' is a person, Christ the Messiah. His anointing, in this connection, is evidently in preparation for His millennial reign which opens at the expiry of the 'seventy weeks'. He was indeed the Anointed One at His birth in Bethlehem, for such is the meaning of the name Christ (Gr. 'Christos', Anointed) acclaimed as such by the angels to the shepherds (*Luke 2*:11). Anointing was administered to the high priest (*Leviticus 8*:12) to sanctify (set apart) him for his holy office as his people's intercessor, and especially to kings (1 *Samuel 15*:1) as the seal of their appointment by God. The Lord Jesus Himself declared (*Luke 4*:18, quoting from *Isaiah 61*:1, already referred to) that He had been anointed by the Spirit to do the various works which He had come on earth to do. Yet there is no good reason to disbelieve that He, having accomplished His earthly mission as man, should be re-anointed as the risen Christ for His present work in Heaven as our great high Priest, and for His future reign as King over the peoples of the world. In fact His anointing as King, at least, is indicated in *Hebrews 1*:8—9:

"Thy throne, O God, is for ever and ever: a sceptre of righteousness is the sceptre of thy kingdom. Thou hast loved righteousness and hated iniquity; therefore God, even thy God, hath *anointed* thee with the oil of gladness above they fellows''.

The whole passage, as quoted from *Psalm 45,* speaks of Christ as *King,* and His anointing evidently occurs after His ascension to the 'right hand of the Majesty on high' (*Hebrews 1*:3). Christ's righteous life on earth, without sin in thought, word or deed, has befitted Him to be received into Heaven as 'the King of glory' (*Psalm 24*:7) to be 'crowned with glory and honour' (*Hebrews 2*:9). Shortly, we believe, He will come again to earth as 'KING OF KINGS, AND LORD OF LORDS' (*Revelation 19*:16). The 'oil of gladness above thy fellows' suggests possibly the delight which God has in His Son for His worthiness to be King, above all earthly kings, because as a man on earth at His first coming He 'loved righteousness and hated iniquity'.

From the above evidence, the 'most Holy' almost certainly refers to the Lord Jesus Christ, anointed as King, to reign over the world in righteousness — the blessed event of *Daniel 9*:24 which will close the Seventy Weeks prophecy ('seal up the vision').

THE CHRIST AND THE ANTICHRIST

Appropriately, before the prophecy concerning the Antichrist — the last prophecy of Daniel (*Daniel 10—11*) — is revealed to him, he has a vision, in direct contrast, of the Christ in His pre-incarnate Person. We shall therefore consider this vision under the title that follows before the main prophecy.

The Man in Linen. In such form does the Son of God appear to the prophet (*Daniel 10*:5—9).

''Then I lifted up mine eyes, and looked, and behold a certain man clothed in linen, whose loins were girded with fine gold of Uphaz: his body was like the beryl, and his face as the appearance of lightning, and his eyes as lamps of fire, and his arms and his feet like in colour to polished brass, and the voice of his words like the voice of a multitude. And I Daniel alone saw the vision: for the men that were with me saw not the vision; but a great quaking fell upon them, so that they fled to hide themselves. Therefore I was left alone, and saw this great vision, and there remained no strength in me: for my comeliness was turned in me to corruption, and I retained no strength. Yet heard the voice of his words, then was I in a deep sleep with my face toward the ground''.

A similar vision later appeared to the apostle John (*Revelation 1*:13—18) concerning 'one like unto the Son of man', a title which Christ repeatedly used of Himself while on earth. Consideration of this vision and its context makes it clear that the Person seen in the vision is in fact that of the Lord Jesus Christ, the Son of God, risen and ascended. Therefore there is every reason to believe that the Man clothed in linen seen in Daniel's vision is a preview of the Son of God *before* His incarnation as Jesus Christ.

Such a glorious vision would have been too much for Daniel if he had not been in the right condition to receive it; he had previously been mourning for the sins of his people and fasting for three 'full weeks' (*Daniel 10*:2—3). Incidentally, this term in the original means 'weeks of days', in contrast perhaps with the 'weeks' in the Seventy Weeks prophecy which were 'weeks' of years, as we have shown. It seems as if we are being informed that ordinary time is now reverted to for the prophecy that is to follow the vision.

Regarding the vision itself, only a few comments need be made. The *face* of the Person seen, as might be expected of Deity, is dazzingly bright. To John, in the later vision, it appeared as 'the sun shineth in his strength'. The *eyes,* as Daniel saw them 'as lamps of fire', would indicate their purifying and convicting effect, as they burned into every heart and conscience, revealing every sinful thought and motive. The *voice* 'like the voice of a multitude', was of infinite power (see *Psalm 29*), that said in the beginning, 'Let there be light: and there was light' (*Genesis 1*:3); that called up Lazarus from the grave after he had been dead four days (*John 5*:43—44), and that will ultimately call up *all* the dead, some to 'the resurrection of life' and some to 'the resurrection of damnation' (*John 5*:28—29). Yet in this day of grace the same voice says to us, in gentle entreaty, 'Come unto me, all ye that labour and are heavy laden, and I will give you rest' (*Matthew 11*:28). Have you, reader, yet responded to His loving invitation?

Although Daniel, by his mourning and fasting, was prepared to some extent for the vision, the effulgent glory of the divine Being sapped his strength and the thunderous sound of His words stupified his senses. No human being can bear to behold the dazzling splendour of the Son of God or to listen to His all-powerful voice. The touch of a hand, the reassurance of a voice helped to revive the prophet — from what follows it was probably an angel (Gabriel?) who had restored him and then tells him: ''Now I am come to make thee understand what shall befall thy people in the latter days' (*Daniel*

10:14). Thus we come to the last prophecy of Daniel, as revealed to him by the angel. It first predicts the rise of certain kings from the time of Cyrus, king of Persia (536—529B.C.), to Antiochus Epiphanes (*Daniel 11*:21—35), king of Syria, whom we have already considered. The prophecy, already fulfilled up to this point with remarkable accuracy, then leaps over the centuries to the time of the end (v.35) and foretells the advent of two prominent persons (vv.36—45). One of them, 'the king of the north', has previously been described under 'The King of Fierce Countenance'; it remains for us to consider the other, referred to only as 'the king' (v.36) but shown from what follows to be the Antichrist. It should be mentioned here that some expositors assert that the Beast is the Antichrist but there is little scriptural evidence for this view. Like Christ, the Antichrist will be a Jew and will be accepted by the apostate Jews as their Messiah and as the king of Israel. The Beast, on the contrary, will be associated with Rome and her religion. It is inconceivable that the Jews in Israel would regard him as a possible Messiah for them.

The King. The career of this evil potentate is described for us as follows (*Daniel 11*:36—40):

"And the king shall do according to his will, and he shall exalt himself, and magnify himself above every god, and shall speak marvellous things against the God of gods, and shall prosper till the indignation be accomplished: for that that is determined shall be done. Neither shall he regard the God of his fathers, nor the desire of women, nor regard any god: for he shall magnify himself above all. But in his estate (i.e. in the place of God) shall he honour the God of forces: and a god whom his fathers knew not shall he honour with gold, and silver, and with precious stones, and with pleasant things. Thus shall he do in the most strong holds with a strange god, whom he shall acknowledge and increase with glory: and he shall cause them to rule over many, and shall divide the land for gain. And at the time of the end shall the king of the south push at him: and the king of the north shall come against him like a whirlwind, with chariots, and with horsemen, and with many ships; and he shall enter into the countries, and shall overflow and pass over".

'The king' is introduced abruptly after vv.32—35 which recount very briefly the history of the *Jews* from the time of Antiochus Epiphanes to the time of the end, when the king will be a ruler in Israel. He will evidently be a Jew, albeit an apostate one not acknowledging 'the God of his fathers' or Christ ('the desire of women'; see later under 'His Virgin Birth'). Like Antiochus, he will be characterised by his self-exaltation; but although he will 'magnify himself above every god' he will yet do honour to a superior potentate, 'the God of forces'. This title aptly fits the Beast who, in *Revelation 13,* takes the position of a god, being worshipped by all the world (v4), and of whom it is asked, 'who is able to make war with him?', and who, as the rider on the white horse 'went forth conquering and to conquer' (*Revelation 6*:2). Also, as the Roman prince (*Daniel 9*:26) he could well be referred to, in the passage we are now studying, as 'a god whom his (the king's) fathers (the Jews) knew not' and as 'a strange god'. The Beast's association with Rome and her church would make him 'strange' (or foreign) to the Jews in respect of both country and religion. Thus 'the God of forces' honoured by the king must be the Beast, who, as the first 'beast' of *Revelation 13,* is made an object of world-worship by the second 'beast' (vv.11—12), who in turn, must be 'the king' of *Daniel 11*:36—40). His other scriptural titles are 'the false prophet' (*Revelation 16*:13), the 'antichrist' (1 *John 2*:18) and 'the idol shepherd that leaveth the flock' (*Zechariah 11*:17). The one referred to in the last title is evidently identical with the Antichrist because, like him, the idol shepherd will be a Jew, as the context indicates. Also, his title is in direct contrast with that of Christ, the 'Good Shepherd' Who 'giveth his life for the sheep' (*John 10*:11). Our Lord doubtless alluded to the idol shepherd when on the occasion of His healing of the impotent man (*John 5*:1—16), He said to the Jews who sought to kill Him, 'Ye have not the love of God in you. I am come in my Father's name, and ye receive me not: if *another* shall come in his own name, him ye will receive' (vv.42—43). The Jews of that day rejected Christ, their true Messiah, but when the Antichrist (the 'another') comes, in self-exaltation ('in his own name') he will be received by Israel at large as her promised Messiah and king. Yet he, the idol shepherd, will have not love for his subjects ('the flock'): he will in truth be as an idol, an object for worship, quite unresponsive to his worshippers. The idolisation of this evil man by the Jews will be regarded by God as the lowest depth of their degradation: 'Thou (Israel) wentest to the king .... and didst debase thyself even to hell' (*Isaiah 57*:9). Where the Jews will descend morally, their ruler will be consigned actually: 'Tophet (hell) is ordained of old; yea, for the king it is prepared' (*Isaiah 30*:33).

Continuing our study of *Daniel 11*,a few details are given (vv.38—39) of the king's relationship with the Beast ('the god of forces') and can be understood as follows. The king as the accepted ruler of Israel, will apparently set up strategic strongholds throughout the country ('the land') to secure the Beast's infiltration. Clearly this will be in the early days of the Beast's career and may well constitute one of the terms of the seven-year pact between him and his ally the king. The strongholds may be controlled either by the Beast's own commanders or by men chosen from the many apostate Jews disloyal to their own country — as the tax-collectors, in the time of Christ, served their Roman overlords. The strongholds could be used not only to prevent a possible uprising among the few faithful Jews, as actually occurred in the days of Antiochus Epiphanes, but also as centres for the collection of much of the country's wealth. Such wealth could be in the form of money ('gold and silver') or even as valuable possessions ('pleasant things'), probably extorted from the public. The king would ensure that this accumulated wealth was placed at the Beast's disposal for his nefarious ends. Only one other incident of the King is recorded in the passage before us (v.40). It occurs at the end of the seven-year period, at the close of this present age. The king, commanding the Israel forces, will be attacked by Egypt ('the king of the south') and then, in much greater strength, by the power believed to be Communist Russia ('the king of the north'). The second attack on Israel will rapidly overwhelm her defences and also those of neighbouring states (v.41), probably Turkey, Syria and Lebanon, but Jordan ('Edom, Moab .... and Ammon') will escape. Further details of the northern assault are recorded in vv.42—45 but these will be considered under a later heading, 'The Battle of Armageddon'.

THE ABOMINATION OF DESOLATION

This incident, in its ultimate fulfilment, is purely future and should, strictly speaking, be described under 'Coming Events' but it is more convenient to give a full account of it here.

All sin is hateful to God. Especially *abominable* to Him however, is idolatry — putting other gods, animate or inanimate, before Him, in flagrant disobedience to His first two commandments (*Exodus 20*:2—5). Yet the most *amazing* act of idolatry will be the assumption of deity by the Beast in Israel's future temple: truly 'the abomination that *astonisheth*'. This is an alternative rendering to 'the abomination that maketh desolate' of *Daniel 11*:31 and *Daniel 12*:11. The former reference to the phrase concerns the desecration of the Jews' sanctuary (i.e. the Holy of holies) by Antiochus Epiphanes, recounted previously. The phrase in the later reference has to do with the yet future profanity which is now being studied, but the meaning of the phrase is not revealed anywhere in the chapter. In fact we have to go to the New Testament for enlightenment; there are two allusions to the profanity.

Firstly, Christ said to His disciples, in reply to their question as to what would be the sign of His coming and of the end of the world (*Matthew 24*:3):

"When ye therefore shall see the *abomination of desolation*, spoken of by Daniel the prophet, stand in the holy place .... then let them which be in Judaea flee into the mountains .... For then shall be great tribulation, such as was not since the beginning of the world to this time, no, nor ever shall be .... Immediately after the tribulation of those days shall the sun be darkened .... and then shall all the tribes of the earth mourn, and they shall see the Son of man coming in the clouds of heaven with power and great glory" (vv.15,16,21,29,30).

In another account (*Mark 13*) of the same occasion it is recorded that our Lord said (v.14), 'But when ye shall see the abomination of desolation, spoken of by Daniel the prophet, *standing where it ought not*'. The striking fact here is that, although in the original Greek the noun 'abomination' in of the neuter gender, its dependent participle 'standing' is not neuter but masculine in form. In English, therefore, the phrase should be 'standing where *he* ought not', showing that the abomination will be a person, not a thing. The second New Testament allusion to the profanity, if not actually to its title ('the abomination of desolation') is evidently made by the apostle Paul (2 *Thessalonians* 2:3—4):

"Let no man deceive you by any means; for that day shall not come, except there come a falling away first, and that *man of sin* be revealed, the son of perditions; who opposeth and exalteth himself above all that is called God, or that is worshipped; so that he as God *sitteth in the temple of God,* showing himself that he is God".

The 'day' refers back to 'the day of Christ' (v.2) which, as the context implies, will be a day of trouble, called in the Old Testament 'the day of the Lord' and referring to Christ's second coming to *earth* in judgment, prior to His millennial reign. At first sight, the self-exaltation of the man of sin, as described above, appears to parallel that of 'the king' (*Daniel 11*:36), except for his sitting in the temple. For the following reasons, however, it is believed that it is the *Beast,* not his ally the 'king' (the Antichrist), who is this man of sin. In our study of the 'seventy weeks' prophecy (*Daniel 9*) we have seen that it is the Roman prince (the Beast) who will 'desolate' the Jews' sanctuary (v.27) — evidently the act indicated by the phrase 'the abomination of desolation'. Moreover, he always takes precedence over his confederate (as 'the king', etc) in the prophecies in which the two persons are mentioned together, the latter being ever ready to do honour to the Beast in one way or another. Also, the Beast would scarcely tolerate his ally being worshipped as God (albeit in the temple in Israel) when he himself is worshipped by the world at large. Finally, of these two evil men, the first to appear on the scene, according to Scripture, will be the Beast. It is therefore very unlikely that the man of sin, referred to in 2 *Thessalonians 2*, would apply to the Beast's partner, completely ignoring his predecessor, the Beast himself.

Reverting to *Daniel 12,* the chapter clearly has to do with the yet future, the opening verses referring to an unprecedented time of trouble for Israel; doubtless the period of the Great Tribulation, occupying, as we have seen, the last three-and-a-half years of this present age. The duration of the period is accurately confirmed in v.7 as 'times, times and a half', i.e. 3½ times, equivalent to, as already explained, 3½ × 360 = 1,260 days, or 3½ luni-solar years. The period will commence from 'the time that the daily sacrifice shall be taken away and the abomination that maketh desolate (or 'that astonisheth') set up' (v.11). This time of trouble will be limited to 1,260 days, and after that, when a further period of 75 days elapses (i.e. 1,335 days from the start of the trouble), a period of blessing is promised (v.12) — the millennial reign of Christ. The 75-day interval will be necessary to accommodate the events of the 'day of the Lord', as described later.

The Moslem Mosque on the Temple Site. Before leaving Daniel's last prophecy concerning the abomination of desolation, just described, it should be mentioned that the 1,335 days may be regarded not only as ordinary 24 hour days but, by analogy with the year-days of the Seventy Weeks prophecy, could conceivably represent 1,335 years. Certainly it is a striking fact that exactly this period, in lunar years (1 year = 354 days) as used by the Mohammedans, elapsed *from* the beginning of their era in A.D. 622 *to* the momentous year A.D. 1917 — the year, as already noted, that saw the Turkish forces driven out of Palestine and the foundation thus laid for Israel's ultimate blessing. It is remarkable, too, that in 1917 the Moslem calendar with its lunar scale was discontinued by the Turks and replaced by our western one (the Gregorian calendar) with its solar scale. That year, by its eastern reckoning, was 1335 but was then changed to 1917. Turkish coins were actually issued with the western date on one side and the eastern date 1335 on the other side. These facts have led some students of prophecy to believe that the Mohammedans have been the scriptural desolator of Israel, and certainly for nearly thirteen centuries it was they who trod down Jerusalem and desolated Palestine. Moreover, their mosque, the Dome of the Rock, which has stood for this period in Jerusalem on the site originally occupied by the Jewish temples, has been thought to represent the abomination of desolation of *Daniel 12*:11. Yet, as we have shown, the 1,335 days will usher in Israel's *final* blessing *at the end of the age* whereas the period, when reckoned as 1,335 years, expired in 1917, which year was only the *beginning* of the end-time. Even when the years are taken as *solar* years, the period is extended only to 1957 and this year, too, is past and gone. The Mohammedan mosque *still* stands to desecrate Israel's temple area; the age is *not* ended and her promised blessing has not materialised. Thus the view, held by some expositers, that the Dome of the Rock is the scriptural abomination of desolation, can be accepted at best as only a *partial* fulfilment of Daniel's prophecy, assuredly not the complete and final one.

In concluding our studies of prophetic revelations recorded in the Old Testament we have occasion to refer to the closing chapter of its last book, in which there is a warning and a promise (*Malachi 4*:1–2):

"For behold, the day cometh, that shall burn as an oven; and all the proud, yea, and all that do wickedly, shall be stubble: and the day that cometh shall burn them up, saith the Lord of hosts, that it shall leave them neither root nor branch. But unto you that fear my name shall the Sun of righteousness arise with healing in his wings".

The 'day' specified is referred to in earlier prophecies (e.g. *Joel 1*:15) as 'the day of the Lord', a day of 'destruction from the

Almighty'. It will commence immediately after the Great Tribulation, when the Lord Jesus Christ will come a second time to participate in the affairs of this world. He came the first time, as described hereafter (Part III), in the form of a lowly man to be our Saviour. He will come the second time in the unveiled splendour of His intrinsic character, first to judge all nations and peoples, with the result — to the proud and to the evil-doers — of the fiery fate predicted in *Malachi 4*:1, and then to reign over mankind. The verse constitutes a solemn warning to this world that there is a day of judgment coming for all the wicked: this will be indeed the dark, if short, aspect of the 'day of the Lord'. Verse 2 promises, however, a brighter prospect of 'the Sun of righteousness' arising, indicating the dawn of the millennial 'day' when Christ begins His righteous rule: a time of blessing to those, said the Lord, 'that fear my name'.

PAST EVENTS

PART III

CHRIST CONQUERS AT CALVARY

CHAPTER 6

THE PROMISED SAVIOUR APPEARS

With the coming of the Son of God into this world to deal at last with the question of sin, the most important event in time was reached, the central point of human history which has divided our calendar (B.C. and A.D.). As the Lord Jesus Christ He was born at Bethlehem in 3 B.C., lived a perfect life for 33½ years, and died a vicarious death, 'that through death He might destroy him that had the power of death, that is, the devil' (*Hebrews 2*:14). Yes, in this way, the long-promised Seed of the woman (*Genesis 3*:15) was to bruise the serpent's head; the greater than David to defeat the greater than Goliath (1 *Samuel 17*); the heavenly Isaac (see *Genesis 22*:1—14) to be sacrificed (as Isaac himself was not) on the cross by *His* Father; the mightier than Moses to deliver not only Israel but the world from the thraldom of a mightier than Pharaoh, through faith in *His* Blood, the Lamb of God. This was God's answer to Satan's attack on our first parents four thousand years previously, an attack which plunged mankind into sin and alienation from their Maker. The problem had been: how could man be restored to favour? God still loved His fallen creatures, but hated and must punish their sin; how could He be just and at the same time justify the sinner? Of course, He knew the solution to the problem even before it arose: an innocent and sinless man must die in the place of the guilty and sinful human race. Since no such perfect substitute could ever be found among the tainted sons of Adam's stock, the sinless Son of God must become the Son of man; the Eternal must step into time; the Glorious One (glimpsed by Daniel in his last vision) must veil His glory in human form; the Immortal must become mortal.

Yet, it was not sufficient that the Son of God should put on humanity and come to the earth as a man, die for our sins and return to Heaven. It was necessary that He should touch our life at all points, from infancy to maturity; that He sould identify Himself with us in all our trials and temptations, which He must endure and overcome without sin. In fact, from the time of His birth to the time of His death, He must be completely sinless: His being born, in the usual way, from tainted human parents, was thus ruled out. The answer was that He should be born of an earthly mother but begotten by His Heavenly Father. The early promise that Christ should be the Seed of the woman would then be fulfilled in this remarkable way. To us, of course, it appears miraculous that He should be born of a virgin, and those who do not believe in miracles would discredit it. If we believe in God and the Bible, which is full of miracles, we must accept them, as His supernatural acts. Even so, some of us may be puzzled as to how Christ could be born sinless from a human mother who, however exceptional, must have a sinful nature inherited from the fallen human race and must, in the normal way, pass it on to her offspring. The answer can only be that Christ was begotten by *God* Who could dominate the chosen mother's sinful nature. All things are possible with Him.

HIS VIRGIN BIRTH

God chose the virgin Mary, a pious young woman living in poor circumstances in the despised town of Nazareth in Galilee, to be the mother of our Lord. Betrothed at the time to a carpenter, Joseph, she was visited by the angel Gabriel who, after allaying her natural fear of him, said:

"Thou shalt conceive .... and bring forth a son, and call his name JESUS. He shall be great, and shall be called the Son of the Highest: and the Lord God shall give unto him the throne of his father David: and he shall reign over the house of Jacob for ever: and of his kingdom there shall be no end" (*Luke 1*:31—33).

Non-Jewish women would scarcely appreciate the thrill with which Mary would receive this announcement. She realised indeed how highly favoured and blessed among women she was, in being thus singled out to be the mother of the Messiah (aptly termed 'the desire of women' *Daniel 11*:37), the One Who was to fulfil Israel's national aspirations and be their King. Her question to the angel, 'How shall this be, seeing I know not a man?' may reveal some of the thoughts which might have flashed through her mind at the time. Would the promised Son be born of her as a result of her later intended marriage to Joseph? She doubtless knew that both she and her husband-to-be were in the direct line of descent from

King David; she through David's son Nathan, and Joseph through David's royal son Solomon. It thus seemed likely that the Son to be born might restore the kingdom to Israel, with Himself as their King by right of His human lineage. She realised, however, that the angel had as yet made no mention at all of Joseph, so she waited with intense interest for Gabriel's reply. He made it clear that Mary had been thinking along the wrong lines:

"The Holy Ghost shall come upon thee, and the power of the Highest shall overshadow thee: therefore also that holy thing which shall be born of thee shall be called the Son of God" (*Luke 1*:35).

She knew now that, in some miraculous way, *God* was to be the Father of the Holy Child. In due time, the Lord Jesus was born in Bethlehem, and His birth was heralded by the angels, announcing that He had come as the Saviour, to champion our cause against Satan and to provide the means whereby we may be freed from his bondage and reconciled to God. This was the essence of the 'good tidings of great joy, which shall be to all people' (*Luke* 2:10—11), as will be explained later.

Meanwhile Satan was not inactive but was seeking to destroy the Lord Jesus, as a child barely two years old, so that His mission would be thwarted at the outset. The Devil inspired Herod, the Roman king of Judaea, to attempt this murder when he heard from the wise men (*Matthew* 2:1—16) that Jesus had been born King of the Jews. We know that Satan was behind this plot by consideration of *Revelation 12*:1—5, where he is depicted as a dragon with seven heads and ten horns waiting for the woman (Israel) to give birth to her man-child (Christ), whom he would then devour. Needless to say, the Devil was not permitted to carry out his wicked purpose through Herod, although it caused the death of many Jewish children in the region of Bethlehem. The king paid the penalty for this mass murder in his own death: history tells us that it was from a loathsome disease.

The early life of our Lord is largely passed over in silence until He reaches thirty years of age, as the Bible is mainly concerned with his last three-and-a-half years, which we shall summarise under the next three headings.

HIS BAPTISM AND TEMPTATION

At thirty years of age, Christ was baptised in the River Jordan by John the Baptist, and when He came out of the water, the Holy Spirit, like a dove, descended upon Him, and a voice from Heaven said (*Matthew 3*:17): 'This is my beloved Son, in whom I am well pleased'. Thus did God publicly proclaim His Son and, at the same time, show His approval of the life which Jesus had thus far lived, evidently *the* perfect life, without spot or stain; sinless in thought, word and deed.

Yet at this stage, when Christ was about to enter upon His public ministry, it was necessary for Him to submit to the most severe testing of His character. For this purpose He went into the wilderness and, after fasting for forty days and nights, allowed Himself to be tempted by the Devil (see *Matthew 4*:1—11). This fast, while weakening Him physically, might well have strengthened Him morally and spiritually to meet the coming trial: but Satan was quick to take advantage of the Lord's hunger as the basis of his first temptation. He said:

"If thou be the Son of God, command that these stones be made bread". Now Jesus had come into the world to carry out God's plans and purposes, which required obedience, at every step, to His Father's will. To have acted independently of God, even for the sake of self-preservation, would have been a sin comparable with that of Adam in eating of the forbidden fruit. Thus Christ replies:

"It is written, Man shall not live by bread alone, but by every word that proceedeth out of the mouth of God".

It is note-worthy that Jesus, even though He was the Son of God, did not use His own words as such but quoted Scripture (*Deuteronomy 8*:3) — and His present followers might do well to copy His example. In the second temptation the Devil is subtle enough to use, or misuse, the sacred word, when he takes Jesus up to a pinnacle of the temple and says:

"If thou be the Son of God, cast thyself down: for it is written, He shall give his angels charge concerning thee: and in their hands they shall bear thee up, lest at any time thou dash thy foot against a stone" (*Psalm 91*:11—12).

Had Christ obeyed Satan in this instance, it would have been tempting God: perhaps an even greater sin than living independently of Him; so our Lord's answer was,

"It is written again, Thou shalt not tempt the Lord thy God" (*Deuteronomy 6*:16).

Satan is here, in effect, telling Jesus to put God to the test, to *prove* that God would do what He had promised in His word; a temptation to distrust God. The last temptation, in which Satan openly shows his hand, is the most blasphemous one. After taking Jesus up into a high mountain to show Him all the kingdoms of this world he said:

"All these things will I give thee, if thou wilt fall down and worship me".

That the Devil is indeed the prince of this world is attested by Scripture, by the Lord Himself in another place (*John 14*:30), and the position was doubtless originally assigned to him by God, Who has not yet seen fit to deprive him of it, in spite of his fall before man's creation, since when Satan and his demon hordes have continued to exercise their evil influence over human souls. Yet, as he faced the Son of God on the mountain top, clearly he had no right, even if he had the power, to barter his kingdoms to such a One for such an infamous purpose. As he asserts his own person, Jesus addresses him by name:

"Get thee hence, Satan; for it is written, Thou shalt worship the Lord thy God, and him only shalt thou serve" (*Deuteronomy 6*:5,13, etc.).

It seems that these temptations, particularly the last one, took place to some extent in the spiritual realm. It is recorded (*Matthew 4*:8) that 'the devil taketh him up into an exceeding high mountain, and sheweth him all the kingdoms of the world' and the parallel account (*Luke 4*:5) adds 'in a moment of time'. Satan, as a spiritual being not subject to physical laws, had the power to do as quoted, the Lord evidently allowing him. We must realise too that Jesus, though truly human, was still truly God, able at any time, if He wished, to exercise divine power and authority. Doubtless he could assume spiritual sight, enabling Him to see the personal form of the Devil and to see 'all the kingdoms of the world in a moment of time'.

When Satan had finished tempting Christ, he 'departed from him for a season'. This was the Devil's second attack on the Lord Jesus since His birth, and ended, like the first one through Herod, in defeat: Christ returned from the scene of battle, victorious.

HIS PUBLIC MINISTRY

One of the Lord's first public acts, after His temptation, was to go into the Jewish synagogue at Nazareth (*Luke 4*.16—21) and to read to the congregation a passage from the book of Isaiah:

"The Spirit of the Lord is upon me, because he hath anointed me to preach the gospel to the poor; he hath sent me to heal the broken-hearted, to preach deliverance to the captives, and recovering the sight of the blind, to set at liberty them that are bruised. To preach the acceptable year of the Lord''. In the prophecy (*Isaiah 61*:1—2) v.2 continues: 'And the day of vengeance of our God', which our Lord deliberatly omitted to read. He stopped in the middle of a sentence, closed the book and added,

''This day is the scripture fulfilled in your ears''.

He had come into the world as *Saviour,* initiating 'the acceptable year of the Lord'. This long period of His grace and favour (A.D.) is still with us today; the 'day of vengeance has not yet dawned and was therefore not mentioned by the Lord Jesus. The prophet's distant preview of what were in fact two separate events, separated by some two thousand years, appeared to him as one continuous happening. Yet as surely as Christ came the first time as Saviour, He will come to this earth a second time as Judge. As One or the Other we must all have to do with Him; what is your choice, reader?

Not only was the Lord Jesus Christ manifested by His own declaration in the synagogue at Nazareth, but also at Bethabara (about twenty miles south east of Nazareth, on the eastern bank of the Jordan) He was publicly acclaimed by John the Baptist to be 'the Lamb of God' which taketh away the sin of the world' (*John 1*:29). The Baptist further attested that he had baptised Jesus and seen the Spirit descending on Him, and that he was thus assured that He was the Son of God (vv.32—34). In this way the Lord Jesus was made known to the people of Palestine, among whom He would move the three years and more, showing to them and through their record to the world the very character of God, lived out in Himself. He first announced that the kingdom of God was at hand (*Mark 1*:15). By this He did *not* mean, as many imagined, that He had come to set up an earthly kingdom, by throwing off the Roman yoke and Himself becoming King of Israel. He meant that, by virtue of his sacrificial death which He was to suffer for the sin of the world, a *spiritual* kingdom would be born. It would consist of all loyal subjects who had obeyed His command, 'Repent ye, and believe the gospel' (v.15). After His death and resurrection, He commissioned His followers (*Mark 16*:15—16) to preach the same gospel. In this way the 'kingdom' (later called 'His church') increased and has since spread throughout the world to this day. Beginning with a small band of fishermen of Galilee, Andrew (Peter's brother), probably being the first to follow Jesus, it has grown into a vast company, people from every tribe and nation, Jew and Gentile, who have owned allegiance to their as-yet invisible King, the Lord Jesus Christ now in Heaven. In the hearts of this great host, Satan has been dethroned and his dominion broken; but alas he is still the prince of this world at large; from the time of Christ to the present day the huge majority have lived and died under the Devil's sway.

Jesus not only preached the gospel: He also taught the principles of godly living, healed the sick, gave sight to the blind, hearing to the deaf and speech to the dumb, and even raised the dead. He cast out demons from those possessed, walked on the sea, stilled the storm at a word, fed five thousand with five loaves and two small fishes, turned water into wine and showed His ability to read the thoughts and discern the inner motives of every individual. All these wonderful works — miracles to us — and many others, recorded in the four Gospels, plainly revealed His deity. Indeed, He repeatedly spoke of God as His Father and even said to Philip (*John 14*:9), in answer to his request to be shown the Father:

"Have I been so long time with you, and yet hast thou not known me, Philip? he that hath seen me hath seen the Father".

In His public ministry, the Lord thus sufficiently manifested God; He was then ready to undertake the *main work* for which He had come into the world: to deal with the sin question, which would necessitate His giving His life as a ransom for all.

HIS DEATH, RESURRECTION AND ASCENSION

The religious leaders of the Jews — the scribes and lawyers, the Pharisees and Sadducees — would not believe that Jesus was what He claimed to be, the Son of God, their Messiah. They plotted to kill Him, and eventually persuaded the Roman governor, Pontius Pilate, to condemn Him to death, after a mock trial in which Pilate found no fault in Him, but the Jewish people themselves gave the deciding voice against Him (*Matthew 27*:20—26). Jesus was beaten with the cruel Roman scourge and subjected to the coarse indignities of the Roman soldiers, who plaited a crown of thorns and thrust it upon His head. He was then led away outside the city wall of Jerusalem, where He was crucified between two thieves on the hill of Calvary. He was on the cross for six hours, from 9 a.m. to 3 p.m., and just before His expiry He cried with a loud voice,

"It is finished", adding "Father, into thy hands I commend my spirit" (*John 19*:30; *Luke 23*:46).

Yes, with a *shout* of victory He dismissed His Spirit, having accomplished the work He came to do — to die for our sins. His death was no ordinary one, it was a sacrificial offering: He said (*John 10*:17—18):

"I lay down my life .... No man taketh it from me, but I lay it down of myself. I have power to lay it down, and I have power to take it again".

It is true that He allowed wicked hands to crucify Him, but it was all part of the pre-determined plan of our salvation. The very day of his crucifixion was fore-ordained to be that of the Jewish passover, Friday the 14th Nisan (A.D. 32). The Jewish leaders, who were primarily responsible for His death, would have preferred it to be on any day but this their special feast day, the annual commemoration of the Passover, when Israel had been delivered from the hands of the Egyptians (1613 B.C.) but God had so decreed it, because Jesus was indeed the true Paschal Lamb. Through faith in His blood, shed on Calvary, we can be delivered from sin and Satan's power.

The body of Jesus was taken down from the cross by one of his followers, Joseph of Arimathea, who put it into his own new sepulchre, hewn out of a rock, and rolled a large stone against the opening. The next day, Saturday, the chief priests and Pharisees obtained Pilate's permission to set a guard at the tomb and seal the stone, on the pretext that His disciples might come to steal His body and make it appear as if He had risen from the dead, for He had said that He would rise the third day. Careful watch was doubtless kept that night, but just before the dawn of Sunday, 'There was a great earthquake: for the angel of the Lord descended from heaven, rolled back the stone .... and sat upon it. His countenance was like lightning, and his raiment white as snow: and for fear of him, the keepers did shake and become as dead men' (*Matthew 28*:2—4). The angel stayed to reassure the two women followers of Christ (Mary Magdalene and Mary, the mother of James and Joses, who had come early to the sepulchre in the hope of putting spices on the body of Jesus) and to tell them that He was risen from the dead. Later the risen Lord Himself appeared to Mary Magdelene, to Peter, to two on a Sunday walk from Jerusalem to Emmaus, and to a group of disciples the same evening. For the next forty days Christ was seen from time to time by His followers and finally, before His ascension, by all the apostles. Having commanded them to preach the gospel to every creature, and promised them the gift of the Holy Spirit to empower them, He was 'taken up and a cloud received him out of their sight' (*Acts 1*:8—11). While they still gazed upward, two angels stood beside them and said.

"This same Jesus, which is taken from you into heaven, shall so come in like manner as ye have seen him go into heaven".

That angelic promise we believe will shortly be fulfilled.

DESCRIPTION OF THE PERSON OF OUR SAVIOUR

The following was taken from a manuscript copied from an original letter of Publius Lentullus, at Rome.

It being the custom of Roman Governors to advertise the Senate and people of such material things as happened in their provinces in the days of Tiberius Caesar, Publius Lentullus, President of Indes, wrote the following letter to the Senate concerning OUR SAVIOUR.

"There appeared in these days a man of great virtue named JESUS CHRIST who is yet living amongst us, and of the Gentiles is accepted for a Prophet of Truth, but his own disciples call him the SON of GOD; he raiseth the dead and cureth all manner of diseases. A man of stature somewhat tall and comely, with very reverent countenance, such as the beholder may both love and fear: his hair of the colour of a chestnut full ripe, plain to his ears whence downwards it is more orient and curling and wavering about his shoulders. In the midst of his head is a seam or partition in his hair, after the manner of the Nazarites. His forehead plain and very delicate; his face without spot or wrinkle, beautified with a lovely red, his nose and mouth so formed that nothing can be reprehended; his beard thickish, in colour like his hair, not very long but forked; his look innocent and mature; his eyes grey, clear and quick. In reproving he is terrible, in admonishing courteous, and fair spoken; pleasant in conversation mixed with gravity. It cannot be remembered that any have seen him laugh, but many have seen him weep. In proportion of body most excellent; his hands and arms most delicate to behold: In speaking very temperate, modest and wise. A man for his singular beauty, surpassing the children of men."

CHAPTER 7

THE GOOD NEWS PREACHED

Now that Christ had died and risen again, the Gospel was to be told by His followers to everybody, beginning at Jerusalem and reaching out in ever-widening circles to the whole world. Readers of the previous six chapters of this book should already have some idea of what is meant by the Gospel. In its simplest form it is the good news to fallen man, born in sin and doomed by a holy God, that 'Christ died for our sins, according to the scriptures; and that he was buried, and that he rose again the third day according to the scriptures' (1 *Corinthians 15*:3—4). Through this fundamental fact we who are lost can be saved, as we shall explain under the next two headings.

THE MEANS OF SALVATION

We must first realise that, by no deeds of our own can we merit salvation: our only hope is in the intervention of God on our behalf. Yet He, in His perfect holiness, could make no contact with sinful man; a suitable mediator was required, able to approach God and man: the Son of God volunteered to act in this capacity. In order to do this, He, Who was co-equal with God, had to become man, and that was not all: He must provide a just basis for man's reconciliation to God. By Adam's disobedience, man had become corrupted by sin; henceforward God passed upon him the following verdict (*Romans 3*:10—18).

"There is none righteous, no, not one: there is none that understandeth, there is none that seeketh after God. They are all gone out of the way, they are together become unprofitable; there is none that doeth good, no, not one. Their throat is an open sepulchre; with their tongues they have used deceit; the poison of asps is under their lips: whose mouth is full of cursing and bitterness: their feet are swift to shed blood: destruction and misery are in their ways: and the way of peace have they not known: there is no fear of God before their eyes''.

The tragedy is that, being born in sin, we cannot see our true condition, we are spiritually blind. Not only are we corrupted by sin but also we are under the control of Satan (*Ephesians* 2:2; 2 *Timothy* 2:26), the prince of the 'power of the air', who forces us to walk in his steps — although, of course, we are quite unaware of it.

Such were the people that Christ must reconcile to His Father, God. Yet, at the same time, they must be freed from the Devil's captivity; a ransom price had to be paid before his prisoners could be offered their release. The cost of our redemption was, in fact, the precious life's Blood of the Lord Jesus Christ, 'as of a lamb without blemish and without spot' (1 *Peter 1*:18—19). He died, 'the Just for the unjust, that he might bring us to God' (1 *Peter 3*:18): the great gulf between us and God, because of the first man's sin, has been bridged. God laid on His Son the sins of the world; the penalty, death, Christ submitted to, and *His* death was sufficient to atone for all the sins of humanity. On God's side everything has been done for the complete justification of every individual. Yet man has a free will, given to him by God, so He will not force our allegiance to Him. By the exercise of his will, in a decisive act against His Maker, Adam was lost and a captive to Satan, whom — instead of God — he had accepted. It must also be by a decisive act of the human will that each of us can be saved and freed from the Devil's domination. What this act is, and some of the blessings it results in, will now be explained.

THE WAY OF SALVATION

The decisive act for salvation involves two steps, 'repentance toward God, and faith toward our Lord Jesus Christ' (*Acts 20*:21). The first step requires a *change* in our attitude to God, a turning to Him, a seeking after Him. Hitherto we followed our own way, astray from God on the broad road that leads to destruction (*Matthew 7*:13). The admission of our sinfulness and our turning to God for pardon constitutes true repentance. 'God .... now *commandeth* all men everywhere to repent' (*Acts 17*:30).

The next step entails our looking to the Lord Jesus Christ, God the *Son*, and a personal belief in him:

'Believe on the Lord Jesus Christ and thou shall be saved' (*Acts*

16:31). 'For God so loved the world, that he gave his only begotten Son, that whosoever believeth in him should not perish (be lost eternally), but have everlasting life' (*John 3*:16). 'Believing' in Him is really *receiving* Him as one's own personal Saviour: 'But as many as received him, to them gave he power to become the sons of God, even to them that believe on his name: which were born, not of blood, nor of the will of the flesh, nor of the will of man, but of God' (*John 1*:12—13). We thus experience a new birth, a spiritual regeneration, which is not a natural birth and is not obtained as a result of any human effort, but is brought about by God Himself. The third Person of the triune God, the Holy Spirit, comes to indwell us and we enter upon a new life, which He empowers us to live in a way that pleases God, profits our neighbour and is a joy to ourselves; moreover, it does not terminate at death but continues in the after-life in Heaven. The new life is imparted to us *as soon as we* believe: He that believeth on the Son *hath* everlasting life' (*John 3*:36). At the same time, we also *receive* Him and with Him comes the life, as He *is* the life: 'He that hath the Son hath life' (1 *John 5*:12). He is depicted as knocking at our heart's door (*Revelation 3*:20):

"Behold, I stand at the door and knock: if any man hear my voice and open the door, I will come into him".

Sad to say, He has been knocking for a very long time at many hearts and is still refused admittance. Holman Hunt, the famous artist, has tried to catch the scene in his painting, 'The Light of the World', where Jesus is shown knocking at a door which has no handle on the outside and which is overgrown by weeds — a proof that it had not been opened for a considerable time.

Certainly Christ will never force His way into our lives; He waits patiently to give us ample time to open to Him. Doubtless, if we do not admit Him Satan will not be dethroned from our hearts and will continue to do his utmost to prevent our letting the Saviour in. The Devil is very strong but he knows that he must relinquish us when the One, Who is stronger than he, is admitted to keep the citadel of our hearts. Satan is a hard taskmaster, and although he is subtle enough to try to make us self satisfied so that we shall wish for no fuller life, which is available for us with Christ as our Master, he has no love whatever for us and will readily crush us to serve his own evil purposes. In complete contrast, the abundant life in Christ is such that 'all things work together for good' (*Romans 8*:28); that in all our troubles we shall be 'more than conquerers through him that loved us' (v.37); that our journey through this mortal life may be increasingly clear until it opens out on the sunlit river of eternity, where our onward course on its smooth waters will be unmistakeable, 'the path of the just is as the shining light, that shineth more and more unto the perfect day' (*Proverbs 4*:18). One of Satan's most plausible arguments, which he will endeavour to put into our minds to deter us from receiving Christ, is that our life will then be too restricted and exacting for us: nothing is farther from the truth; our Lord Himself said (*Matthew 11*:28—29):

"Come unto me, all ye that labour and are heavy laden, and I will give you *rest*. Take my yoke upon you, and learn of me; for I am meek and lowly in heart: and ye shall find rest in your souls. For my yoke is *easy* and my burden is *light*".

Receiving Him results in our being yoked to Him, so that He will always bear the heavy end. These are some of the benefits which are promised to us in the Gospel of our Lord Jesus Christ as soon as we are willing to repent and believe and are saved.

The first to preach the 'Good News' was the apostle Peter in Jerusalem on the day of Pentecost (Whitsunday) in A.D. 32 to a multitude of Jews from 'every nation under heaven' (*Acts* 2:5), doubtless having come to the city for the Feast. Peter made the most of this opportunity, given by God, to speak to this great gathering, with the result that 3,000 'gladly received his word' (v.41) and initiated the church of Christ. They were all baptized, met together in the temple, and 'continued steadfastly in the apostles' doctrine and fellowship, and in breaking of bread, and in prayers', etc. (see vv.42—47). This early Church increased daily and when Peter again preached, on the occasion of the healing of the lame man outside the temple (*Acts 3*), about 5,000 believed (*Acts 4*:4). If the conversions of such multitudes marked the opening of the Gospel era, the salvation of even larger numbers in our own times (mainly as a result of great evangelistic crusades) may be a sign that the era is almost at its close, such being gathered in before it is too late. If 'the acceptable year of the Lord' is indeed nearly over, 'the day of vengeance' fast approaches and 'How shall we escape if we neglect so great salvation' (*Hebrews* 2:3).

Although Satan suffered an overthrow by Christ's conquest at Calvary, he is still active behind the scenes and is waiting to manifest himself publicly as soon as the Church is complete and translated to Heaven. He cannot reveal himself until she is out of the way and her purifying and restraining influence on the world is removed, and we shall now describe this latter occurrence under 'Coming Events'. This section deals with 'things which must shortly come to pass' (*Revelation 1*:1), and constitutes perhaps the major part of the present work. The sole source of information on the subject is of course the Bible (particularly *The Revelation*), because its Author, God, is the only One Who can know the future.

COMING EVENTS

CHAPTER 8

THE DAY OF JESUS CHRIST IN HEAVEN

The 'day' opens with the coming of our Lord for all his saints to take them to be with Himself in Heaven, where it proceeds concurrently with the Beast's rule on earth during the last seven years of the age, the 'day' thus denoting this period of time. The day is first mentioned by the apostle Paul who, writing to the local church at Corinth, expresses the hope that she may be 'blameless in *the day of our Lord Jesus Christ*' (1 *Corinthians 1*:8). He later explains what he means by this, as follows:

"For we must all appear before the judgment seat of Christ, that every one may receive the things done in his body, whether it be good or bad" (2 *Corinthians 5*:10).

Evidently he is referring to a future time when he and the members of this local church, together with all the saints throughout the ages, will be assembled before Christ to give an account of what they have done on earth. This judgment is the first *recorded* event of 'the day of our Lord Jesus Christ', but it clearly presupposes that all those judged have been resurrected or, if alive, transformed, and the combined group translated to Heaven. We shall therefore consider the translation of the saints as the first actual event of 'the day'. Certainly the gathering together of all His saints to be for ever with Him will, for Christ, be at least a joyous precursor of His 'day' in Heaven.

THE TRANSLATION OF THE SAINTS

This event may occur at any time in the near future; there is nothing earlier, predicted in Scripture, that has yet to be fulfilled. In the Old Testament there is no direct reference to it, but it is symbolised in the life of *Enoch,* the seventh from Adam (see *Genesis 5*). The relevant incident (v.24) is pin-pointed in the New Testament catalogue of the faithful (*Hebrews 11*):

"By faith Enoch was translated that he sould not see death: and was not found, because God had translated him: for before his translation he had this testimony, that he pleased God" (v.5).

Referring back to the original record (*Genesis 5*:21—24):

"And Enoch lived sixty and five years and begat Methuselah: and Enoch walked with God after he begat Methuselah three hundred years, and begat sons and daughters: and all the days of Enoch were three hundred sixty and five years: and Enoch walked with God: and he was not; for God took him".

His age was very great by our standards, but had he not been translated he might well have reached the far greater age of early mankind approximately to 900 years; certainly his son Methuselah attained to 969 years, the oldest man of all time. The first man, Adam, lived to 930 years, and in fact might never have died, apart from mortal injury if he had not sinned. God had told him that, concerning the forbidden tree, 'in *the day* that thou eatest thereof thou shalt surely die'. Satan, deliberately taking 'the day' in the literal sense, contradicted the Lord's assertion; but it was true, even literally, from His point of view in which 'one day is with the Lord as a thousand years, and a thousand years as one day' (2 *Peter 3*:8). Nobody, not even Methuselah, was allowed to reach the age of a thousand years, and gradually the age of man, as his corrupt nature developed, declined to the present level of around seventy years.

In the case of Enoch there was a change in his character afer the birth of Methuselah, which induced him to 'walk with God'. Before then, presumably, he had walked his own way in independence of his Maker, just as we do by nature until, if ever, we experience a change of heart. We are given no clue as to the reason for Enoch's transformation except that it was in some way connected with the birth of his son, Methuselah. A study of the name affords us some information on the subject. We know that names were then more significant than they are now; they were frequently given to denote some special incident in the life of the parent such was the case with 'Cain', the first son to be born into this world (see *Genesis 4*:1). 'Methuselah' means 'when he is dead it shall come'. Apparently Enoch had a revelation from God that some catastrophe was approaching, but that it would not occur until the death of the son just born to him. Enoch was so impressed with this divine communication that he incorporated it into the name of his son as a continuous reminder of it to him. Such a contact with God could well have been the cause of Enoch's change of life — to one of unbroken fellowship with the Lord that would last for three hundred years, as far as his mortal existence was concerned. Thereafter, God decided to call him up to Heaven so that, in a newly-given spiritual body, the fellowship would continue for ever. In the meantime, as revealed to him at the birth of his son, a catastrophe *did* occur when Methuselah died; it was no less than the Flood, already described. Moreover, reference to the chronology of the period (Table 1, Appendix III) proves that this deluge came upon the earth *in the very year* of Methuselah's death, thus fulfilling God's revelation to Enoch. It is characteristic of God's long-suffering that, having declared that the catastrophe would not take place until Methuselah died, this man's life was prolonged (to reach 969, the highest age of mankind) so that the Flood would be deferred as long as possible.

In the case of the translation of *all* the saints — of whom Enoch was one, translated before the time — it will obviously include *the faithful, like Enoch, of Old Testament times.* A few of these worthies, beginning with Abel, are listed in the passage already referred to (*Hebrews 11*), those singled out by name: Enoch, Noah, Abraham and Sarah (his wife), Isaac, Jacob, Joseph, Moses, Rahab (see *Joshua 2; 6*:23,25), Gideon, Barak, Samson, Jepthah (see *Judges 11*), David and Samuel. Many others, unnamed but illustrious for their deeds of faith, are added to this gallery of the faithful. For example, Daniel in the lion's den can be recognised, as also his three friends in the burning fiery furnace; see *Daniel 6* and *3* respectively. The writer to the Hebrews calls these earlier representatives of the faith 'the elders' (*Hebrews 11*:2) and he concludes with the words (vv.39—40):

"And these all, having obtained a good report through faith, received not the promise: God having provided some better thing (the Church) for us (members of the Church), that they (all the saints of the Old Testament, pre-Church era) without us should not be made perfect".

Evidently then, both Old Testament and New Testament saints will be translated ('made perfect') together, but it does not follow that both are included in the Church. The dividing line comes, in fact, with John the Baptist, of whom Christ said (*Matthew 11*:11):

"Among them that are born of women there hath not risen a greater than John the Baptist: notwithstanding he that is least in the kingdom of heaven (the Church, essentially) is greater than he''.

John was the last representative of the Old Testament saints; Christ proclaimed the inauguration of a new kingdom, a new order of believers, His Church which He Himself would build 'upon the foundation of the apostles and prophets' (*Ephesians 2*:20; see also *3*:5). The apostles were the first representatives of the Church, and the 'prophets' were gifted with a new type of prophecy, not in the Old Testament sense of foretelling the future or of directly communicating the mind of God with their 'Thus saith the Lord'; but in expounding the Scripture, under the inspiration of God, to the building up of the Church. Thus these New Testament prophets are coupled with the apostles as occupying the basic position of the new kingdom, which, corporately, would be a 'kingdom of priests': every member would have the responsibility of offering praise to God and of petitioning Him on behalf of the people.

The translation of the combined groups of Old Testament and New Testament believers, symbolised together as *twenty four elders*, is seen in the apostle John's vision as having just occurred along with his own translation (in spirit) to Heaven (*Revelation 4*:1—4).

''After this I looked, and behold, a door was opened in heaven: and the first voice which I heard was as it were of a trumpet talking with me; which said, Come up hither, and I will show thee things which must be hereafter. And immediately I was in the spirit: and, behold, a throne was set in heaven, and one sat on the throne. And he that sat was to look upon like a jasper and a sardine stone: and there was a rainbow round the throne, in sight like an emerald. And round about the throne were four and twenty seats (thrones): and upon the seats I saw four and twenty elders sitting, clothed in white raiment; and they had on their heads crowns of gold''.

This vision is seen immediately after the one depicting the complete course of the Church from her foundation to her translation (*Revelation 2—3*). It is hence reasonable to conclude that she is thereafter in Heaven. Yet the Church, as such, disappears from the scene from Ch.4 onwards. This is understandable if, as we believe, she is translated not alone but in company with the Old Testament saints — the twenty four elders fittingly portray the united assembly. We have already seen that the Old Testament saints in the catalogue of the faithful (*Hebrews 11*), are represented by 'the elders'. Also, the first apostles (originally the twelve disciples) of the Church are classed as 'the elders' (see *Acts 11*:30; *21*:18; 1 *Peter* 5:1; 2 *John 1*). The term was thereafter used, collectively, for those who governed every local church (*Acts 14*:23); each church did not have *one* man in charge, as is the rule in Christendom today; Christ *only* was the invisible Head of the church, and the members, including the elders, were corporately the Body. From all the foregoing considerations we must conclude that the Old Testament saints will participate in the translation as well as the Church of the present age and that the combined groups in Heaven are represented by the twenty four elders. The common view that the Church only will be translated is untenable. *It is inconceivable that she should be taken and the Old Testament saints who have, as it were, waited so long for Christ's coming, should be left behind.*

We come now to the few *direct* references to the translation in the New Testament; there are only a few because the event will doubtless be a secret one, like Enoch's translation. The world at large will not see it happen; they will but be aware, very soon, that a very large company of people have suddenly disappeared from their midst. The first allusion to it is by our Lord (*John 14*:1—4), addressing His disciples privately at the Last Supper:

"Let not your heart be troubled; ye believe in God, believe also in me. In my Father's house are many mansions: if it were not so, I would have told you. And if I go and prepare a place for you. *I will come again,* and receive you unto myself; that where I am, there ye may be also".

Further light is thrown on the event, by Paul, writing to the Gentile churches at Corinth and Thessalonica:

"Behold, I show you a mystery; we shall not all sleep (die), but we shall all be changed, in a moment, in the twinkling of an eye, at the last trump: for the trumpet shall sound, and the dead shall be *raised incorruptible, and we (the living) shall be changed. For this corruption must put on incorruption, and this mortal must put on immortality*" (1 *Corinthians 15*:51—53); and "For this we say unto you by the word of the Lord, that we which are alive and remain unto the coming of the Lord shall not prevent (precede) them which are asleep. For the Lord himself shall descend from heaven *with a shout, with the voice of the archangel,* and with the trump of God: and the dead in Christ shall rise first: then we which are alive and remain *shall be caught up together with them in the clouds, to meet the Lord in the air:* and so shall we ever be with the Lord" (1 *Thessalonians 4*:15—17).

The italicised sections of the above two passages provide successively new information, following the brief 'I will come again and receive you unto myself' of Christ. Putting all these facts together we learn that when the Lord Jesus Christ comes again, in fulfilment of His promise to His disciples, He will descend from Heaven with a summons which will first raise from the dead all who are classed as 'in Christ'. At first sight these may appear to be the members of His Church only, from the earliest disciples to the last believer of these closing days. In another passage, however, He refers to His 'sheep' (*John 10*:1—29), which constitute those for whom He died (v.15), who follow Him and to whom He gives eternal life (vv.27—28). None of these sheep will 'perish' (v.28); they are all safely enclosed in the double grasp of both Christ and His Father (vv.28—29). Thus all the sheep are 'in Christ' and as such they all will be translated. Yet, evidently (v.16), His sheep include more than one category: those existing before He came into the world, and the 'other sheep' which He would bring into the one fold. The latter evidently denote all the members of His Church but the former 'sheep' doubtless embrace all His pre-Church followers, both Jews and Gentiles. The two companies, united in 'one fold' with its full complement of 'sheep', will together be called for by the Good Shepherd when He comes again.

The 'shout' of the descending Lord, having brought to life the dead 'in Christ', then transforms the living, both being given immortal bodies. Respecting the dead, their spirits which have been in Paradise will be united to their resurrected bodies. Paradise is the place of the departed spirits of the Lord's 'sheep', to which His spirit went after His death on the cross. He had said to the repentant thief, crucified with Him:

"Verily I say unto thee, Today shalt thou be with me in paradise" (*Luke 23*:43).

Our Lord had previously (*Luke 16*:22) spoken of the place as 'Abraham's bosom', to indicate that the spirit of the patriarch, presiding there, would be a source of comfort to the other inmates, notably to the newly admitted spirits such as Lazarus the erstwhile beggar (vv.23,25). Apparently Paradise (Gr. for 'garden'), like Eden's garden in the beginning but in a spiritual sense, will be a region of enjoyment, in fellowship with the Spirit of Christ Who will reign there; for Paul said (2 *Corinthians 5*:8) that 'to be absent from the body' was 'to be present with the Lord'. The place is presumably in Heaven, within the same region — 'under the altar' (*Revelation 6*:9) — as the abiding-place of the souls of the post-Church saints, those who will suffer presecution and martydom under the Beast during the last seven years of the age.

Almost simultaneously to the Lord's shout, come the 'voice of the archangel and the trump of God', perhaps to marshal and call upwards the saints whom the Lord, a moment before, had raised or changed. The angel's mission may also be to escort the ordered host to meet the Lord in the clouds and thence to the 'Father's house' (Heaven), to the 'many mansions' prepared for them by Christ.

THE JUDGMENT SEAT OF CHRIST

Judgment, on any occasion, is God's 'strange work' (*Isaiah 28*:21), foreign to His character of love and mercy; Christ Himself, while on earth, was full of compassion (*Matthew 9*:36 etc.). Yet, consistent with His holiness, justice must be administered. When it is necessary the judgment is usually executed speedily, and doubtless that of His saints at His judgment seat will be no exception, occurring soon after their translation. Of course, there will be no question of any one here being punished for an offence because 'Jesus .... was delivered (to death) for our offences, and was raised again for our justification' (*Romans 4*:24—25), that is, for us who believe (His Church) as well as for the Old Testament saints like Abraham (vv.3, 16—23). To them and to us, at the judgment seat, no sin at all can be imputed; all believers are counted righteous (vv.3—8); but all will be held responsible, from the point of view of receiving a reward or not, for 'the things done in his body' (2 *Corinthians 5*:10, previously quoted in full on p.73), that is, while on earth.

The judgment seat (Gr. 'bema') is first mentioned by Paul when writing to the church in Rome (*Romans 14*:10,12):

"But why dost thou judge thy brother (in the faith) or why dost thou set at nought thy brother? for we shall all stand before the judgment seat of Christ .... So then every one of us shall give account of himself to God".

To the church at Corinth he writes (1 *Corinthians 4*:5):

"Therefore judge nothing before the time, until the Lord come, who both will bring to light the hidden things of darkness, and will make manifest the counsels of the hearts: and then shall every man have praise of God".

These are certainly words for Christians today; it is so easy to judge other Christians, more often than not wrongfully because their actuating motives cannot be fully discerned — only the Lord knows them. If such unjust criticisms and mistaken attitudes are not exposed and confessed in this life — and they seldom are — it is only just that they should be made public in the after-life, and the wrong made right.

Another obvious reference to the judgment seat of Christ, although not actually thus named, is made by the apostle, again addressing the church in Corinth (1 *Corinthians 3*:9—17):

"For we are labourers together with God .... ye are God's building. According to the grace of God which is given unto me, as a wise master builder, I have laid the foundation, and another buildeth thereon. But let every man take heed how he buildeth thereupon. For other foundation can no man lay than that is laid, which is Jesus Christ. Now if any man build upon this foundation gold, silver, precious stones, wood, hay, stubble; every man's work shall be made manifest: for *the day* (i.e. of Jesus Christ) shall declare it, because it shall be revealed by fire; and the fire shall try every man's work of what sort it is. If any man's work abide which he has built thereupon, he shall receive a reward. If any man's work shall be burned, he shall suffer loss: but *he himself shall be saved;* yet so as by fire. Know ye not that ye are the temple of God, and that the Spirit of God dwelleth in you? If any man defile (corrupt) the temple of God, him shall God destroy; for the temple of God is holy, which temple ye are".

These remarks, like Paul's others on the subject, were to local churches in particular and to the Church in general, to all the members throughout the Christian era. Clearly he could have no message for the past and gone Old Testament saints, who will nevertheless be judged according to the same principles.

Of course, in the spiritual realm of Heaven there will be no literal fire; the word is used as a symbol of the fiery judgment of Christ's all-searching eyes, which are elsewhere depicted (*Revelation 1*:14) in fact as 'a flame of fire'. The 'work' of each saint present before Him will be critically assessed and revealed as it really is, to be recompensed or brought to nothing as the case may be. It is portrayed as that of a builder constructing a house: perhaps the simple children's chorus will explain this:

"We are building day by day in our work and in our play;
Building a house not made with hands,
Following Jesu's perfect plans;
Little builders all are we, building for eternity"

The foundation of our Christian 'building' is the Lord Jesus Himself, Who comes into our life as soon as we accept Him as our personal Saviour; if any other Christian is the means of our conversion, he will be regarded as laying the foundation (like Paul, the 'wise master-builder') and will get the credit for it. With the foundation laid, then, we immediately — consciously or unconsciously — begin to build thereon the 'house', our Christian life; the things we think and say and do. Our house, in one sense our body, has a new tenant, formerly Satan, now Christ, Who enables us by His Spirit to live as we should. Yet the building material we erect on the foundation — reverting to the original figure — may be good or bad. The good is represented as 'gold, silver, precious stones'; the bad as 'wood, hay, stubble'. The former are durable substances, the latter perishable. According to scriptural typology, gold, silver and precious stones could symbolise the nature of God, the redemption of man and individual members of Christ's Church respectively. Whatever we do for the glory of God, towards the redemption of our fellows and by actually winning them for Christ will be rewarded by Him at His judgment seat. Wood, hay and stubble (the worthless stalks left after harvesting the corn) may denote the human nature of man, his transient glory and the wicked (i.e. the unbelieving) as individuals, respectively. What we do, as Christians, from purely humanitarian purposes, from a desire to glorify man, and in association with unbelievers, would thus be adjudged as of no value.

The passage emphasises that even the saint with least to show, with all his work 'burnt up', will *himself* never be rejected — he is saved for time and for eternity, as already pointed out. Yet Paul has to warn the Corinthian believers of the danger of any one being cut off in one's mortal life on account of one's defiling the 'temple of God' (here, the local church at Corinth). The apostle evidently had in mind the particular case reported to them later (1 *Corinthian* 5:1—5), which the church had condoned rather than condemned — Corinth was notorious for its immorality, which had infected even the church. The principle emerges that if a saint should sin (a contradiction in terms, but it is sadly possible) he must be punished for it in *this* life, not in the hereafter. A sin sufficiently grave could be punishable by death: in the above instance, a deliverance into the hand of Satan 'for the destruction of the flesh, that the spirit may be saved in the day of the Lord Jesus' (v.5). Of course, the principle enunciated does not apply in the case of a sin that is confessed to God: 'If we confess our sins, he is faithful and just to forgive us our sins, and to cleanse us from all unrighteousness' (1 *John 1*:9). This passage alludes only to believers in Christ (see 1 *John 5*:13). For His sake their sins, when confessed to God, are forgiven forthwith and the cleansing follows in due time, doubtless involving the forsaking of the sin in question (*Proverbs 28*:13).

LIFE IN HEAVEN DURING THE DAY OF CHRIST

We have seen that the saints, as soon as they are translated to Heaven — an event frequently known as 'the rapture', because they are 'caught-up' — are depicted as *twenty four elders*. It is under this title, therefore, that we must look for information about them in Heaven during the course of their seven years there. Since the title occurs only between *Revelation 4*:4, already quoted, and *Revelation 19*:4, we shall consider the relevant passages within this section. The first reference to the twenty four elders indicates, by the use of the terms 'crowns' and 'thrones', that they will occupy a position of kingly authority in Heaven, around the throne of God Himself. Their 'white raiment', symbolic of righteousness — purity, rightness of thought and behaviour; Christlikeness, in a word — is fitting 'apparel'for the presence of God.

They serve and worship Him, as the succeeding verses and chapters show, in close co-operation with *four Beings* who are God's constant attendants, capable of executing His purposes with all speed and intelligence — typified by their each having 'six wings' and being 'full of eyes'. The seer, John, designates them as 'beasts' because they appear to him largely in such forms: 'And the first beast was like a lion, and the second beast was like a calf, and the third beast had a face like a man, and the fourth beast was like a flying eagle'. The four 'living creatures' of Ezekiel's version (*Ezekiel 1*:4—24) undoubtedly represent the same Beings but with more detail and complexity: only a few features can be considered here. The first thing to be noticed is that the 'creatures' are under the direct control of the 'spirit' (evidently the Holy Spirit of God), and move as 'a flash of lightning' and in perfect union to carry out their commission without any possible deviation. This undeflected movement is further emphasised by the 'wheels' with which the creatures are connected; in fact, the spirit of each of them is said to be *in* the wheels, as if their thoughts are automatically transmitted to action. The colour of the wheels, like 'a *beryl*', links these Beings with Christ in His pre-incarnate form, as the man clothed in linen and whose body was like the beryl (*Daniel 10*:6). It may be that they are under His immediate control, as it were His executive, He being the divine *Operator* of the Trinity, as we stated at the beginning of this book. Yet, they are energized by the Holy Spirit, as already seen, and are always in contact with God (the Father) from Whom the divine plans originate. Thus these Beings appear to be an integral part of the Triune Godhead as far as the carrying out of the divine Will is concerned, but they evidently have their own personality in regard to their voluntary worship of God, in which they are joined by the twenty four elders, as noted.

As we further consider these elders in Heaven, as seen in vision by John, the scene moves to focus our attention on the Lamb (*Revelation 5*), the Lord Jesus Christ Himself, especially on His worthiness to open the 'book .... sealed with seven seals', in the right hand of God seated on the throne:

"In the midst of the throne and of the four beasts, and in the midst of the elders, stood a Lamb as it had been slain, having seven horns and seven eyes, which are the seven Spirits of God sent forth into all the earth. And he came and took the book out of the right hand of him that sat upon the throne. And when he had taken the book, the four beasts and four and twenty elders fell down before the Lamb, having every one of them harps, and golden vials full of odours, which are the prayers of saints. and they sang a new song, saying, Thou are worthy to take the book, and to open the seals thereof: for thou was slain, and hast redeemed us to God by thy blood out of every kindred, and tongue, and people, and nation; and hast made us unto our God kings and priests: and we shall reign on the earth" (vv.6—10).

A few comments will explain this passage. The characters are plain enough at this stage of our studies. The Lord Jesus appearing as a Lamb in this setting is to emphasise the importance of His sacrificial death at Calvary, which the elders fittingly affirm has been the means of their redemption, and which is the ground of Christ's worthiness to open the book. Of course, the forms in which the characters appear in the vision must be symbolic. Christ cannot be conceived as looking like an actual lamb, any more than those we have termed the 'four Beings' will really be four beasts, or the translated saints twenty four elders. Concerning the other features of the passage, the 'golden vials full of odours (incense)' are, in fact, stated as signifying 'the prayers of saints'. These saints are evidently those of the post-Church period: appropriately, their agonising petitions are mediated by their fellow-saints (the twenty four elders) in Heaven. The 'harps' possessed by these 'elders' doubtless produce heavenly music on a much grander — because spiritual — scale than any earthly melody. Indubitably, harmony and peace and unalloyed joy have always reigned in Heaven, but the presence of the saints there will bring added bliss. Accompanied on their 'harps', they burst into a *new* song, never heard in Heaven before, because it is a song of thanksgiving and praise to Christ, the Lamb, for His work of redemption on their behalf. This note struck by the saints is the signal for countless angels to join in worshipping the Lamb, leading to a universal ascription of 'blessing, and honour, and glory, and power' to both God and the Lamb.

The scene now reverts to the seven-sealed book which the Lamb had taken from the hand of His Father, God, and now proceeds to break the seals. A study of *Revelation 6—11* makes it clear that the 'book' is not just a programme of the things coming to pass during the last seven years of the age — a series of calamities under the Beast's reign of terror — but consists, in symbol form of those calamities themselves, successively unleashed upon the world at the opening of each seal. It is evident that these events, although some of them will be brought about by the Beast (as we shall see), are all under the ultimate control of God and transpire at the precise moment of His timing. The opening of the fifth seal (*Revelation 6*:9—11) brings before us a scene which, unlike those of the other seals, comes to pass exclusively in Heaven, so we shall describe it as this point.

The Fifth Seal. This relates to the disembodied souls of 'them that were slain for the word of God, and for the testimony which they held', probably those who would not worship the Beast during the first half of his seven-year rule. Their souls are seen 'under the altar' (v.9), presumably 'the golden altar' in Heaven (*Revelation 8*:3). They are given 'white robes' and told 'to rest yet for a little season, until their fellowservants also and their brethren should be killed as they were, should be fulfilled' (*Revelation 6*:11). Apparently these later martyrs are those of *Revelation 7*:9—17, who are seen, after death, also as a white-robed company but with 'palms in their hands' and having come 'out of great tribulation' — evidently the latter 3½-year period of the last septennium. The words of consolation (cited above) would doubtless be addressed to both companies, possibly by the twenty four elders who as already mentioned, may be able to hear 'the prayers of saints' (*Revelation* 5:8).

Regarding the other seals — relating to events on *earth* during the last septennium of the age — these will be considered, along with other events occurring in the period (*Revelation 12—18*), in our chapters 9—11 which follow. Before these, however, we shall describe 'the marriage supper of the Lamb' which will be the last event *in Heaven* before or Lord's return at the end of the age (*Revelation 19*:7—9).

THE MARRIAGE SUPPER OF THE LAMB

The twenty four elders continue to appear on the scene, serving and worshipping God in Heaven, until their seven years there are almost completed and preparations are made for the marriage of the Lamb. At this point (*Revelation 19*:4), when they worship God for the last time as a group of 'elders', they are seen no more as such but experience a division into their two original companies: the Old Testament saints, as we have termed them, and the Church, comprising all the saints of this present era (A.D.). The Church becomes the Bride of the Lamb, as Paul makes clear (*Ephesians* 5:22—23,25,31—32):

"Wives, submit yourselves unto your own husbands, as unto the Lord. For the husband is the head of the wife, even as Christ is the head of the church .... Husbands, love your wives, even as Christ loved the church, and gave himself for it .... For this cause shall a man leave his father and mother, and shall be joined unto his wife, and they shall be one flesh. This is a great mystery: but I speak concerning Christ and the church".

If then, at the marriage of the Lamb, the Church is His Bride — and she undoubtedly is — the saints of the pre-Church age must be 'they which are called unto the marriage of the Lamb', whom we term the 'wedding guests'. These saints will have been in close fellowship with the Church in Heaven from the time they were translated together with her, seven years previously: most fittingly therefore would they be invited to the wedding.

The Bride. She is introduced, as it were, by the 'voice of a great multitude', saying (*Revelation 19*:6—7):

"Alleluia: for the Lord God Omnipotent reigneth. Let us be glad and rejoice, and give honour to him: for the marriage of the Lamb is come, and his wife hath made herself ready''; and we are further informed, ''And to her was granted that she should be arrayed in fine linen, clean and white: for the fine linen is the righteousness of saints'' (v.8).

As we should expect, it is a scene of great rejoicing in Heaven and the bride has made adequate preparation for the ceremony, probably referring to the 'raiment of needlework' (*Psalm 45*:14) which she has stitched for herself to please her Lord and King, symbolic perhaps of the things done for Christ on earth by individual members of the Church, which combine to adorn her after she is translated to Heaven to become the Bride. Of course, in that spiritual sphere it is the *character* will be manifested, just as form and clothing are seen to the human eye in the physical world; although, doubtless, there will then be the outward attractiveness, too.

If the 'raiment of needlework' represents what the Bride has provided for herself, the 'fine linen, clean and white', which is 'the righteousness of saints', would signify what Christ has done for her, as the Church, imputing righteousness, by virtue of His redemptive work, to her and the Old Testament saints as well (e.g. *Romans 4*:9). Concerning the Church, this truth is elaborated by Paul (*Ephesians 5*:25—27):

''Christ also loved the church, and gave himself for it; that he might sanctify and cleanse it .... that he might present it to himself a glorious church, not having spot, or wrinkle, or any such thing, but that it should be holy and without blemish''.

In addition to her own raiment of needlework and Christ's provision of the fine linen for her, the Bride will have, underlying as it were, 'clothing of wrought gold' which will make her 'all glorious within' (*Psalm 45*:13) — signifying, according to Bible typology, what *God has wrought* within her while on earth. Again Paul explains (*Philippians 2*:12—13):

''Work out your own salvation with fear and trembling. For it is *God which worketh in you* (i.e. the members of the Church) both to will and to do of his good pleasure''.

The Wedding Guests. These are they who are 'blessed' by being 'called unto the marriage supper of the Lamb', undoubtedly the saints of the pre-Christian era, probably from Abel to John the Baptist. Nothing more than the words quoted is recorded about them in that passage: we have to go to the Gospels to find further information about them. Two of our Lord's parables may well refer to them: those concerning the marriage of a king's son (*Matthew* 22:1—14), and the ten virgins (*Matthew* 25:1—13). The former parable is described thus:

"The kingdom of heaven is like unto a certain king (i.e. God), which made a marriage for his son (Jesus Christ), and sent his servants to call them that were bidden (the wedding guests?) to the wedding: and they would not come (i.e. the unbelieving *Jews* in the first instance). Again he sent forth other servants, saying, Tell them which were bidden, Behold, I have prepared my dinner (an earlier meal than a supper): my oxen and my fatlings are killed, and all things are ready: come unto the marriage. But they made light of it, and went their ways, one to his farm, another to his merchandise: and the remnant took his servants, and entreated them spitefully, and slew them. But when the king heard thereof, he was wroth: and he sent forth his armies (especially those of Nebuchadnezzar?), and destroyed these murderers (Israel as a whole who had killed many of the Old Testament prophets, the messengers of God), and burned up their city (Jerusalem, in 587 B.C.)".

It is convenient to break off at this point — where Israel, as the first 'invited guests', was rejected — to emphasise that the parable has nothing whatever to say about the bride of the marriage. Doubtless, the reason for the omission is that she, as the Church, had then (at the time of Christ) scarcely come into existence. The parable is purely concerned with the wedding guests. Of course, God had in mind from the beginning the marriage of His Son, and had planned to choose first the wedding guests, from the people living before Christ; and the Bride next, from those of the present age (A.D.). Perhaps to indicate that the former group was the earlier of the two in point of time, the parable refers to its marriage feast as a 'dinner' whereas later, in John's vision of the actual marriage of the Lamb, it is regarded as a 'supper'.

Continuing the parable (*Matthew* 22:8—14): "Then saith he (the king) to his servants, The wedding is ready, but they which were bidden were not worthy. Go ye therefore into the highways, and as many as ye shall find, bid to the marriage. So those servants went out into the highways, and gathered together all as many as they found, both bad and good: and the wedding was furnished with guests. And when the king came in to see the guests, he saw there a man which had not on a wedding garment: and he saith unto him, Friend, how camest thou in hither not having a wedding garment?

And he was speechless. Then said the king to his servants, Bind him hand and foot, and take him away, and cast him into outer darkness; there shall be weeping and gnashing of teeth. For many are called, but few are chosen''.

The first invitation having been rejected or neglected by those bidden — probably representing all the unbelieving of Israel up to the time of Christ — a second invitation is sent out to all others who were willing to accept it. These latter would depict the Gentiles, of whom only the believing were chosen as the wedding guests. The unbelieving, represented by the man without a wedding garment (i.e. the fine linen of the righteousness of Christ), are rejected and meet the doom of all unbelievers of all time.

Thus the wedding guests for the marriage supper of the Lamb were chosen from among all those who lived up to the time of Christ, the number being completed, representatively, by John the Baptist (see *Matthew 11*:11). The whole company, like him (*John 3*:29), can be regarded as a *friend* of the Bridegroom; such friendship might well be expected of wedding guests.

In the second parable, that of *the ten virgins* (*Matthew 25*:10—13), it is the virgins who are the invited guests at the marriage, and again there is no mention of the bride:

''Then shall the kingdom of heaven be likened unto ten virgins, which took their lamps, and went forth to meet the bridegroom. And five of them were wise and five were foolish. They that were foolish took their lamps, and took no oil with them: but the wise took oil in their vessels with their lamps. While the bridegroom (Christ) tarried, they all slumbered and slept. And at midnight there was a cry made, Behold the bridegroom cometh; go ye out to meet him. Then all those virgins arose, and trimmed their lamps. And the foolish said unto the wise, Give us of your oil; for our lamps are gone out. But the wise answered, saying, Not so; lest there be not enough for us and you: but go ye rather to them that sell, and buy for yourselves. And while they went to buy, the bridegroom came, and they that were ready went with him to the marriage: and the door was shut. Afterward there came also the other virgins, saying, Lord, Lord open to us. But he answered and said, Verily I say unto you, I know you not. Watch therefore, for ye know neither the day nor the hour wherein the Son of man cometh''.

Whereas the wedding guests in the first parable (the marriage of the king's son) might represent the friends of the Bridegroom, the wise virgins in the second parable would rather denote the companions of His Bride, in keeping with *Psalm 45*:14—15: 'The virgins her (the bride's) companions that follow her shall be brought unto thee (the bridegroom, the king). With gladness and rejoicing shall they be brought: they shall enter into the king's palace'. The 'king' here is clearly the Lord Jesus (see vv.1—8); His Bride is depicted both as 'the queen in gold of Ophir' (v.9) and also as 'the King's daughter' (v.13 — see 2 *Corinthians 6*:18); the 'king's palace' portrays Heaven. The virgins here (*Psalm 45*) are all, without exception, received *along with the bride* into the king's palace — confirming our belief that the wedding guests at the marriage of the Lamb are the Old Testament saints and *are translated into Heaven along with the Church* (His Bride).

Reverting to the second parable of the ten virgins (*Matthew 25*), five out of the ten were shut out from the marriage because they had no oil (type of the Holy Spirit) in their lamps (mere profession of Christianity?). The inspired apostle affirms categorically (*Romans 8*:9): '*Now if any man have not* the Spirit of Christ (synonymous with the Spirit of God and the Holy Spirit), he is none of his'. The five wise virgins had oil in their lamps and went into the wedding. They picture, as already indicated, the Old Testament saints who will become the wedding guests at the marriage of the Lamb. Clearly these saints must have been at least sealed with the Spirit (*Ephesians 1*:13), although the Holy Spirit could not come — officially, as it were — on believers until Christ had actually carried out His work of redemption. Yet that work was evidently effective for all believers (like, for example, Abraham) who lived *before* Christ.

With further reference to the parable of the ten virgins, its main relevance to the marriage of the Lamb is that it indicates the close friendship which will exist between the wedding guests and the Bride, evidently after their joint translation to Heaven and their living together there during the seven years leading up to the marriage. It is noticeable in the parable that the marriage took place soon after midnight; any ensuing fast would thus be in the nature of a *supper*, as will be the case at the marriage supper of the Lamb.

Recapitulating, 'they which are called unto the marriage supper of the Lamb' — whom we have termed the 'wedding guests' — will include all the faithful of Old Testament times, up to John the Baptist. While on earth, their faithfulness, like that of John, was regarded as friendship with the Bridegroom (Christ). When translated to Heaven, that friendship will clearly deepen, as also will their companionship with the Bride. In both respects they will be fitted to be the wedding guests at the marriage supper of the Lamb.

CHAPTER 9

SATAN'S SWAY ON EARTH

As we have said, the Day of Jesus Christ in Heaven runs concurrently with the last septennium of the age on earth. Although Satan, manifested as the Beast, will appear to be in absolute control of the world during these years, everything will transpire according to the permissive will of God, unfolded out of the 'seven-sealed book' by the Lord Jesus Christ. In effect God will be giving humanity a 'man' of their own heart to reign over them, the one (Satan) whom they had obeyed in the garden of Eden at the dawn of their history and whom they, apart from a minority faithful to God, have ever since obeyed, although he has remained unseen. What more could they desire than to have him appear in human — or better still, superhuman — form for them to worship as their god! Nevertheless, the seven-year period of his rule as the Beast will have been ordained of God to punish the world for rejecting His Son, Jesus Christ, in *the day of salvation;* with which, by contrast, the final septennium is referred to as '*the day of vengeance of our God*' (*Isaiah 61*:2). It will be recalled that the Lord Jesus, in the synagogue at Nazareth, read the passage (vv.1—2) up to this phrase, closing the book of the prophet after reading 'the acceptable year of the Lord' (*Luke 4*:19—20). The closing of the 'book' was a symbolic act, indicating that it would not be opened again until the 'year of the Lord' (the 'day of salvation' — 2 *Corinthians 6*:2) ended and the 'day of vengeance' came — symbolised, in turn, by Christ's opening the 'book' (of seven seals) in Heaven. The breaking of the first seal (*Revelation 6*:1—2) reveals the opening scene of the 'day of vengeance': the coming into the world of the Beast, Satan's man, depicted as a conqueror riding 'a white horse'; he carries 'a bow', and 'a crown' is given to him. These quoted features betoken the *speed* and *power* with which he achieves his conquests, and the *high authority* which he quickly attains and which is really that given to him by the Devil himself, who, under God, is indeed the prince of this world. The Beast, Satan's *alter ego* (other self), will now be described in detail.

THE BEAST WITH SEVEN HEADS

We have already had much to say about this evil genius, because he is mentioned frequently in the Old Testament in one form or another, chiefly in the prophecies of Daniel. Briefly recapitulating, we understand that the Beast will appear in the world at the time of the existence of a ten-kingdom union in the area of the old Roman empire. In his rapid rise to power he will subdue three of these states, possibly Luxembourg, Belgium and the Netherlands — the smaller countries of the present Common Market (the European Economic Community, based on the Treaty of Rome, 1955) which may be assumed to develop into the combine of ten kingdoms envisaged in Bible prophecy. For seven years he will be in authority, perhaps at Rome initially (Scripture indicates that he is a *Roman* 'prince'). At the beginning of this period he will make a seven-year pact with Israel under the false prophet (or Antichrist) by which, apparently, he will permit her to re-establish in her new temple her ancient system of sacrificial offerings to God, repugnant as these would naturally be to the Satan-inspired Beast. Yet, in exchange, the false prophet will enable him to set up strongholds at strategic points in Israel and will give him much of the country's wealth, in the form of money and produce. Half-way through the seven-year period the Beast will break the pact and compel the Jews to discontinue their temple offerings. At the same time he will show his real purpose in this act of treachery: it is that he himself may sit in the temple and be worshipped as God. He may even occupy the 'mercy seat' in the most holy place of the temple, a seat originally reserved for the presence of God.

We turn now to what the New Testament has to say about the Beast, described in the book of the Revelation; he is first seen, in John's visions, as 'a beast' rising up from 'the sea' (*Revelation 13*:1—10).

"And I stood upon the sand of the sea (the Mediterranean), and I saw a beast rise up out of the sea, having *seven heads* and *ten horns*, and upon his horns ten crowns, and upon his heads the name of blasphemy. And the beast which I saw was like a *leopard*, and his feet were as the feet of a *bear*, and his mouth as the mouth of a *lion*, and the dragon (Satan) gave him his power, and his seat (or throne), and great authority. And I saw one of his heads as it were wounded to death; and his deadly wound was healed: and all the world wondered after the beast'' (vv.1—3).

It is evident from the italicised elements of the beast that he incorporates the combined features of the four great beasts of Daniel's vision: between them they had seven heads and ten horns; individually they were like a lion, a bear, a leopard and a monster respectively. The Beast (we revert to the use of a capital initial letter for the sake of distinction) of John's vision is himself a monster, and we would call special attention to the point that the apostle sees the three features (of leopard, bear and lion) of his Beast in the reverse order to that in which Daniel's first three beasts appear (lion, bear and leopard) to the prophet. The main reason for John's reversal of the original sequence will be understood when we come to consider his later vision in which the Beast is seen in a different setting.

Regarding the present vision it may be noted that there is no separate portrayal of the Roman empire as there was in Daniel's vision (as the fourth beast), probably because in John's time (*circa A.D.90*) that empire was then in existence and he follows on, so to speak, from there. Nor is he, apparently, much concerned with the intermediate empires of Grecia and Medo-Persia, symbolised (to be consistent with Daniel's vision) by the leopard and bear features (in this order) of John's Beast. Of course these two ancient empires, historically, had preceded that of Rome and had long since passed away, but their *characteristics,* it seems, will be incorporated in the Beast and his world kingdom: the leopard's speed and stealth in attack, and the bear's ferocity. Yet, when the Beast, by virtue of these characteristics, attains supreme authority he will show especially the features of the *lion* — pride and power, and loud-voiced utterances — the first beast of Daniel's vision, depicting the empire of Babylon. Thus, the Beast's empire, in God's view, will be a revival of Babylon; not geographically — because Scripture asserts that the capital city of the ancient empire, now lying beneath the desert sand, will never be rebuilt (*Isaiah 13*:19—22) — but morally and spiritually. Doubtless this is what is meant by the healing of the 'deadly wound' in one of the Beast's seven heads. Ancient Babylon suffered this 'wound' when her empire fell in 538 B.C., but all her sinful pride and glory will reappear in a worse form in the coming empire of the Beast. The belief that the healing of the wounded head refers to the revival of the Roman empire is not in keeping with *all* the scriptural symbolism on the subject —

here and elsewhere (see under the next heading). That the Beast's kingdom will in fact constitute the final *phase* of the old Roman empire cannot be denied, for Scripture itself affirms, as we have shown, that it will spring from a union of ten kingdoms in the region of what once was Roman territory. This may perhaps be regarded in a geographical sense as a revival of Rome's empire, but as such it is not the fulfilment of Bible prophecy, which, as previously indicated and presently confirmed, views the Beast's kingdom as proceeding without a break from the old Roman empire. This unbroken sequence is especially seen in the great image of Nebuchadnezzar's deam. The ten toes depicting the ten kingdoms to come, are an *integral* part, of course, of the feet and legs, portraying the old Roman empire. In fact the whole image is *intact* when the stone (Christ, at His coming) smites it and causes its disintegration, suggesting that the Beast's kingdom, in God's sight, will be an embodiment of the four ancient empires, but appearing finally in the reverse order. First, the ten kingdoms based on Rome, which then develop quickly through the characters of ancient Grecia and Medo-Persia into the empire of Babylon revived, when the whole world kingdom will be present — as it were, the original great image, whose head of gold is the Beast who will dominate and personify the whole.

Thus in John's vision, the Beast is seen as a composite form of the four beasts of Daniel's vision: the monster with seven heads and ten horns, which we have described. Further information about him is given in the apostle's vision (*Revelation 13*:4—10).

"And they (the world, v.3) worshipped the dragon which gave power unto the beast: and they worshipped the beast, saying, Who is like unto the beast? who is able to make war with him? And there was given unto him a mouth (like a lion's, v.2) speaking great things and blasphemies; and power was given unto him to continue (or, to make war) forty and two months. And he opened his mouth in blasphemy against God, to blaspheme his name, and his tabernacle, and them that dwell in heaven. And it was given unto him to make war with the saints, and to over-come them: and power was given him over all kindreds, and tongues, and nations. And all that dwell upon the earth shall worship him, whose names are not written in the book of life of the Lamb slain from the foundation of the world. If any man have an ear, let him hear. He that leadeth into captivity shall go into captivity: he that killeth with the sword must be killed with the sword. Here is the patience and the faith of saints".

Evidently the world will know that Satan is the real power behind the Beast, but they will worship the Beast, too, for his person and for his invincibility in war. Concerning his person, he may well show much of the original beauty and wisdom of his master Satan before his fall, as depicted by the King of Tyrus (*Ezekiel 28*:12—15). The *prince* of Tyrus (vv.2—10) probably portrays the Beast himself. The Beast may also be considerably above the average height; we may recall that his master, the Devil, is typified by the giant, Goliath. With respect to the Beast's war-like activities, he could receive no higher tribute than to be called 'the god of forces' (*Daniel 11*:38) by his ally 'the king' (the Antichrist), as we have seen. The world will indeed rightly say of the Beast, 'who is able to make war with him? (*Revelation 13*:4); like Alexander the Great he will be irresistible. In the space of three-and-a-half years ('forty and two months', v.5) he will, presumably, have conquered the world. It is during this *first* half of his septennial existence on earth that he will also 'make war with the saints' (v.7) and put them to death ('overcome them') — certainly their disembodied souls are seen in Heaven *preceding* those of the martyrs of the Great Tribulation, the latter half of the seven-year period, as previously demonstrated. Presumably these later martyrs will have met their death not directly from the Beast, as in the case of the earlier martyrs, but by refusing to worship his image (see p.103). All who do worship it, or indeed the Beast himself, will have their names excluded from the 'book of life' (v.8), being doomed to everlasting destruction. The passage concludes (v.9) by indicating that the blood of the martyrs (of both groups) will be avenged and their faith and patience will be rewarded.

The Seven Heads and 'He' the Eighth. In a later vision (*Revelation 17*) further information about the Beast is revealed:

"So he carried me away in spirit into the wilderness: and I saw a woman sit upon a scarlet coloured beast, full of names and blasphemy, having seven heads and ten horns" v.3).

We shall consider the 'woman' under the next heading: suffice it here to mention that 'she' will be closely associated with the Beast at the time, or soon after his appearing. Evidently it is to him that the 'beast .... having seven heads and ten horns' refers. The scarlet colour might indicate something of his character: deep-dyed in sin (cf. *Isaiah 1*:18); swift to shed blood? Certainly such a one he will show himself to be, from what we have already learned of him from other scriptures.

Following further details concerning the 'woman', the angel then explains to John the 'mystery' of the Beast (*Revelation 17*:7—11), especially with regard to his seven heads and the order in which, as seven 'kings', they make their appearance. Strangely enough, as far as the present writer is aware, no expositer has hitherto been able to elucidate the 'mystery' of the 'seven heads' from the clues provided by the angel. The explanations put forward have failed because, one and all, they have been in conflict with the interpretation of at least one other prophecy connected with the Beast. In some cases, where the conflicting evidence is ignored or unnoticed, support is sought from sources outside Scripture, as we shall shortly demonstrate. First, however, we must quote the passage in question (vv.8—11):

"The beast that thou sawest was, and is not; and shall ascend out of the bottomless pit, and go into perdition: and they that dwell on the earth shall wonder, whose names are not written in the book of life from the foundation of the world, when they behold the beast that was, and is not, and yet is. And here is the mind that hath wisdom. The seven heads are seven mountains, on which the woman sitteth. And there are *seven kings: five are fallen, and one is, and the other is not yet come; and when he cometh, he must continue a short space.* And the beast that was, and is not, even *he is the eighth, and is of the seven,* and goeth into perdition".

Before dealing with the italicised portions of the above passage, which will be the main object of our study here, we have a few comments on what goes before. It is clear that 'the beast' in this connection has a dual significance. Firstly it represents something (ancient Babylon?) that existed in the past ('was') and then ceased to exist ('is not'); and secondly someone (certainly a person), from the abode of demons (the 'bottomless pit'), who will appear in the world and be an object of wonder to all, before he finally meets his doom. Of course we know that this person is the Beast, the coming ruler of this world during the last seven years of this present age, and his world kingdom will partake largely of the character of ancient Babylon. His portrayal with seven heads and ten horns show, in the first instance, his close affinity with Satan himself who is seen in a previous vision. (*Revelation 12*:3) as 'a great red dragon, having seven heads and ten horns', typical of his high spiritual authority and superabundant power used for destructive purposes. The seven heads, according to the angelic interpretation, symbolised both seven mountains and seven kings (or kingdoms). The seven mountains evidently denote the city of the seven hills, Rome, with which the Beast (as well as the 'woman') will be intimately connected, as already shown.

We come now to the consideration of the seven kings and the other italicised portions of the passage, especially those in v.10. Perhaps the most popular and reasonable of past interpretations of this verse has been the view that the seven kings (depicted by the seven heads) stand for seven *empires*, the 'five fallen' being those of Assyria, Egypt, Babylon, Medo-Persia and Greece, the 'one is' that of Rome, and 'the other' to come that of Rome revived. Unfortunately for this theory, the seven heads of the Beast in John's two visions (*Revelation 13* and *17*), being evidently a composite form of those of the four beasts of Daniel's vision (*Daniel 7*), do *not* represent seven empires but only *four*, those of Babylon, Medo-Persia, Greece and Rome. The number of kingdoms is brought up to seven by reason of the fact that the Grecian empire (symbolised by the leopard with *four* heads) is regarded as consisting, not of one kingdom (like the other three empires) but of four, as it actually did at Alexander's death. Thus, according to Scripture, there are only four empires but they are viewed by the seer, John, as seven kingdoms, or seven 'kings' as the angel describes them. The idea that there are seven empires requires that two empires (Assyria and Egypt), *outside* the scope of the prophecies, be brought in to bolster it up. This view must therefore be rejected on these grounds alone, and in other ways it conflicts with Scripture, as will be apparent from what follows.

Of the seven kingdoms, the 'five fallen', if we take the order in which Daniel's four beasts appeared, would be first Babylon (*one* head of the lion), second Medo-Persia (*one* head of the bear), and then *three* of the four kingdoms of Grecia (three of the four heads of the leopard). This order, however, would leave the sixth kingdom of John's prophecy to be the remaining fourth kingdom of the Grecian empire, which did not exist in John's day (the time of Christ). Whereas we know that the sixth kingdom of his prophecy, depicted as the 'one is' in the verse (*Revelation 17*:7) we are studying, evidently existed in his day and was in fact the *Roman* empire.

In our consideration of John's first vision of the seven-headed beast (*Revelation 13*:1—10) we noted it bore, in some of its features, the likeness of a leopard, a bear and a lion, in that order, which was remarkably the reverse order of that in which the same three beasts appeared in Daniel's vision (*Daniel* 7:4—6). We are now in a position to see the reason for this. If we view the 'five fallen' kings as proceeding in Daniel's sequence, it leads us, as we have just seen, to an impossible interpretation of the sixth king. If, on the other hand, we take John's own order for his 'five fallen' all is clear and consistent. Thus the five would stand for the successive empires of Greece, counted as *four* kingdoms (from the four heads of the leopard), and Medo-Persia, reckoned as *one* kingdom (from the one head of the bear). Two empires remain, those of Babylon and Rome, each counted as one kingdom (from the one head of the lion and the one of the unspecified beast — *Daniel* 7.4,7). Of these the 'one is' (i.e. the one present in John's life) clearly refers to the Roman empire, while 'the other', who is to come and 'must continue a short space', must be that of Babylon — the sixth and seventh kingdoms respectively. All the evidence we have presented so far goes to prove that this seventh kingdom will be that of the Beast, and that it will be a revival, in character but not in situation, of Babylon. Concerning the duration of his kingdom, seven years (Daniel's 70th 'week'), it is aptly portrayed as a 'short space' — a brief period indeed when compared, for example, with that of the Roman empire which existed for over four centuries. In fact, as already explained in Ch.4 (see under 'The Four Great Beasts'), that ancient empire is regarded in prophecy as existing uninterruptly, from the time of its rise to the future end of the age. It will then, as the sixth kingdom (the 'one is'), exist along with the seventh kingdom ('the other') — as it were, 'Babylon revived' superimposed on 'Rome continued'. The resulting world state under the Beast will be characterised by the ruthlessness of ancient Rome combined with the despotic power and blasphemous pride of ancient Babylon, concentrated in the world's ruler, the Beast himself — as was Babylon in the person of her first emperor, Nebuchadnezzar; the 'head of gold' of his dream image. In the Beast and in his kingdom, in fact, will be embodied the outstanding features of *all four* empires (seven kingdoms), as already noted. Thus John could finally say of him (*Revelation 17*:11): 'And the Beast that was, and is not, even he is the eighth, and is *of the seven,* and goeth into perdition' — the 'eighth' here representing, not so much a kingdom as the actual person of the king, the Beast himself.

THE GREAT WHORE — RELIGIOUS BABYLON

As the Beast and his empire are viewed by God as the revival of *political* Babylon in all its pride and power, so 'the great whore that sitteth upon many waters' (*Revelation 17*:1) is regarded as a revival of *religious* Babylon, in all its idolatrous corruption. Evidence will be adduced, as we proceed, to show that she will be an apostate world church based on Rome — analogous but in vivid contrast to the true Church of Christ which will then have been translated to Heaven and later will become His Bride.

The idolatry of ancient Babylon can be seen in the feast of Belshazzar (*Daniel 5*) who used the sacred vessels taken by his grand father Nebuchadnezzar from the temple at Jerusalem and drank wine out of them praising the 'gods of gold, silver, brass, iron, wood and stone' (v.4). The variety of these gods worshipped by ancient Babylon may well typify the many false cults and religions in the world today, amalgamated into the coming world church. The whore 'sitting on *many waters*', symbolising (according to Bible typology) that *many nations* will be under her control, would confirm the idea of a future world church. In this connection, perhaps one of the most significant trends of the present century is a desire to unite the various churches of the world, the so-called ecumenical movement, leading in 1948 to the formation of the World Council of Churches (W.C.C.) at Amsterdam. The ultimate aim of the W.C.C. is to create a One World Church, including the Roman Catholic Church. In 1962, Dr. Ramsey, the Archbishop of Canterbury, declared his support of this aim, and in March 1966, paid a visit to Rome, evidently as a step to uniting the Church of England with that of Rome. Yet Pope John XXIII had before made it clear that, in any union with other churches, he would expect them to accept the principles and practices of his church; in effect that Rome would be head of the confederation.

Scripture demonstrates (*Revelation 19*:9,18) that the future world church will be based on Rome (the seven-hilled city) who will dominate the kingdoms of the world, as the Roman Church of the past used to do to a large extent. Many other details concerning the 'woman' confirm that the coming church will be strongly associated with Roman Catholicism, thus: 'And the woman was arrayed in purple and scarlet colour, and decked with gold and precious stones and pearls, having a golden cup in her hand full of abominations and filthiness of her fornication' (v.4). The colours are those of the garments of the popes and cardinals; the other details, too, could portray the characteristics of Romanism throughout the ages: her gaudy display and costly trappings, her worship of images and relics ('abominations') and her immorality. It is indeed a fitting name which the woman bears on her forehead (v.5):

"MYSTERY,

BABYLON THE GREAT,

THE MOTHER OF HARLOTS AND ABOMINATIONS

OF THE EARTH."

The 'mystery' attached to the woman's title, 'Babylon the Great', is probably to inform us that the name is not to be taken as literal but as symbolic — of Rome, as we have demonstrated. As to her being called 'the Great', the epithet, in the first instance, would aptly describe the Roman Church during her long history: great in age, power, corruption and, in times past, cruelty, in persecuting to the death millions of martyrs. 'And I saw the woman drunken with the blood of the martyrs of Jesus: and when I saw her, I wondered with great admiration' (v.6). If the word 'great' could be applied to the Roman Church of the past, much more will it be true of the coming church, greater in extent and authority and with everything that appeals to the eye and to the gratification of fleshly lust and greed (*Revelation 18*:3,12—16). Well might it invoke the wonder and great admiration of the seer! Yet, outwardly grand, the false church will be 'the habitation of devils,and the hold of every foul spirit, and a cage of every unclean and hateful bird' (v.2). From this description we can scarcely imagine to what depth of unholiness and uncleanness the future church will sink; spiritism, very prevalent today, may set the stage for such iniquity.

Her Destruction. The world church, unlike that of Rome with her age-long history, will be short-lived. Rising with the Beast at the beginning of the last septennium of this age, she will be suffered by him to exist for only half that period. As explained earlier, after 3½ years he will break his 7-year covenant with Israel and put an end to her revived religious system. At the same time he will take the opportunity to encompass the total destruction of the world church, so that now he may be the sole object of world worship. Doubtless he will think that it is the right time to take this step, having made himself by conquest the ruler of the world. With the church eliminated and Israel's temple ritual abolished, the Beast will be alone responsible for both the politics and religion of the world — political and religious Babylon revived. The destruction of the church, actually carried out by the ten states of the European union where the church will presumably be most strongly represented — will be sudden and drastic; thus: 'Therefore shall her plagues come in one day, death, and mourning, and famine; and she shall be utterly burned with fire; for strong is the Lord God who judgeth her' (*Revelation 18*:8). Her downfall, although sorely lamented throughout the world by rulers (v.9), merchants (vv.11—16) and ship-owners (vv.17—19) who have enjoyed illicit pleasure or have been made rich by her existence, will be an occasion of great rejoicing in Heaven over the fall of one who has shed the blood of so many saints (vv.20—24; ch.19:1—3)

THE FALSE PROPHET

This is the final name in Scripture and the most meaningful for the third person of the evil trinity, namely, the dragon (Satan), the Beast and the *false prophet* (*Revelation 16*:13). His previous designations, in order of mention are: the king (*Daniel 11*:36), the idol shepherd (*Zechariah 11*:17), the Antichrist (1 *John 2*:18) and the *second*beast of *Revelation 13*:11—18. We have already considered the false prophet under all except the last title, the second beast, which is described as follows (vv.11—12).

"And I (John) beheld another beast coming up out of *the earth;* and he had two horns like a lamb, and he spake as a dragon. And he exercised all the power of the first beast before him, and causeth the earth and them which dwell therein to worship the first beast, whose deadly wound was healed".

The 'first beast' is, of course, he whom we have hitherto termed the Beast, and we have frequently referred to most of the verses (1—10) which relate to him here. At this point, however, it is convenient to indicate that he rises from 'the sea' (v.1) whereas the second beast comes up from 'the earth'. To avoid confusion, we shall call the former the Beast (as usual) and the latter the false prophet. The 'sea' from which the Beast comes would typify the Gentile nations of the world, unordered from God's point of view, like the troubled sea (*Isaiah 57*:20); whereas the 'earth' would represent the nation of Israel, the only *earthly* people (the Church of Christ is regarded in Scripture as a heavenly people) subject at least nominally to the laws of God and therefore ordered and settled like the earth (in contrast to the restless sea). Apparently, in the same symbolic sense, the 'earth' and the 'sea' are linked together in *Revelation 12*:12: 'Woe to the inhabiters of the earth and of the sea! for the devil is come down unto you, having great wrath, because he knoweth that he hath but a short time'. Certainly Satan will manifest himself with destructive intent in the person of the Beast among the Gentiles, and in that of the false prophet among the Jews in Israel. They will accept the false prophet as their king, as shown earlier, and he will pose (in the figure of a two-horned lamb) as their Messiah, being in fact acknowledged as such by the great majority. The two horns give some indication of his power which will indeed be great, as we shall see, but clearly he is not the true Messiah, the *all*-powerful Son of God, depicted as the *seven*-horned Lamb. Moreoever, his dragon's voice belies his lamb-like appearance; he will have none of the meek and gentle qualities of the Lord Jesus, but will be self-assertive and destructive like Satan himself.

It is to be noted that the false prophet 'exerciseth all the power (Gr. authority) of the first beast *before him*' (*Revelation 13*:12). This sentence suggests that what follows in the chapter confirms that the false prophet is subordinate to the Beast, who gives him the power to perform miracles and whom the world worships in consequence; the Beast is always present when the miracles are performed. The passage continues (vv.13—15):

"And he (the false prophet) doeth great wonders, so that he maketh fire come down from heaven on the earth in the sight of men, and deceiveth them that dwell on the earth by the means of the miracles which he had power (Gr. which was given to him) to do in the sight of the beast; saying to them that dwell on the earth, that they should make an image of the beast, which had the wound by a sword, and did live. And he had power (Gr. it was given him) to give life unto the image of the beast, that the image of the beast should both speak, and cause that as many as would not worship the image of the beast should be killed".

The particular miracle which wins acclaim — *making fire come down from heaven* — is one that was frequently performed by God Himself (*Genesis 19*:24; *Leviticus 10*:2; 1 *Kings 18*:38; 2 *Chronicles 7*:1, are instances). Doubtless those who see this and other wonders performed will be aware, or will be made aware, that it is the Beast who is really responsible for them, and they will be quite ready at the false prophet's command to make an image of the Beast 'which had the wound by a sword, and did live'. The last quotation again reminds us that the Beast, representing his empire, will be a revived form of that of ancient Babylon, which was indeed struck down by the 'sword' when the armies of Medo-Persia overthrew her in 538 B.C. Concerning the *Beast's image,* no details are recorded as to its size or as to where it will be set up. It may well be a colossus, at least as imposing as the hundred-foot (30 m.) golden image erected by Nebuchadnezzar *(Daniel 3*:1), Babylon's first emperor. It seems probable that it will be set up in the region of Jerusalem because the false prophet, then ruler in Israel, will be responsible for its construction. A suitable site would be the temple area of the capital itself. The Moslem mosques (notably the Dome of the Rock) now occupy a commanding position in that area, and it is where the Jews' third temple will doubtless be built; the wailing wall is all that is left of their second temple. A convenient time for the erection of the image would be as soon as possible after the destruction of the apostate church and the abolition of the Jews' temple offerings, at the mid-point of the last seven years of the age. These two forms of religion could then forthwith be replaced by the universal worship not only of the Beast himself, but also of his image. From this time forward it is therefore evident that he will assume deity and occupy the temple, perhaps sitting in the mercy seat of the Holy of Holies (2 *Thessalonians 2*:4). He would thus, too, be in close proximity to the image — assuming it to be in the temple area, as seems quite likely — to superintend its worship. The false prophet's power to give life to the image is apparently limited to making it speak and enabling it to kill those who refuse to do to it the required homage. Yet this latter capacity is sufficiently terrible to enforce obedience on the vast majority of the people who come (freely or by compulsion) from all parts of the globe to worship the image or die.

THE MARK OF THE BEAST

The Beast's further glorification by the false prophet is thus described (*Revelation 13*:16—18):

"And he causeth all, both small and great, rich and poor, free and bond, to receive a mark in their right hand, or in their foreheads: and that no man might buy or sell, save he that had the mark, or the name of the beast, or the number of his name. Here is wisdom.

Let him that hath understanding count the number of the beast: for it is the number of a man: and his number is Six hundred threescore and six''.

In the original Greek of this passage, the number is not given in words as in the English translation, but in two letters and one symbol, standing for 600,60 and 6 respectively (see Appendix IV). Of course we cannot be at all sure that the triple Greek sign representing the three numbers, will itself be the mark with which all but a few of the people will be branded in the last three and a half years of the present age; it may well be in ordinary Arabic numerals (666) or in some secret cypher. For those who refuse to bear the mark of the Beast it will certainly be difficult to avoid starvation, as they will be unable to buy food. Also one can easily imagine that many other privations will be theirs because of their inability to buy or sell, making life almost impossible for them, not to mention persecution from those carrying the mark.

CHAPTER 10

THE GREAT TRIBULATION

This will be a time of *unprecedented* trial which will involve the whole world during the last three and a half years of the present age. It is indeed referred to (*Revelation 3*:10) as 'the hour of temptation' for all the earth and, in so far as it affects Israel, as 'the time of Jacob's trouble (*Jeremiah 30*:7). It will commence, as intimated, with 'the abomination of desolation', when the Beast will occupy the holy place of the temple, claiming to be God Himself; with the setting up of the Beast's image and its compulsory worship, and with the imposition of his mark on the persons of his followers. All this will initiate an intensification of his oppression of the world in general and the Jews in particular, whose daily sacrifices he will have stopped. The persecution during the previous three and a half years of his reign will have been mainly directed against those among the *Gentiles* who refused to associate with the world church, under his control of course. These martyrs of the earlier period are those whose souls are seen 'under the altar' (in Heaven) by John in his vision, as already related — the faithful among the *Jews* will have their lives preserved by God during both this and the following period of the Great Tribulation, as we shall show.

In the Great Tribulation the affliction falling on mankind will not only arise because of Satan's rule but will also result from the chastisement of God Himself. in a series of terryfying visitations upon the earth-dwellers — the angelic judgments, described, along with the culminating battle of Armageddon, later in the chapter. It is small wonder that the period will impose on humanity the most terrible trial of all time, as our Lord said (*Matthew 24*:21): 'For then shall be great tribulation, such as was not since the beginning of the world to this time, no, nor ever shall be'.

THE SEALING OF THE ELECT OF ISRAEL

"And I saw another angel ascending from the east (from the region of Israel?), having the seal of the living God: and he cried with a loud voice to the four angels, to whom it was given to hurt the earth (Israel?) and the sea (the Gentile nations?) saying, Hurt not the earth, neither the sea, nor the trees (faithful Jewish leaders?), till we have sealed the servants of God in their foreheads. And I heard the number of them which were sealed: and there were sealed an hundred and forty and four thousand of all the tribes of the children of Israel" (*Revelation* 7:2—4).

Twelve thousand from each of the twelve tribes: Judah, Reuben, Gad, Asher, Naphtali, Manasseh, Simeon, Levi, Issachar, Zebulon, Joseph and Benjamin (see vv.5—8). It may be recalled that, of these twelve tribes, only two (Judah and Benjamin) constitute the Jews who people the State of Israel today. The other ten tribes of Israel, after their captivity to Assyria in 720 B.C., mingled with the surrounding nations and ultimately lost their identity. Yet, although these tribes are still unknown to man they are evidently, from the above passage, intimately known to God and, before the Tribulation begins, He will 'seal' a proportion of each of the ten tribes as well as of the Jews' two tribes.

In setting His seal upon the elect of the twelve tribes, God is virtually marking this chosen company out as His own, just as today He seals each member of His Church with His Holy Spirit. Similarly also he has a special purpose for the elect of Israel: it is, as all the evidence goes to show, that they should be *the nucleus of the new nation of Israel in the Millennium* and be the progenitors, during that age, of her innumerable future members. It follows too that the sealed ones of Israel, if they are to be alive at the end of the age to populate the new nation, must be protected by God so as to survive the rigours of the preceding septennium under the Beast's misrule, especially the final three and a half years of the Great Tribulation in which the Jews will be the main object of his attack.

With respect to the *number* of those sealed — 144,000 in all; 12,000 in each tribe — the figures cannot be taken literally, as we shall show presently. In Scripture numbers are frequently symbolic, and the significance of a particular number is usually revealed in the passage where it is first mentioned. Thus 'twelve' occurs first in *Genesis 14*:4, where we read: 'Twelve years they served Chedorlaomer', indicating that it is the number of government.

Twelve times twelve, a hundred and forty four, could therefore represent *governmental perfection,* which will surely be true of the new Israel in the Millennium, when Christ reigns and all the world will in fact come under His perfect rule. The number is in thousands, doubtless in order to suggest profusion, and such will certainly characterise the ultimate population of Israel at the *close* of the Millennium. The population at the start of this period may be roughly estimated as follows. The number of Jews in Israel (1979) was 3.2 million, which we will assume may reach 4.5 million when the Lord returns at the battle of Armageddon. At this battle, described later, two-thirds of these Jews will be 'cut off and die' (see *Zechariah 13*:8) in unbelief, leaving 1.5 million of the faithful (v.9) as part of the total of the 'sealed' of Israel. The number of Jews in the rest of the world (1981) was about 12 million, increasing to (say) 15 million at the time of Christ's coming to earth. Of these, if the proportion of the faithful is the same as that in Israel, there would be 5 million 'sealed', making, with those in Israel, a total of 6.5 million. All these are Jews, i.e. the two tribes, Judah and Benjamin. Assuming the other ten tribes of Israel, scattered throughout the world, number five times that of the two tribes of the Jews and that the proportion of the faithful is the same, there would be 32½ million of the faithful among the ten tribes. These, with the faithful Jews, would total *39 million* of the 'sealed' members of the twelve tribes of Israel throughout the world, preserved to populate the new land of Israel at the opening of the Millennium. This figure, of course, can be only very approximate and probably minimal but is far in excess of the '144,000', proving that the scriptural number is a representative rather than an actual one.

The 'sealing' of the faithful will doubtless be a secret operation of which even they themselves are unaware. Yet, of course, their godly behaviour would single them out to their neighbours, even in the 3½ years before their 'sealing' — by their not worshipping the Beast or joining his church. In the last 3½ years of the Tribulation, their refusal to worship his image would normally be fatal, but their lives *will* be spared, for if there is to be a new Israel, formed by Christ, of mortal beings who turn to Him in repentance when He returns — as Scripture asserts (see *Ezekiel 37*:21—22; *Zechariah 12*:10) — it can only consist of the sealed ones who have not worshipped the Beast's image and yet have been divinely preserved from death. In the danger zone (round Jerusalem) many may escape death by fleeing from the neighbourhood to the 'mountains'

(*Mark 14*:14) or into the 'wilderness' (*Revelation 12*:14).

THE GENTILE MARTYRS OF THE PERIOD

If the faithful of Israel, by God's protection, survive the Great Tribulation (as they surely will), many of the faithful Gentiles will have to forfeit their lives, and these are seen by John (*Revelation 7*:9—17) as a great company in Heaven:

"After this I beheld, and, lo, a great multitude, which no man can number, of all nations and kindreds, and people, and tongues, stood before the throne, and before the Lamb (Christ), clothed in white robes (symbolising purity), and palms (typifying victory) in their hands; and cried with a loud voice, saying, Salvation to our God which sitteth upon the throne, and unto the Lamb. And all the angels stood round about the throne, and about the elders and the four beasts, and fell before the throne on their faces, and worshipped God, saying, Amen: Blessing, and glory, and wisdom, and thanksgiving, and honour, and power, and might, but unto our God for ever and ever. Amen. And one of the elders answered, saying unto me, What are these which are arrayed in white robes? and when came they? And I said unto him, Sir, thou knowest. And he said unto me, These are they which came out of great tribulation, and have washed their robes, and made them white in the blood of the Lamb. Therefore are they before the throne of God, and serve him day and night in his temple: and he that sitteth on the throne shall dwell among them. They shall hunger no more, neither thirst any more; neither shall the sun light on them, nor any heat. For the Lamb which is in the midst of the throne shall feed them, and shall lead them unto living fountains of water: and God shall wipe away all tears from their eyes".

The passage gives some idea of the privations and anguish endured by the Gentile martyrs before they are finally done to death — most of them, probably, when brought before the image of the Beast during the course of the Tribulation period. These privations, such as hunger and thirst, would doubtless come upon them soon after the start of the period, assuming that the world-wide branding of the mark of the Beast will then be enforced. Refusing to be so branded, the faithful would be unable to buy or sell and would thus find it difficult to maintain life. For most of them, confrontation with the Beast's image — if localised in the vicinity of Jerusalem, where the image will probably be set up — would not occur for some considerable time after the start of the Tribulation, time enough for them to become destitute before being killed by the image. If the suffering of these martyrs while on earth has been great, their bliss in the after-life will be more than compensation for them, as the passage indicates. Should they have any regret at all in their heavenly habitation, it would surely be that they had neglected to receive the Lord Jesus Christ as their Saviour in this present day of grace, when they could have been spared the anguish and death which they had in fact suffered. Yet a considerable number of faithful Gentiles will escape death during the whole period because, as we shall see later, they live to be rewarded when Christ comes to judge the nations — evidently through God's providential mercy.

THE EVERLASTING GOSPEL

This is to be proclaimed to the world by the angel (*Revelation 14*:6—13) just before the Tribulation, the opening words being as follows (v.7):

"Fear God, and give glory to him, for the hour of his judgment is come: and worship him that made heaven and earth, and the sea, and the fountains of water".

The good news of this 'gospel' is apparently not revealed until the closing words (v.13) of the passage:

"Blessed are the dead which die in the Lord from henceforth: Yea, saith the Spirit, that they may rest from their labours; and their works do follow them".

Evidently the 'everlasting gospel', as its name implies, promises blessing for the eternal hereafter rather than for the present life, which will have to be sacrificed by the Gentiles who 'fear God .... and *worship him*' (v.7) and who thus, when brought before the image, refuse to worship it. This 'gospel' then is quite distinct from that which has been preached since the time of Christ until the present day: 'the gospel of the grace of God' (*Acts 20*:24), which offers to the believer in Christ blessing not only in the life to come, but also here and now, as previously explained. The latter gospel was evidently that which was first preached by Christ Himself because it contains the same two conditions of blessing, 'repent and believe':

"Jesus came into Galilee, preaching the *gospel of the kingdom* of God, and saying, The time is fulfilled, and the kingdom of God is at hand: repent ye, and believe the gospel" (*Mark 1*:14—15).

Many expositors have thought that this 'gospel of the kingdom' differs from the 'gospel of the grace of God'. They argue that the 'kingdom' refers to the millennial kingdom to be set up on earth by Christ, but *that* kingdom could not plainly be stated to be 'at hand' when He spoke the words cited above, nearly two thousand years ago. Surely it is much more logical to believe that the kingdom He referred to was the Church which He was about to set up: a kingdom in 'mystery' perhaps, but still a kingdom in very truth. The parables about the kingdom of heaven (*Matthew 13*:1—52) all speak of the Church. The other allusion to the 'gospel of the kingdom', apparently in a different setting, is as follows (*Matthew 24*:14):

"And this gospel of the kingdom shall be preached in all the world for a witness unto all nations: and then shall the end come".

At first sight 'this' gospel is the same as that preached by our Lord at the beginning of His public ministry (*Matthew 3*:2 and, as cited above, *Mark 1*:14—15), but it is referred to in the context of the coming Tribulation seemingly just before the end of the age. Yet the message of this gospel would have no real application to the time after the Church is translated, and the opportunity for repentance is past — when, indeed, only the everlasting gospel will have meaning. We can only conclude that this gospel of the kingdom is the same gospel as our Lord preached and as the gospel of the grace of God, and that it will be preached only until the translation of the Church — to the end of the day of grace, some seven years short of the end of the age.

Reverting to the everlasting gospel, it not only promises blessing to the obedient but also gives warning to the world at large, first of the more immediate coming of the Great Tribulation ('the hour of his judgment' — *Revelation 14*:7) with a reminder of the then recent fall of the apostate world church ('Babylon', v.8) as an example of God's judgment on the wicked, and then of the much more terrible punishment of hell fire, the final fate of all those who disobey the commands of the everlasting gospel. This last warning is so solemn that we must quote the angel's words (vv.9—11) in full:

"If any man worship the beast and his image, and receive his mark in his forehead, or in his hand, the same shall drink of the wine of the wrath of god, which is poured out without measure into the cup of his indignation; and he shall be tormented with fire and brimstone in the presence of the holy angels, and in the presence of the Lamb: and they have no rest day or night, who worship the beast and his image, and whosoever receiveth the mark of his name''.

Evidently this warning will be given *before* the setting up of the Beast's image at the outset of the Tribulation and *after* the destruction of the apostate church, which confirms that the events will occur in this order.

THE TWO WITNESSES

Another important feature of the Tribulation will be the presence of God's two 'witnesses' on earth through the period, to speak and act for Him (*Revelation 11*:1—12).

''And I will give power unto my two witnesses, and they shall prophesy a thousand two hundred and three score days'' (v.3).

This period, equivalent to 3½ luni-solar years, is that of the Tribulation, during which, as the previous verse indicates, Jerusalem ('the holy city') will be under the heel of the Gentiles. The Beast, after abolishing the Jewish sacrifices in the temple there, may then perhaps make the city his headquarters, in order to enable him to supervise the construction of the image and to watch its worship, assuming that it will be erected in the area.

The witnesses are clad in sackcloth (v.3), signifying their grief at the prevailing wickedness, against which they evidently testify *daily* throughout the Tribulation — its duration is here given in *days* (1260). In contrast, the same period, when applied to the downtreading of Jerusalem, is measured in *months* (42 months), perhaps to bring home to the Jews the extent of their loss from a religious point of view — their holy days were frequently associated with the new moons.

The identity of the two witnesses can be deduced from vv.4—6:

''These are the *two olive trees,* and *the two candlesticks standing before the God of the earth.* And if any man will hurt them, *fire proceedeth out of their mouth, and devoureth their enemies:* and if any man shall hurt them, he must in this matter (i.e. by fire) be killed. These have power to *shut heaven, that it rain not* in the days of their prophecy: and have *power over waters to turn them to blood,* and *to smite the earth with all plagues,* as often as they will''.

The italicised phrases, as we shall show, make it reasonably certain that the two witnesses will be Moses and Elijah reincarnated. The 'two olive trees' take us back to an Old Testament prophecy (*Zechariah 4*:1—14) in which is recorded a vision: 'Behold a candlestick all of gold .... and two olive trees by it' (v.2—3).

The interpretation, in its initial application (vv.5—10), indicates that the two olive trees which supplied oil to the candlestick (in the *singular*) represent the Holy Spirit in Zerubbabel, who was thus empowered to lead the Jewish captives back to Jerusalem (see *Ezra 2*). The oil-fed candlestick (complete of course, with wick), is used in Scripture generally to denote a God-inspired witness: a nation (Israel), a local church (in the New Testament sense) or an individual, as in the case of Zerubbabel.

The prophetic vision, however, goes beyond Zerubbabel and has in view *two* individuals who are so filled with the Spirit that they themselves are depicted as the two olive trees. 'What are these two olive trees', says the prophet (*Zechariah 4*:11); 'These', replied the angel (v.14), 'are the two anointed ones, that stand by the Lord of the whole earth'. The *position* of the two, as stated in the last clause, suggests that they are the two witnesses of *Revelation 11,* who occupy virtually the same position (v.4, quoted above). Moreover, basically the same phrase, 'standing before the God of the earth' — except that 'of the earth' is omitted — is used in special connection with both Moses and Eljah. When Moses and the children of Israel stood before Mount Sinai to receive the ten commandments, the occasion is referred to (*Deuteronomy 4*:10) as 'the day that thou *stoodest before the Lord thy God* in Horeb'. Elijah introduces himself in the Bible, as he addresses Ahab, with the words (1 *Kings 17*:1): 'As the Lord God of Israel liveth, *before whom I stand,* there shall not be dew or rain these years, but according to my word'. Later Elijah is in Horeb (as was Moses) forty days and forty nights sustained by God (again true of Moses, *Exodus 24*:18), and he receives the command: 'Go forth, and *stand* upon the mount *before the Lord*'. (1 *Kings 19*:11). Long after, in the time of our Lord, the two men *together,* in glorified bodies, 'stood with him' on the mount of transfiguration (*Luke 9*:32).

In further support of the belief that the two witnesses will be Moses and Elijah, the special miracles associated with the old prophets are seen again in the case of the two witnesses. Thus, Elijah had the power by prayer to command that there should be no rain or dew on the land for three and a half years (1 *Kings 17*:1; *James 5*:17); it is significant that this period is also that of the Tribulation during which the witnesses, too, have the power to stop rain. The prophet was able, in addition, to call down fire from heaven to destroy those sent to take him (2 *Kings 1*:9—12); in the case of the two witnesses, fire from their mouths automatically kills those who would harm them — an even greater miracle. Moses was the instrument in God's hand of turning the waters of Egypt into blood and of bringing the subsequent plagues on the Egyptians (*Exodus* 7:14—20; *Exodus 8—10*): the witnesses are *themselves* able to turn water to blood and to 'smite the earth with *all* plagues *as often as they will*'. Clearly the two witnesses will have more power than Moses and Elijah, but this is to be expected from beings who have passed from this mortal life. Elijah, in fact, had never died but was taken up to heaven in 'a chariot of fire .... by a whirlwind'. (2 *Kings* 2:11). Moreover, Moses' death and buriel were decidedly unusual:

"So Moses the servant of the Lord died there in the land of Moab, according to the word of the Lord. And he (i.e. the Lord) buried him in a valley in the land of Moab .... but no man knoweth of his sepulchre unto this day. And Moses was an hundred and twenty years old when he died: *his eye* was *not dim, nor his natural force abated*" (*Deuteronomy 34*:5—7).

Evidently he did not die of old age and infirmity; presumably God terminated his life by His command on the day when the prophet had led the people of Israel to the very border of the promised land, after their forty years' wandering in the wilderness.

"And the Lord spake unto Moses that self-same day, saying, Get thee up into this mountain Abarim, unto mount Nebo .... and behold the land of Canaan, which I give unto the children of Israel for a possession: and die in the mount whither thou goest up .... because ye trespassed against me among the children of Israel at the waters of Meribah-Kadesh .... Yet thou shalt see the land before thee; but thou shalt not go thither unto the land which I give to the children of Israel" (*Deuteronomy 32*:50—52).

Ages afterwards, as we have shown, Moses and Elijah appeared with our Lord on the mount of transfiguration in the sight of three of His disciples. On this occasion, presumably, both the prophets had spiritual bodies but later, when they again come to earth as the two witnesses — if they are in truth such — their bodies, while still super-human, will be invested with a kind of mortality because, when their work is finished (but not until then), they will allow themselves to be killed by the Beast:

"And when they have finished their testimony, the beast that ascendeth out of the bottomless pit shall make war against them, and shall overcome them, and kill them" (*Revelation 11*:7).

Doubtless the Beast, their implacable enemy by reason of their fearless testimony against him, will have frequently sought their death but, until the Tribulation comes to its close, is unable to achieve his object because those sent for the purpose are repeatedly destroyed by the fire from the witnesses, just as in the case of Elijah of old.

What transpires after their death is vividly portrayed in the verses that follow (8—13). Apparently, at this time Jerusalem is a metropolis of the world and the seat of the Beast since the start of the Tribulation. The city will have become notorious for immorality (like Sodom in the days of Lot) and for religious persecution, especially towards the Jews (as in the Egyptian oppression in the days of Moses). The Beast's image may have been set up *in the vicinity* because, as we have seen, the accepted ruler *in Israel* (the false prophet) is responsible for its erection; and the immorality and persecution may well be centred around its worship. With such wickedness abounding, which the two witnesses will have constantly exposed, it is small wonder that there is general rejoicing when they are killed and their bodies lie unburied in a thoroughfare of Jerusalem. People from all parts of the earth flock to the city to see the dead bodies, perhaps to convince themselves that such supernatural beings had really died and possible also to gloat over their death as a seeming triumph of evil over good. It was an occasion even for sending gifts to one another and for making merry, because the witnesses had been a source of 'torment' to these and all evil-doers — torment to their consciences as well as to their bodies by the plagues inflicted. Yet their triumph is short lived: in three and a half days from the death of the two witnesses they have a spectacular resurrection: 'the Spirit of life from God entered into them, and they stood upon their feet; and great fear fell upon them that saw them' (v.11). The hearts of the evil-doers had at last been moved; what the witnesses could not achieve in their life they had done by their death and resurrection. Their history concludes thus (vv.12—13):

"And they (the onlookers) heard a great voice from heaven saying .... Come up hither. And they (the witnesses) ascended up to heaven in a cloud; and their enemies beheld them. And the same hour was there a great earthquake, and the tenth part of the city fell, and in the earthquake were slain *of men* seven thousand: and the remnant were affrighted, and gave glory to the God of heaven".

The original Greek for 'of men' means, literally, 'names of men' and would suggest that the people slain were those whom God had singled out (by name, as it were) for destruction, as being beyond redemption. Even this calamity was an act of God's mercy, to inspire such fear in those unharmed by the earthquake that they are constrained at least to acknowledge Him. Well does Scripture assert, 'The *fear of the Lord* is the *beginning* of wisdom' (*Psalm 111*:10; *Proverbs 9*:10), and it says of the wicked, 'There is no fear of God before their eyes' (*Romans 3*:18). Fear of God, however, is not sufficient by itself; it must be followed by repentance and faith in order to obtain salvation, and there is no indication that such was the case with the spared remnant.

THE SEVEN JUDGMENTS

As we have shown, it is ever God's way to endeavour to bring the wicked to repentance, and even His acts of judgment are designed with this end in view. We shall see evidence of this as we consider the series of divine punishments inflicted upon the earth during the period of the Great Tribulation. They will resemble the ten plagues of Egypt but will be much more severe and widespread. As seen in John's vision, there are two apparently *successive* groups of judgments: the first group introduced by seven angels with seven trumpets; the second group by seven angels with seven vials (full of the wrath of God), also called the seven last plagues — see *Revelation 8,9,11* (vv.15—19) and *16.* Yet, as we study the two groups, each of seven judgments, we perceive that the groups are *coterminous* at the end of the present age. It is therefore clear that the vial' judgments do not begin with the 'trumpet' judgments have all finished, as would appear from the visions — two visions, of course, cannot be seen together although their fulfilments may in fact be concurrent. We believe that this is largely the case with the two sets of judgments. The circumstances connected with a particular 'trumpet' are very much the same as those of the corresponding 'vial' (or 'plague', as we shall now refer to it). Thus, the first trumpet goes with the first plague, the second trumpet with the second plague, and so on. Yet the corresponding pairs are not exactly contemporaneous: there must be an interval of time, in some instances at least, between the trumpet and the plague, the trumpet giving the signal perhaps for a *partial* judgment as a warning which, if ignored, is followed by the full punishment of the plague.

In the accompanying table, 'The Seven Judgments', an attempt has been made to summarise the judgments in an orderly and intelligible fashion. Each trumpet and its corresponding plague are represented as two successive phases of one judgment: thus, there are only *seven* judgments, not fourteen. As already said, the

THE SEVEN JUDGMENTS

Judgment	Stage	Area	Instrument	Result
First	1st. Trumpet	Earth	Hail & fire, with blood	1/3 of trees and all grass burnt
	1st. Plague	Earth	Vial poured on earth	Noisome & grievous sore falls on men having the mark of the Beast.
Second	2nd. Trumpet	Sea	'Mountain' cast into sea	1/3 sea becomes blood, 1/3 sea creatures die, 1/3 ships destroyed
	2nd. Plague	Sea	Vial poured into sea	Sea becomes as the blood of a dead man; all life in sea is destroyed
Third	3rd. Trumpet	Rivers	Star falls into waters	1/3 of waters made bitter; many die of the waters
	3rd. Plague	Ditto	Vial poured into waters	Waters become blood
Fourth	4th. Trumpet	Sun & c.	Smitten	1/3 of sun, moon & stars darkened; 1/3 of day & night darkened.
	4th. Plague	Sun	Vial poured upon sun	Men scorched with great heat, blasphemed name of God, & repented not
Fifth	5th. Trumpet (1st woe)		'Locusts' from bottomless pit, led by Apollyon	All those who have not God's seal in their foreheads are stung by the locusts for 5 months & seek death in vain.
	5th. Plague	Seat of Beast	Vial poured on seat of Beast	Beast's kingdom darkened (by locusts?); his subjects, in pain, repent not
Sixth	6th. Trumpet (2nd woe)	River Euph-rates	200,000,000 'horsemen' from Euphrates	This judgment, 'prepared for the hour, day, month & year to slay the 1/3 part of men', is by fire & c. from the horses mouths & by injury from their tails. Rest of mankind repented not.
	6th. Plague	Ditto	Vial poured on Euphrates. Kings of the East freed	Activities of 'kings of the east' (China?) - by their 'horsemen' (an air armada?) - culminate in the Battle of Armageddon.
	7th. Trumpet (3rd woe)	Air & Earth	Lightnings... great hail & earthquake	'Great voices in heaven saying, The kingdoms of this world are become the kingdoms of our Lord... and He shall reign for ever and ever'. Thy wrath is come.
Seventh	7th. Plague	Ditto	Vial poured into air	'Great voice out of heaven saying, It is done'. Earthquake (greatest ever) causes triple division of Jerusalem & fall of 'cities of the nations'. Heavy hail. 'Every island fled away & the mountains were not found'. Great Babylon (the anti-God kingdoms of this world) is visited by God's wrath.

trumpet gives, in most instances, a warning judgment preparatory to the 'complete' plague to follow. For example, the second trumpet blast causes one third of the sea to turn to blood and one third of the sea creatures to die, whereas the second plague results in the *whole* of the sea turning to blood and in the death of *all* living things in the sea. The infliction is similarly fractional in the case of the first, third, fourth and sixth trumpets, but not in the corresponding plagues, which are more severe. Although there is no such fraction involved with the fifth trumpet, there is instead a time limit (5 months) for the judgment heralded by it — the period, perhaps, between this trumpet and the fifth plague. The sixth trumpet too seems to sound a progressive warning in terms of time: 'hour, day, month and year', indicating that the infliction would only be extended according as it continued to produce no change of heart. Alas! after the full extension, 'the rest of the men which were not killed by these plagues (i.e. of the sixth trumpet) repented not' (*Revelation 9*:20): how hard is the heart of man!

A survey of the table will show that many of the judgments to be poured upon this earth involve phenomena outside present human experience, but they should not, on that account, be allegorised — it will be a time of *unprecedented* trial, as Scripture emphasises. We have thought fit to take most of the judgments literally, as recorded; where there is a hidden meaning the context usually reveals what it is. Many fanciful, even farcical, interpretations of the visions we are studying and, indeed of all *The Revelation,* have been put forward by those who allegorise everything that is difficult to explain.

As we consider the table in more detail we notice that, whereas in the first four judgments (of both trumpets and plagues) people suffer *indirectly* from the effects of providential visitations in the realm of nature (earth, sea, rivers, and sun), at the fifth trumpet they are made the more direct object of attack — only the 'sealed' ones being exempt. In fact when this trumpet sounds, all the ensuing judgments take on a more terrible form as forewarned by the angel (*Revelation 8*:13): 'Woe, woe, woe, to the inhabiters of the earth by reason of the voices of the three angels, which are yet to sound'.

We propose now to comment briefly on each of the judgments in sequence. At the *first trumpet* there is a violent storm of hail and fire (lightning?) — 'mingled with blood' suggests that it is destructive to human and animal life if exposed, as well as to the plant life which is stated to burn up. No doubt this will be a severe blow to the world, similar to the plague of hail and fire which came upon ancient Egypt and brought Pharaoh to his knees (*Exodus* 9:23—28). *That* was indeed a storm the like of which had never before been seen in the land (v.24); if the future storm encompasses the earth, as seems probable, how much more terrible it will be! In the *first plague* the point of attack is not on the plant world but on mankind, those who have the mark of the Beast or who have worshipped his image. The 'sore' with which they are smitten, like the plague of boils in Egypt (*Exodus* 9:8—11), is evidently caused by something dispersed in the air, in this case by the angel with the vial — some irritant, or infecting organism, for example, to which the rest of humanity is in some way immune. The sore, apparently a very painful ulcer, should do much to convince the adherents of the Beast — presumably quite early in the Tribulation, soon after they have received his mark — that God is a force to be reckoned with.

The *second judgment,* turning the sea to blood, will doubtless be just as real as was the first plague in Egypt (the inland waters turned to blood, *Exodus* 7:19—21), with the same fatal effect on the living creatures of the water so transformed. The seaside resorts in the area will not be very popular and sea-fishing will stop but, more seriously, ships — presumably with their crews — will be destroyed in the affected seas.

The *third judgement,* upon the inland waters, touches mankind more closely than did the second judgment; the contaminant bitterness, in the warning stage (in the case of the third trumpet), causes many deaths by drinking the water; in the later stage (the third plague) in which the waters become blood, the hand of God would be more apparent to every one and the water would be equally undrinkable (as were the smitten waters of Egypt). The net result of this judgment, apart from numerous side-effects inevitably incurred, would be increasing suffering from the thirst until the contaminant — bitterness or blood — was gradually washed away from the flowing waters.

If the finger of God is seen in the spectacular act of turning water to blood — and this cannot be regarded as symbolic any more than the corresponding plague of Egypt, as already indicated — it will be even more apparent in the *fourth judgment* in which the bodies in *the heavens* are affected; a region in which man can play little or no part. In the trumpet stage, while the stated effect of the judgment — a third part of the day and night darkened — is fairly intelligible, the way in which it is said to be brought about (by a third part of the sun, moon and stars being darkened) is scarcely understandable to the finite mind. In the plague stage the angel's vial poured upon the sun evidently increases its output of heat but, although earth dwellers are 'scorched' by it, it causes them in general only to blaspheme and to remain unrepentant.

With the *fifth trumpet* blast the first woe begins, and for a period of five months all men except those having 'the seal of God in their foreheads' (*Revelation* 9:4, Israel's sealed ones of *Revelation* 7:3 are inflicted with such torment as makes them long (in vain) for death. The instrument of this woe, the 'locusts' — also of that which follows, the 'horsemen' — must, in these two exceptional instances, be taken symbolically, as the context shows. The locusts' place of origin, the bottomless pit, the prison-house of demons, at once proclaims them as a horde of these evil beings. Their king, Apollyon (Gr.) or Abaddon (Heb.) — both words mean the destroyer — is the angel of the bottomless pit (Gr. the abyss) and is apparently Satan himself, the 'star' who falls 'from heaven to the earth: and to him was given the key of the bottomless pit' (*Revelation* 9:1). Previous to this he will have already opened the abyss for the Beast to come out and manifest himself on the earth at the start of the Tribulation. Earlier still, during this present era and even before, there have been demon spirits on the earth, presumably let out of the pit by Satan, to do his wicked work and to seek possession of human souls when they can.

On the occasion of the fifth judgment, however, the demon army from the pit attacks the subjects of the Beast (Satan's man), those who have worshipped his image or have borne his mark. Virtually it will be a case of Satan against Satan: apparently he has not the power, even if he has the will, to prevent his demon horde's assault on his human followers — indeed, he has little regard for any person but himself. With respect to the *form* in which the demons appear we should first mention that originally they were angels who, with Satan, fell from grace. As such they would have spiritual bodies which are normally invisible to the human eye but, whereas angels have occasionally been made visible to certain human beings, there is no record in Scripture that demons have so appeared. The case of our Lord's temptation in the wilderness in confrontation with Satan is scarcely in the same category, as of course Christ had spiritual sight, along with other superhuman qualities, which He could exercise at will. The demons of the fifth judgment will presumably be seen by man for the first time in history, and the seer's view of them at least makes it clear that they will appear in a particularly terrifying form — we shall not attempt to interpret its obviously symbolic features.

In the *plague* phase of the fifth judgment, although the demons (the 'locusts') are not directly mentioned — as they are in the trumpet phase — they are evidently present because the Beast's kingdom if 'full of darkness' (locusts can darken the sky) when the angel's vial is poured upon his 'seat' (or throne) — *Revelation 16*:10. In spite of the excrutiating pain inflicted on his subjects (they 'gnawed their tongues') by the demons in this fifth plague, the tragedy is that the sufferers still do not repent but even blaspheme the God of Heaven (v.11). At least they are in no doubt that it is He Who is responsible for their tribulation.

The *sixth judgment*, in both trumpet and plague stages, appears to be concentrated in the Middle East region ('the great river Euphrates' — *Revelation 9*:14), leading up to the battle of Armageddon. Before the battle itself vast armies of 'horseman' will be on the move for a whole year in the area (vv.15—16) and cause innumerable casualties (v.18). The description of the 'horsemen' (vv.17—19) strongly suggests that they will in fact be aircraft. Doubtless the survivors of these progressively intensive air raids will be terribly shaken, but they still do not repent of their worship of devils and images, nor of their murders, sorceries, fornication and thefts (vv.20—21). In the plague stage of the judgment, taking us right up to Armageddon itself, the emphasis seems to be on 'the kings of the east' (*Revelation 16*:12), probably a Chinese confederacy. They may well have been responsible for the above-mentioned air attacks in the Middle East and now their troops are on the march that way, perhaps to occupy Israel. The reference to the drying up of the Euphrates, if it is not to be taken literally, may signify the breaking down of resistance in the area by these air raids. Meanwhile the rest of the world, inspired by the Beast and false prophet (under the influence of Satan, the 'dragon', vv.13—16), will have been mustering its forces perhaps to counter the threatened Chinese entry into Israel. In fact, a considerable part of the Beast's armies may have already been in the land and, having been decimated by the air attacks, now await reinforcements. At this juncture Russia, deciding perhaps at the last moment to act independently of the Beast, may anticipate the Chinese move and herself launch an attack on Israel, as intimated in our previous studies. The battle of Armageddon, now initiated, will be described under the heading that follows.

In the *seventh judgment*, which brings us to the close of the age, no direct reference is made as to the course of the battle, but its climax — notably the *earthquake* and *hailstorm* — is disclosed in both the trumpet and plague phases of the judgment. In the case of the trumpet (*Revelation 11*:19), the severity of the two calamities is not stressed, suggesting that this phase— as in previous judgments —will be less dramatic than the plague. In the latter (*Revelation 16*:17—21), the earthquake is described as 'such as was not since men were upon the earth, so mighty an earthquake, and so great', and its effect on the world (vv.19—20, summarised in the table) proves the truth of this statement. The severity of the hail is also expressed (v.21); one can easily imagine the damage and injury, probably throughout the earth, caused by hailstones weighing about a hundred-weight (50 kg.) each! As we have indicated, this disaster will be the climax of Armageddon which starts at the close of the sixth plague and culminates at the end of the seventh plague. In describing the battle itself we are now in a position to bring together all the scriptural information on the subject, some of which has already been mentioned previously.

THE BATTLE OF ARMAGEDDON

Essentially this is a battle between God, in the person of Christ (the Lamb), and Satan, in the person of the Beast. It will commence, practically at the close of the age, with an attack by the 'king of the south' (Egypt and her allies — an Arab confederacy?) on Israel under her ruler, 'the king' (the false prophet, the Antichrist). The 'king of the north' (Russia), who has long had designs on Israel since she has been re-established as a nation, will also come against her with all his forces, probably including a naval squadron ('many ships' — *Daniel 11*:40) via the Black Sea, a huge air armada ('like a cloud over the land' — *Ezekiel 38*:9), and doubtless with every armament of modern warfare. Of Israeli resistance to these onslaughts from the south and north nothing is told us in the relevant prophecies, possibly because their main purpose is not to chronicle a battle but to issue a warning: firstly to Israel, as to what is in store for her from her neighbours (their assault on her is in fact a divine punishment on her for accepting the false prophet as her king); and secondly to her would-be invaders, as to what their fate will be at the hands of God if they harm his people. Since only brief mention is made (*Daniel 11*:40) of the southern attack on Israel we may infer that she succeeds in warding it off. The northern aggression, frequently alluded to in much detail in Scripture, is clearly much more formidable, and Israel, if she is then as well informed as we should expect her to be — in spite of or perhaps because of the 1974 Arab assault on her, for which she plainly was not fully prepared — will have deployed her main forces to meet it. Also she may well be strongly supported, if not actually led, by the Beast who, as we have suggested, may have a strong garrison of western troops in the land and may too have ordered reinforcements from the west. The garrison may have already been used to repel the southern attack, which, incidentally, implies that at this time Egypt, as well as Russia, will throw off the Beast's yoke.

Apparently the combined western and Israel army will advance northward by way of the valley of Jordan or perhaps through the coastal plain of Sharon (the more direct route for sea-borne contigents landing in the south of the country), to reach the plain of Esdraelon (or Jezreel) near Megiddo. This ancient fortress town, which gives its name to the battle (Armageddon = hill of Megiddo), commanded the pass through the mountains between the plains of Sharon and Esdraelon. In the latter plain, the scene of many an ancient conflict, the forces from the south may well seek to halt the nothern aggressor: if so, the outcome of this first phase of the battle of Armageddon can be in no doubt because we know that the northern foe continues his rapid march southwards and storms Jerusalem (*Joel 2*:1—11). The plight of the inhabitants is terrible in the extreme (*Zechariah 14*:2), half of them being taken captive. Meanwhile the invader sweeps onward to Egypt, which he subjugates with great vigour (*Isaiah 19*:4), and appropriates her wealth (*Daniel 11*:43). He is supported in this campaign by the Lybians and Ethiopians who will previously have made an alliance with him (*Ezekiel 38*:5—6). Also in league with him are Persia and '*Gomer .... and Togarmah of the north quarters, and all his bands*'.

We have no certain knowledge as to the identity of the tribes which originally sprang from Gomer and his son Togarmah (*Genesis 10*:2—3), and settled in the north of what was later Canaan and then Israel, and as such they do not really concern us here. What is important to us is that we should get to know, if possible, what nations these particular names represent to *us in these last days,* to which the prophecy clearly applies (see *Ezekiel 38*:8). A possible clue is that the ancient name Gomer, embodied also in 'Togarmah' is basically similar to our word German and in fact to its equivalent in many important languages since the time of the Romans, who called thepeople on their northern border Germani (=neighbours), and their country Germania: the words are essentially the same, for example, in Greek, English, Russian and Hebrew. On these grounds, then, it is suggested that the names Gomer and Togarmah together indicated the nation of *Germany* as an ally of Russia at the battle of Armageddon. Indeed this interpretation of the prophetic names has already been partly verified inasmuch as East Germany (Togarmah?) is even now under Russian control. It remains for West Germany (Gomer?) in the future, by persuasion if not be compulsion, to join forces with the U.S.S.R. Of course, both she and Russia for most of the last septennium in which the Beast is in power, will be subject nations to him, but towards the close of the period — when many states will break away from him, as already indicated, she may well, in collusion with Russia, act against him.

The northern aggressor, at the climax of his triumphant advance through Israel and into Egypt, hears disturbing news from the north and east (*Daniel 11*:44) and swiftly returns northward in great fury, bent on crushing any further opposition. Yet he sees fit to encamp at Jerusalem, perhaps because his expected enemies, from the north and east, are reported to be approaching the city. From the north, presumably, come the scattered remnants of the defeated army in Esdraelon, regrouped and reinforced to renew the battle; from the east the troops of the assumed Chinese confederacy are at last nearing the city.

It is not recorded whether the armies thus gathered round Jerusalem — and they will include those of all the world powers (*Zechariah 14*:2), allied with or separate from those actually named above — eventually clash or not. They probably do *not,* as we know that they are reserved for the direct judgment of the Lord Jesus Christ at His return with His saints — it is a battle, as already indicated, between the kingdoms of this world, led by the evil trinity, and the kingdoms of our Lord. In fact all the nations have been gathered round Jerusalem for this final issue. Yet before it occurs, their movements will be halted by the inflictions of the seventh judgment, especially those of the later plague stage. Its greatest of all earthquakes, as we have seen, divides Jerusalem into three parts, and the heavy hail adds to the disaster, causing casualities to both combatants and civilians alike. The scene is set for the personal intervention of Christ in the battle, but as this 'climax of Armageddon' occurs at our Lord's coming to earth it will be considered in the next chapter.

CHAPTER 11

THE DAY OF THE LORD

This is very different from the Day of Jesus Christ, previously described. That 'day', as we may recall, will be the 7-year period in which the translated saints are with Christ in Heaven and which closes with the marriage supper of the Lamb. As that 'day' of bliss in Heaven ends, then the Day of the Lord begins on earth. It is much alluded to in the Old Testament as a day to be dreaded, for example (*Joel 2*:31):

"The sun shall be turned to darkness, and the moon into blood, before that great and terrible day of the Lord come".

The 'day' is so much to be feared that God will give an unmistakable warning of its approach by signs in the heavens: signs in the sun and moon, cited above and confirmed and added to by our Lord (*Matthew 24*:29):

"Immediately after the tribulation of those days shall the sun be darkened and the moon shall not give her light, and the stars shall fall from heaven, and the powers of the heavens shall be shaken".

Linking these two passages together, we learn that these celestial signs occur immediately *after* the Tribulation and *before* the Day of the Lord. The 'day' will probably be a brief period of seventy five days (see *Daniel 12*:7,12): 1,335 days less 1,260 (3½ times — v.7) days. The seven major events of such a period must therefore follow one another in fairly rapid succession — they are described under the headings which follow. They are given in chronological order, as far as can be ascertained by diligently comparing the relevant scriptures.

Preceding this sign, as intimated above, the heavens will be disordered, so much so that in another passage, evidently relating to the same occasion, we are told:

"There was a great earthquake; and the sun became black as sackcloth of hair, and the moon became as blood: and the stars of heaven fell unto the earth, even as a fig tree casteth her untimely figs, when she is shaken of a mighty wind. And the *heaven departed as a scroll* when it is rolled together; and every mountain and island were moved out of their places. And the kings of the earth, and the great men, and the rich men, and the chief captains, and the mighty men, and every bondman, and every free man, hid themselves in the dens and in the rocks of the mountains; and said to the mountains and rocks, Fall on us, and hide us from the face of him that sitteth on the throne, and from the wrath of the Lamb: for the great day of his wrath is come; and who shall be able to stand?'' (*Revelation 6*:12—17).

The earthquake mentioned here is doubtless the greatest ever one of the last plague, in wich 'every island fled away and the mountains were not found' (*Revelation 16*:20). It is evidently the final event of the Tribulation because it immediately precedes the signs which herald the Day of the Lord.

A further item of information, however, to which we wish to draw special attention in connection with these celestial signs, is the one italicised in the above passage, 'the heaven departed as a scroll'. Clearly it could not mean what it would seem to say, namely the *complete* destruction of the heavenly bodies, because this will not take place until *after* the Millennium, as we shall show later. Yet, preceded as it is by the star-fall and the shaking of the powers of the heavens (*Matthew 24*:29, previously quoted), this phenomenon here ('the heaven departed as a scroll when it is rolled together') must involve the disappearance of at least part of the material heavens, possibly all the bodies near enough to the earth to be seen by the unaided eye before their dissolution. The sun and moon, if not completely destroyed, will no longer function as light-bearers, as we shall show. At this point, when the material heavens cease to be seen of man, the spiritual Heaven is opened to his eye and he beholds the 'sign of the Son of man', (appearing, in some way, as a Lamb) by the throne of God His Father. The dazzling spectacle brings terror to humanity and they call on the mountains — seen not long before in violent agitation as a result of the earthquake — to hide the sight, by falling on them. The very mountains bringing death are less to be feared than the gaze of a holy God and the righteous anger of His Son.

THE LORD'S COMING TO EARTH

The sign of the Son of man in heaven is quickly followed by His coming to earth 'with power and great glory' (*Matthew 24*:30): 'Every eye shall see him, and they also which pierced him: and all kindreds of the earth shall wail because of him' (*Revelation 1*:7). Accompanying Him in His triumphal descent will be the translated saints, portrayed as 'the armies which were in heaven in another view of the scene, which is recorded as follows (*Revelation 19*:11—17):

"And I saw heaven opened, and behold a white horse; and he that sat upon him was called Faithful and True, and in righteousness he doth judge and make war. His eyes were as a flame of fire, and on his head were many crowns; and he had a name written, that no man knew, but he himself. And he was clothed with a vesture dipped in blood: and his name is called the Word of God. And the armies which were in heaven followed him upon white horses, clothed in fine linen, white and clean. And out of his mouth goeth a sharp sword, that with it he should smite the nations: and he shall rule them with a rod of iron: and he treadeth the winepress of the fierceness and wrath of Almighty God. And he hath on his vesture and on his thigh a name written, KING OF KINGS, AND LORD OF LORDS. And I saw an angel standing in the sun (seen by all?); and he cried with a loud voice, saying to all the fowls that fly in the midst of heaven, Come and gather yourselves together unto the supper of the great God".

Considering the earlier part of the above quotation, we learn that the One Who first came to this earth as the meek and lowly Jesus, despised and rejected by the world and mockingly crowned with thorns, will come the second time, with many diadems on His brow: He Who came to save the world now comes to judge it. His blood-red garment, symbolic of His mission of judgment, is in striking contrast with the pure white robes of 'fine linen' worn by His followers. Their apparel proves that they are the saints (v.8). Like their Leader, they are mounted on 'white horses', which could signify that they are to engage in a battle and will conquer not only by their power but by their purity of purpose and character — it is in *righteousness* that their Lord Himself will 'judge and make war'. His eyes, like fire, burn into every heart and conscience, and read every thought and motive. The sword from His mouth, not in His hand, shows that His spoken word both pronounces and *executes* judgment. It is sufficient for Him to give the command and the thing is done, just as in the beginning of creation (see *Genesis 1*) He said, for example, 'Let there be light and there was light' (v.3). Reason is that Christ should be called the Word (*John 1*:1) and that, in the passage here studied (*Revelation 19*:11—17), 'his name is called The Word of God'. Thus the Lord, descending from Heaven, will 'smite the nations', i.e. the armies gathered round Jerusalem, and He will bring to a climax the battle of Armageddon, as described under the following heading.

THE CLIMAX OF ARMAGEDDON

As Christ is seen, coming down with His saints from Heaven towards Jerusalem, the armies round the city are apparently impelled by the demonic Beast to join forces for an impious attack on the heavenly host when it reaches earth (*Revelation 19*:19). Let the words of Scripture recount the sequel (vv.20—21):

"And the beast was taken, and with him the false prophet that wrought miracles before him, with which he deceived them that had received the mark of the beast and them that worshipped his image. These both were cast alive into a lake burning with brimstone. And the remnant (of the armies) were slain with the sword of him (Christ) that sat upon the horse, which sword proceeded out of his mouth: and all the fowls were filled with their flesh".

Although the destruction of this vast multitude is initiated at the command of the Lord, it proceeds in a gruesome way:

"Their flesh shall consume away while they stand upon their feet, and their eyes shall consume away in their holes, and their tongues shall consume away in their mouth"(*Zechariah 14*:12).

Their annihilation is completed by their own hands:

"A great tumult from the Lord shall be among them; and they shall lay hold every one on the hand of his neighbour, and his hand shall rise up against the hand of his neighbour" (v.13).

This carnage, the food for the 'fowls' (*Revelation 19*:21), had previously been referred to by Christ when speaking to His disciples concerning the end of the age: 'Wheresoever the body is, thither will the eagles be gathered together' (*Luke 17*:37). The 'body' and the 'eagles' respectively depict the corpses of the slain at Armageddon and the carrion-eating birds ready, as by divine appointment, to feed on the flesh (*Revelation 19*:17—18).

THE JUDGMENT OF THE PEOPLE OF ISRAEL

We have shown (see Ch.10, the section 'The Sealing of the Elect of Israel') that at the beginning of the Great Tribulation a considerable number of people will be chosen by God out of all the twelve tribes of Israel. These 'elect' will be kept providentially from death and injury during the 3½-year period so that they may live to populate the New Israel in the millennial reign of Christ. Evidently they must also have been preserved during the previous 3½-year period when they would doubtless have proved their faithfulness to God by not worshipping the Beast — which, if it came to his knowledge, would provoke his wrath. During this earlier period, as already shown, the apostate world church would be in existence, and refusal to join it might well be fatal. Happily, however, the Jews — at least those living in Israel, as we have seen — will not be called upon to become members of that church because they will be permitted to have their own temple services. Presumably this exemption will apply to the Jews and the other ten tribes in the rest of the world, assuming the latter will be able to identify themselves as true Israelis. In any event, those among the twelve tribes *not* chosen and 'sealed' will fall under God's judgment at the close of Armageddon. Their fate may well be typified by that of the Jews in Israel, thus (*Zechariah 13*:8):

"And it shall come to pass, that in all the land, saith the Lord, two parts therein shall be cut off and die; but the third part (the 'elect') shall be left therein".

Further details of the same event presumably are given by Christ (*Luke 17*:34—36):

"I tell you, in that night, there shall be two men in one bed' the one shall be taken and the other shall be left. Two women shall be grinding (corn) together; the one shall be taken and the other left".

These two verses may illustrate what will happen, for example, in Jerusalem (see vv.31 and 37), the latter verse alluding to the slaughter at the battle of Armageddon. Those 'taken' typify the two-thirds 'cut-off', and those 'left' the one third preserved. Clearly the 'cutting off' occurs suddenly; there is no record of any preliminary trial of those summarily executed. There is in fact no need for such a trial. The doomed two-thirds of Israel will have already proved their guilt by acknowledging the false prophet as their Messiah; by worshipping the Beast and his image, and by receiving his mark. The remaining one third are chosen for blessing because they have *not* done these things but have been faithful to God during the whole seven-year period, although it meant much hardship and persecution for them especially in the latter half of the period. Their trial is aptly depicted in *Zechariah 13*:9:

"And I will bring the third part through the fire, and will refine them as silver is refined, and will try them as gold is tried: they shall call on my name, and I will hear them: I will say, It is my people: and they shall say, The Lord is my God".

THE CAPTIVITY OF SATAN AND THE FIRST RESURRECTION

The Beast and false prophet having been disposed of, the chief of the evil trinity, Satan, is now dealt with (*Revelation 20*:1—3):

"And I saw an angel coming down from heaven, having the key of the bottomless pit and a great chain in his hand. And he laid hold on the dragon, that old serpent, which is the Devil, and Satan, and bound him a thousand years, and cast him into the bottomless pit, and shut him up, and set a seal upon him, that he should deceive the nations no more, till the thousand years should be fulfilled: and after that he must be loosed a little season".

The passage cited above continues thus (vv.4—6):

"And I saw thrones, and they sat upon them, and judgment was given unto them: and I saw the souls of them that were beheaded for the witness of Jesus, and for the word of God, and which had not worshipped the beast, neither his image, neither had received his mark upon their foreheads, or in their hands; and they lived and reigned with Christ a thousand years. But the rest of the dead lived not again until the thousand years were finished. This is *the first resurrection.* Blessed and holy is he that hath part in the first resurrection: on such the second death hath no power, but they shall be priests of God and of Christ, and shall reign with him a thousand years".

It is clear from this account that the first resurrection is so called because it precedes the Millennium whereas the second resurrection, or 'the second death' as it is more appropriately termed in the text, occurs after this period. The first resurrection, in contrast to the second 'death' (considered later)', leads to *life* in its true and fullest sense, an eternity of happiness and holiness and satisfying service to God and Christ. Included in the first resurrection are not only the saints of the post-Church era, directly specified in the passage, but also, by implication, those raised at the Rapture, seven years previously. The Rapture, as we have seen, embodies a change of the living as well as a resurrection of the dead: nevertheless the resurrection phase must be regarded as part of the first resurrection, although separated in point of time. There are only *two* resurrections specified as such in Scripture, as, for example, those described by our Lord (*John 5*:28—29):

"Marvel not at this: for the hour is coming, in the which all that are in the graves shall hear his (Christ's) voice, and shall come forth; they that have done good, unto the resurrection of life; and they that have done evil, unto the resurrection of damnation".

Reverting to *Revelation 20*:4, the souls of the martyr saints, existing in Heaven since their death (by decapitation) during the Beast's rule in the last septennium of the age, are re-emobdied immortally by Christ, apparently just before He descends to earth.

THE 'HEALING' OF THE DEAD SEA

The territory of the present state of Israel has some physical defects, notably the excessive saltiness of the Dead Sea: it contains 20—27% (by weight) of salt, whereas normal sea water has about 6% salt. This is, of course, due to its position in the deepest depression on the earth's surface (1,292 feet — 395 m. — below sea level), and as it has no outlet when the river Jordan flows into it, the river salt, small though it is, continually builds up in the Dead Sea — the excess water is disposed of by evaporation in the hot atmosphere. From the beginning of its existence it would not take very long for the water of the Dead Sea to become saturated with salt, and it has necessarily remained so ever since, further incoming salt being deposited from solution. As a result of its high salinity the Dead Sea, as its name implies, has no fish living in it, and its arid briny atmosphere scarcely supports plant life on its shores. When Christ reaches earth He will correct this situation in the following marvellous way (*Zechariah 14*:8,9):

"And his feet shall stand in that day on the mount of Olives, which is before Jerusalem on the east, and the mount of Olives shall cleave in the midst thereof toward the east and toward the west, and there shall be a very great valley; and half of the mountain shall remove toward the north, and half of it toward the south .... And it shall be in that day, that living waters shall go out from Jerusalem; half of them toward the former sea (the Dead Sea), and half of them toward the hinder sea (the Mediterranean) .... And the Lord shall be king over all the earth''.

This cataclysm will cause the waters of the Mediterranean Sea to pour into the depression of the Dead Sea and continue northward to flood the Jordan valley to the Sea of Galilee (at present, 682 feet — 208 m. — below sea level) and beyond, almost to Lake Huleh (7 feet — 2.1 m. — above sea level); and southward from the Dead Sea to the Gulf of Akaba. Thus would be formed a great inland sea, some 200 miles (322 km.) long and 15 miles (23 km.) broad, with outlets to the Mediterranean and the Gulf of Akaba; in the early Glacial Period a frozen lake probably covered much the same area. It may well be, however, that the great earthquake of the seventh plague will have so altered the topography of the land as to make the position of the inland sea different from what we have depicted in Map 1 and Map 2 (on a larger scale), assuming unchanged topography. The main effect of the influx of sea water into the Dead Sea will be to reduce its salt content to that of the ocean or even less, as the fresh waters of the upper Jordan pour into it. Thus, as predicted in the Bible (*Ezekiel 47*:10):

"…. The waters *shall be healed* and …. there shall be a very great multitude of fish …. and it shall come to pass, that the fishers shall stand upon it (i.e. the shore of the Dead Sea) from Engedi (on the middle W. bank) even unto Eneglaim (on the N. shore); they shall be a place to spread forth nets; their fish shall be according to their kinds, as the fish of the great sea (the Mediterranean), exceeding many''.

The once dead waters will teem with life, and fishing will become a thriving industry there. Another great improvement, resulting from the cataclysm, might be a navigable water-way from Jerusalem to the Mediterranean Sea and to the Red Sea.

THE OCCUPYING OF THE LAND

The new land of Israel, thus prepared by our Lord, will be peopled, as previously indicated, by the 'elect': those among all the twelve tribes who will have kept faithful to God during the last seven years of all the age, the 70th 'week' of Daniel. Their trials will be particularly severe in the last 3½ years of that period of the Great Tribulation, when they will refuse to worship the Beast or his image. Although God will preserve (by 'sealing') these elect from death and injury, their sufferings will have the effect of refining them, to befit them to occupy their new land in the Millennium, as we shall see. In the sub-sections that follow we shall show how they are assembled in the land, something of their character and of the work they will do for God (their 'fruit-bearing').

The Gathering of the Elect. 'And he (Christ) shall send his angel with a great sound of a trumpet, and they shall gather together his elect from the four winds, from one end of heaven to the other' (*Matthew 24*:32), or 'from the uttermost part of the earth to the uttermost part of heaven' (*Mark 13*:27). Evidently, in a moment of time from all nations of the world, the elect will be picked out by the angels and transported to Israel:

"Thus saith the Lord God; Behold, I will take the children of Israel from among the heathen, whither they be gone, and I will gather them on every side, and bring them into their own land: and I will make them one nation in the land upon the mountains of Israel; and one king (Christ) shall be king to them all: and they shall no more be two nations, neither shall they be divided into two kingdoms any more at all" (*Ezekiel 37*:21—22).

The two kingdoms refer of course to that of Judah (including Benjamin: two tribes, the Jews) and that of the other ten tribes (originally called 'Israel' or 'Ephraim'). These two kingdoms will be united again — as they were under Solomon — to form the new Israel in the Millennium. Then shall be answered (in the affirmative) the question (*Isaish 66*:8): 'Shall the earth be made to bring forth *in one day?* or shall a nation be born at once?'.

The Character of the Elect. "And I (John, the seer) looked, and, lo, a Lamb (Christ) stood on mount Sion, and with him an hundred forty and four thousand, having his Father's name written in their foreheads .... These are they which were not defiled with women; for they are virgins. These are they which follow the Lamb whithersoever he goeth. These were redeemed from among men, being the firstfruits unto God and to the Lamb. And in their mouth was found no guile: for they are without fault before the throne of God" (*Revelation 14*:1,4—5).

These '144,000' are evidently the same people as those seen in the earlier vision (*Revelation 7*:4—8), the 'sealed' ones of Israel, considered in the preceding chapter. In both cases the number is identical and they are similarly marked in their foreheads. The people of the earlier vision are *stated* to be of the twelve tribes of Israel, so those of the later vision evidently belong to the same nation, being assembled *in her land* (on 'mount Sion' — Jerusalem). They must, in fact, be the elect who have been gathered by the angels from all parts of the world (as just described) and are now seen assembled together with the Lord in their promised land. A large area would be required to accommodate such a host; we have estimated that there might be some 39 million. Mount Zion in Jerusalem, as we know it today, would itself be far too small for the purpose. Possibly, the 'mount Sion' in the above passage might be representative of the whole country; the prophet's reference (*Ezekiel 37*:22, previously cited) to the same occasion gives 'one nation .... upon the *mountains of Israel*', which supports this idea.

Concerning the character of the elect, their 'chastity' is to be taken rather in a spiritual than in a moral sense, indicating their refusal to hold any association with the 'harlot' church and her 'fornication'. The assertion that they 'follow the Lamb' will be true of them only from the moment they see Christ on His descent to earth bearing the marks of His passion (*Zechariah 12*:10; *Revelation 1*:7). In the present 'year of the Lord' they will have refused to believe that He was their Messiah and have thus not been translated with the Church. During the last septennium they will have been faithful to God as such, but their unbelief in Christ will continue until they see Him on His return to earth at the close of the age. They will be like Thomas who would not believe in his risen Lord until he saw the marks of His crucifixion (*John 20*:25).

The elect are further said to be 'without fault' and to speak 'no guile'. This feature of their character is evidently referred to also in the Old Testament (*Zephaniah 3*:13): 'The remnant of Israel shall do no iniquity, nor speak lies; neither shall a deceitful tongue be found in their mouth'. Hitherto the nation has acted in the way described by our Lord (*Matthew 15*:8). 'This people draweth nigh unto me with their mouth, and honour me with their lips; but their heart is far from me'.

Finally, the elect are described as being the '*firstfruits* unto God and to the Lamb'. Israel, up to this time, when the new nation will be formed — has never, as a nation, borne any fruit to God or to Christ: to God, in Old Testament times, for choosing her from other nations to be a people for Himself, to serve and honour Him; to Christ the Lamb of Calvary, for coming as her Messiah to sacrifice His life for her and the world in general. We shall proceed to show, under the next heading, what will constitute her 'fruit' during the Millennium.

The Fruit of the Elect. In the plant kingdom, it is the nature of the tree that determines the kind of fruit it will produce. In a similar way, a person must be indwelt by the Spirit of God in order to bear fruit for Him, i.e. to manifest something of His character and to serve Him acceptably. *All* the elect, collectively, will have the Holy Spirit poured upon them when they are gathered together with the Lord on 'mount Sion' (*Ezekiel 36*:24—28. *Joel* 2:28—29). The *partial* fulfilment of the latter prophecy occurred at Pentecost when the eleven apostles and other followers of Christ (probably 120 in all) were endued with the Spirit (*Acts 1*:15 with *Acts 2*:1—4). The complete and final fulfilment of the prophecy is yet future, on the occasion we are now studying (*Revelation 14*1,4—5), when *every* member of the new Israel (39 million people in all?) will be filled with the Spirit. The apostle Paul also refers to this occurrence (*Romans 11*:26—27):

"And so *all* Israel shall be saved: as it is written, There shall come out of Sion the Deliverer, and shall turn away ungodliness from Jacob (i.e. Israel); for this is my covenant unto them, when I shall take away their sins".

This 'all Israel' has been widely thought to mean that every member of the nation, faithful or *unfaithful,* will ultimately be saved. Yet this idea is contrary to all the teaching of Scripture, e.g. 'without faith it is impossible to please God' (*Hebrews 11*:6). Moreover we have shown that, in fact, only the faithful one-third of the people of Israel will be saved to occupy her land; the other two-thirds will be cut off in unbelief (*Zechariah 13*:8—9). It is to this one-third that Paul alludes when he says 'all Israel shall be saved'. In his further statement it is to be noted that he uses the word *Sion,* just as in the passage we are considering (*Revelation 14*:1, 4—5) in which the '144,000' elect are seen on mount Sion, suggesting that both passages refer to the same event.

The new Israel will thus be fully equipped by the Holy Spirit to enable her to bear 'fruit' for God. This fruit will consist of *a special work* she will do for Him among the nations of the world in the Millennium, which will be explained in the next paragraph.

In the present age, the work of the Church is to '*go* into all the world and preach the gospel' with the object of saving souls. The work of the future Israel will be the *teaching of the Law in her own land,* with the object of educating all nations (who will come to her training schools — see Ch.12) in the Word and Will of God; this constitutes His Law in its basic sense and in its widest connotation. Thus, for example:

"But in the last days it shall come to pass that .... the house of the Lord shall be established in the top of the mountains, and it shall be exalted above the hills; and people shall flow into it. And many nations shall *come,* and say, Come, let us go up to the mountains of the Lord, and to the house of the God of Jacob; and he will teach us his ways, and we will walk in his paths: for the law shall go forth of Zion, and the word of the Lord from Jerusalem" (*Micah 4*:1—2).

We have emphasised that the nations will *come* to Israel, whereas, in this age, the Church is commanded to *go* to the nations. A further reference to Israel's work reads thus (*Isaiah 60*:1,3):

"Arise, shine; for thy light is come, and the glory of the Lord is risen upon thee .... And the Gentiles shall come to thy light, and kings to the brightness of thy rising".

The previous chapter (*Isaiah 59*:20) makes it clear that it is the elect of Israel ('Jacob') who are being addressed in the above quotation, at a time when 'the Redeemer shall come to Zion'. Plainly it is the same occasion as that already alluded to, when the Lamb shall stand on mount Sion (the same as Zion) with the '144,000', but *Isaiah 59*:21 further indicates that the *descendants* of the latter, throughout the Millennium, will be similarly endued with the Holy Spirit and be, like the first elect, His continual witnesses.

Witnessing for God is depicted in Scripture as light-bearing. Thus, for example, the Church in this age is represented (*Revelation 1*:12,20) as seven candlesticks, bearing the light of the Gospel to this spiritually dark and godless world. Israel's elect are symbolised as four trees bearing fruit in different ways. Of these, perhaps the *olive* tree portrays her witness: it yielded the pure oil (type of the Holy Spirit) which was used to keep the candlestick light burning in her tabernacle of old. Thus her elect will be inspired to show the light of God's Law (rather than the Gospel) to the Gentiles, in particular to unfold God's Word (the Bible) to them during the Millennium — salvation will then be by works rather than by faith. As the *vine,* planted and nurtured by God (*Isaiah 5*:2, etc.), Israel's 'fruit' will be to bring pleasure to His heart, just as the grapes from the vine yield wine which 'maketh glad the heart of man' (*Psalm 104*:15). The *fig-tree,* in Scripture, is characterised by its sweetness (*Judges 9*:11), and Israel's 'fruit' will be sweet especially to Christ when the elect 'follow the Lamb whithersoever he goeth'. When on earth, on one occasion He looked for fruit on a fig-tree and found none, signifying that Israel had never yet borne any fruit for Him. Thereupon He said to the tree, 'No man eat fruit of thee hereafter for ever', and it soon withered away (*Mark 11*:12—14, 20—21). Thus, symbolically, was Israel set aside in God's purposes and as His people, until the new Israel should appear. As the *pomegranate* she will bear fruit for God by reason of her priestly and other services connected with her new temple in the Millennium. The fruit figured on the high priest's robe which he was required to put on when about to exercise his office in the tabernacle (*Exodus 28*:33—34), and also on the two brazen pillars at the porch of Solomon's temple (1 *Kings 7*:42).

The Harvest of the Earth. While on the subject of fruit-bearing it is fitting that we should consider 'the harvest of the earth' (*Revelation 14*:14—20) reaped first by the Lord ('the Son of man', v.14) and then by an angel, the 'firstfruits' in the same vision having already been gathered as the '144,000' on 'mount Sion'. Since these elect are all that are left of Israel after the preceding judgment of that nation (previously described), the 'harvest' is presumably confined to the Gentiles. Here is the text of the above reference:

"And I looked, and behold a white cloud, and upon the cloud one sat like unto the Son of man, having on his head a golden crown, and in his hand a sharp sickle. And another angel came out of the temple, crying with a loud voice to him that sat on the cloud, Thrust in thy sickle, and reap: for the time is come for thee to reap; for the harvest of the earth is ripe. And he that sat on the cloud thrust in his sickle on the earth; and the earth was reaped. And another angel came out of the temple which is in heaven, he also having a sharp sickle. And another angel came out from the altar, which had power over fire; and cried with a loud cry to him that had the sharp sickle, saying, Thrust in thy sharp sickle, and gather the clusters of the vine of the earth; for her grapes are fully ripe. And the angel thrust in his sickle into the earth, and gathered the vine of the earth, and cast it into the great winepress of the wrath of God. And the winepress was trodden without the city, and blood came out of the winepress, even unto the horse bridles, by the space of a thousand and six hundred furlongs".

This is perhaps a preview, in graphic symbolism, of the same event narrated in plain language by our Lord (*Matthew 25*:31—46) and described under the next heading. Here we shall consider the additional details afforded by the passage quoted above. The first *reaping* (by Christ) would signify the setting aside for blessing of those who are judged worthy (the 'sheep' in *Matthew 25*). The 'reaping' in this connection becomes more meaningful in the light of perhaps a third reference to this occasion (*Matthew 3*:12), in which those who are blessed are called the 'wheat', to be gathered by the Lord into the 'garner' (granary), but the 'chaff' He will burn 'with unquenchable fire'. Evidently, the worthless chaff will be those who, as the 'grapes' in the passage we are studying, are gathered by the *angel* reaper and cast into the 'winepress' of the wrath of God. The terrible carnage depicted by the phrase 'blood .... unto the horse bridles, by the space of a thousand and six hundred furlongs (200 miles — 322 km.)' might well apply to the destruction of the Gentile armies round Jerusalem at the battle of Armageddon, as well as to that of their civilians later at the judgment of the nations, also occurring in such a space *round* the city, as we shall show in the section that follows.

THE JUDGMENT OF THE GENTILE NATIONS

The Gentile peoples from all over the world will be assembled for judgment in the valley of Jehoshaphat (*Joel 3*:1—2), apparently the vast plain (*Zechariah 14*:10) extending north and (mainly) south of Jerusalem, from 'Geba' (6 miles — 10 km. — N.N.E. of the city) to 'Rimmon' (9 miles — 15 km. N. of Beersheba). The distance from north to south would thus be about 45 miles (73 km.). If we assume the distance from east to west to be of the same order, the area (and position) would approximate to that of the province of Judaea (in our Lord's time), a mountainous region. That it will be a *plain* at Christ's second coming to earth (v.9) may be explained by the fact of the great earthquake of the seventh plague, as a result of which 'every island fled away, and the *mountains were not found.* (*Revelation 16*:20). The plain would be capable of holding a very large number of people — we calculate standing room, at least, for the whole world, especially as its normal population will have been considerably reduced by the decimations of the seven judgments. Presiding as Judge at the great gathering will be the Son of man, the *Lord Jesus Christ,* then enthroned as King of the World. Further details of this grand assize (*Matthew 25*:31—46) are as follows. With the Lord are all *the 'holy angels'*,probably positioned with Him well above the ground, not being subject to the Law of

Gravity. With Him too, though not mentioned in the text, are *all the resurrected saints* (*Jude 14—15*) including His erstwhile Church (see 1 *Corinthians 6*:2) now His Bride, who all evidently share in the judgment. Present, finally, will be *the elect of Israel,* to whom the Judge repeatedly refers as 'My brethren' (*Matthew 25*:40,45); they, as human beings still, will be on the ground, perhaps together in the centre of the Gentile host. Never before on earth will there have been anything like it: the serried ranks of people, stretching as far as from London to Brighton; the sky full of saints and angels, whose immortal bodies will doubtless be rendered visible to every eye (as were the angels at Christ's birth in Bethlehem, *Luke* 2:13); and last, but before all, the uplifted throne bearing the Son of God, the King of Kings in all His glory.

The Great Separation. Christ's first judicial act is to divide the vast throng into two companies (*Matthew* 25:32—33), as ' a shepherd divideth his sheep from the goats' — the sheep, as always in the Gospels, represent those who are blessed, and the goats those who are condemned. The Lord (the *first* 'reaper', as we have seen) is personally responsible for the separation, picking out His own to stand 'on his right', the remainder being relegated to His left; a line of demarcation between the two groups extending to the horizon.

The blessing pronounced on the 'sheep' is that they are to 'inherit the kingdom prepared for you from the foundation of the world', i.e. come into the benefits of the millennial reign of Christ, just begun but planned before the creation of the world. The criterion of their blessing is that they showed mercy and charity to His 'brethren', the elect of Israel, during the period of the Beast's power, especially in the Great Tribulation when they will have been the particular object of his persecution. The Judge regards this kind treatment shown to His elect as done to Himself, thus He says to the 'sheep' at His right:

"For I was an hungred, and ye gave me meat: I was thirsty, and ye gave me drink: I was a stranger, and ye took me in: naked, and ye clothed me: I was sick, and ye visited me: I was in prison, and ye came unto me".

When the 'righteous' (i.e. the 'sheep' of the Gentiles) ask Him how they could have thus befriended Him, He replies:

"Verily I say unto you, Inasmuch as ye have done it unto one of the least of these my brethren, ye have done it unto me".

The deeds specified give some indication of the privations which the elect of Israel will have to endure at the hands of the Beast and his subjects; and the Gentiles who sought to alleviate their sufferings would doubtless do so at their peril. Incidentally, these Gentiles themselves could not have worshipped the Beast or his image, or received his mark — to have done so would forfeit all possibility of their being blessed at all.

The Gentiles who are condemned (the 'goats') are judged by the same criteria as are those who are blessed and — because they *failed* to minister to Israel's elect in the way specified — are sentenced to 'everlasting fire, prepared for the devil and his angels'. This would have been their ultimate fate in any case, because of their worshipping the Beast and his image, or of receiving his mark; but the Judge chooses that the immediate ground of their condemnation must be their treatment of His elect. The wholesale destruction of these Gentile 'goats' is immediately effected (by the angels — *Matthew 13*:39,41) throughout the vast plain: the resulting carnage is well depicted by the expression 'blood .... unto the horse bridles, by the space of a thousand and six hundred furlongs' (*Revelation 14*:20).

Thus is our Lord's kingdom, at its commencement, cleansed from all evil-doers, as predicted by Him (*Matthew 13*:41—42):

"The Son of man shall send forth his angels, and they shall gather out of his kingdom all things that offend, and them which do iniquity; and they shall cast them into a furnace of fire: there shall be wailing and gnashing of teeth".

First to be eliminated, as intimated earlier, will have been the Beast and false prophet; then the *military* forces of political 'Babylon', the last great world-system of Gentile powers during the closing septennium of the present age, at Armageddon; next the unfaithful of Israel. then Satan himself ('bound' in the abyss for a thousand years); and, finally, those among the *civil* population of the world (the Gentiles) condemned at the judgment described above.

The passage in *Matthew 14* continues thus (v.43): 'Then shall the righteous shine forth as the sun in the kingdom of their Father', depicting the dawn of the grand millennial 'day' when Christ will reign with His saints, as set forth in the next chapter.

CHAPTER 12

THE MILLENNIAL REIGN OF CHRIST

In the record of the creation of the universe (*Genesis 1*) the seventh day was appointed by God as a day of rest (*Genesis*2:2—3), typifying the Millennium, the long Sabbath of this world, truly a time of rest for God and His creatures. All the lower orders of creation will again be subject to man, as they were before his fall, and will serve him without let or hindrance — and man, unopposed by Satan, will be free to serve God.

NATURE RESTORED

In the *plant* kingdom, the ground will no longer yield harmful and unwanted products: 'Instead of the thorn shall come up the fir tree, and instead of the brier shall come up the myrtle tree: and it shall be to the Lord for a name, for an everlasting sign that shall not be cut off' (*Isaiah* 55:13). What better sign than the two evergreens could there be? A *perpetual* reminder to God that His curse on the earth had been for *ever* removed; to man that he should now be *always* praising the name of the Lord for His deliverance, in which, indeed, all nature is regarded as participating. 'The mountains and the hills shall break forth before you into singing, and all the trees of the field shall clap their hands' (v.21). Doubtless, along with the thorns and briers and suchlike, all poisonous plants will be eradicated.

The *animal* kingdom shall no more be 'red in tooth and claw'. ''The wolf also shall dwell with the lamb, and the leopard shall lie down with the kid; and the calf and the young lion and the fatling (young animal fattened for the table or for the temple sacrifices) together; and a little child shall lead them. And the cow and the bear shall feed; their young ones shall lie down together;

and the lion shall eat straw like the ox. And the sucking child shall play on the hole of the asp, and the weaned child shall put his hand on the cockatrice' (or adder's) den. *They shall not hurt nor destroy* in all my holy mountain: for the earth shall be full of the knowledge of the Lord, as the waters cover the sea'' (*Isaiah 11*:6—9).

The italicised expression will of course apply to all kinds of animal and plant life, including insects and other small creatures as well as micro-organisms (bacteria, etc.). Many of these are now harmful and destructive; they, and all living things will then be helpful and peaceable.

Human life will be lengthened to at least what it was originally, in the period from Adam to Noah; thus most people will live through the Millennium. The death of a man a hundred years old will then be regarded as that of a child (*Isaiah 65*:20), and a wrong-doer of that age will be as unusual as a hardened child sinner is today and will be the object of even greater contempt. With so few deaths in the world at that time, patently the population — relatively small at first as a result of the drastic 'weeding out' by the 'sickle' of the angelic 'harvester' — will increase at a high rate and the earth will soon teem with people. Yet there will be ample food for all; the fertility promised for Israel's land (*Isaiah 35*:1,6) will doubtless apply to the world at large: 'The wilderness .... shall be glad for them: and the desert shall rejoice and blossom as the rose .... for in the wilderness shall waters break out, and streams in the desert. And the parched ground shall become a pool, and the thirsty land springs of water'. Certainly, in order to sustain the vast populations that will eventually develop, the land masses of the earth will need to have their maximum fertility. This may well be achieved, partly by the previous land displacement due to the great earthquake — resulting in a most efficient river system throughout the world, especially in the present desert areas — and partly by a better rainfall distribution, perhaps due to a re-positioning of the seas and an alteration of the earth's contours. Virtually there will be a new earth and — as a result of the star-fall and planetary changes preceding the Lord's coming — new heavens (*Isaiah 65*.17); in both there will be a new look and new functions, in keeping with the start of a new civilisation.

CHANGES IN THE HEAVENS AND THE EARTH

Most noticeable from the earth will be the *absence of the sun and moon* from the sky: 'The sun shall be no more thy light by day: neither for brightness shall the moon give light .... but the Lord shall be unto thee an everlasting light, and thy God thy glory' (*Isaiah 60*:19—20).

This statement from Holy Writ raises a number of problems which cannot be solved by known physical laws. Apparently the solar system, as we know it, will be no more and time will be measured differently. In some supernatural way, our globe will be illuminated from the light which emanates from Christ, but we do not know how earth will be warmed or what its course will be in space — that everything will be ideal for man's environment cannot be doubted. The intensity of the perpetual daylight is indicated in an earlier part of the prophecy (*Isaiah 30*:26) as being *seven times the sun's* light. This dazzling brightness from the Lord during the Millennium will doubtless be diffused throughout the world in a way that will render it perfectly suitable to the human eye.

THE NEW ISRAEL

In the Millennium, Israel will be the leading nation of the world: 'For the nation and kingdom that will not serve thee (Israel) shall perish; yea, those nations shall be utterly destroyed' (*Isaiah 60*:12). *A new city* 'Jehovah-Shammah' ('The Lord is there' — *Ezekiel 48*:35), will replace Jerusalem as the seat of world government under Christ the King. Israel's *territory* will be far more extensive than at present (including the land she won in June, 1967) and will stretch from the Nile to the Euphrates, in fulfilment of God's promise to Abraham nearly 4,000 years ago: 'Unto thy seed (descendants) have I given this land from the river of Egypt to the great river, the river Euphrates' (*Genesis 15*:18).

In order to appreciate the extent of this promise, we must look into Abraham's previous journeyings. The city of Ur, of which he was a native, was then at or near the mouth of the Euphrates — the site of the former city, excavated in 1923 by Sir Charles Leonard Woolley, is now some 150 miles (241 km.) from the present river's mouth. In Ur, Abraham received a call from God (*Genesis 12*:1—3):

''Get thee out of thy country, and from thy kindred, and from thy father's house, unto a land that I will show thee: and I will make of thee a great nation, and I will bless thee, and make thy name great; and thou shalt be a blessing .... and in thee shall all the families of the earth be blessed''.

In obedience to the command, Abraham (then called Abram) and his family left Ur and travelled first to Haran (see Map 1, lat. 37°, long. 40° approx), probably following the course of the Euphrates for some 700 miles (1,130 km.). Staying at this city (as it was then) until the death of his father, Terah, he turned south to cross the river and to proceed towards Canaan, the country to which God directed him and which was to be Israel's home. After he had traversed the land to its southern limit, a severe famine, doubtless ordained by God, caused him and his family to enter Egypt, where they remained for a time and then returned to live in Canaan. Not long after, when he had separated from his nephew Lot, he received the above-cited promise of the country which, with his long journey from Ur to Egypt in mind, he might well expect to extend to the limit of his travels. If we interpret the promise in this broad sense, Israel in the Millennium would possess about 200,000 square miles (520,000 sq. km.) of territory (as in Map 1), comparable to that of France. On this interpretation, as we see from the map, the eastern border is assumed to follow the course of the Euphrates, from a point S.W. of Haran, namely at Tiphsah (now Thapsacus), right down to Basra, near the river mouth. Tipsah (= ford) was the most important crossing place in the middle course of the river and was doubtless used as such by Abraham in his journey from Haran southwards. In Solomon's time it had probably become a town and marked the northern extremity of his empire, where it touched the Euphrates (1 *Kings 4*:24). It seems reasonable therefore to assume that the site of this ancient crossing will also mark the point where the north border of the new Israel will touch the Euphrates. Of course Solomon's empire, although more extensive than the territory of any other king of Israel — possibly occupying as much as 50,000 square miles (130,000 sq. km.), was small in area compared with what her future land will be.

The division of the new Israel among the twelve tribes, as shown in Map 1, is based on the prophecy of *Ezekiel 48.* This chapter informs us that their portions of territory, 'from the east side unto the west side' (vv.2, 3 etc.), will consist of tribal strips whose north and south borders follow parallels of latitude, as in the map. It will be noticed that the strips increase in length as they go from north to south — owing to the S.E. course of the Euphrates. To compensate for this as far as possible and give an equal allotment to each

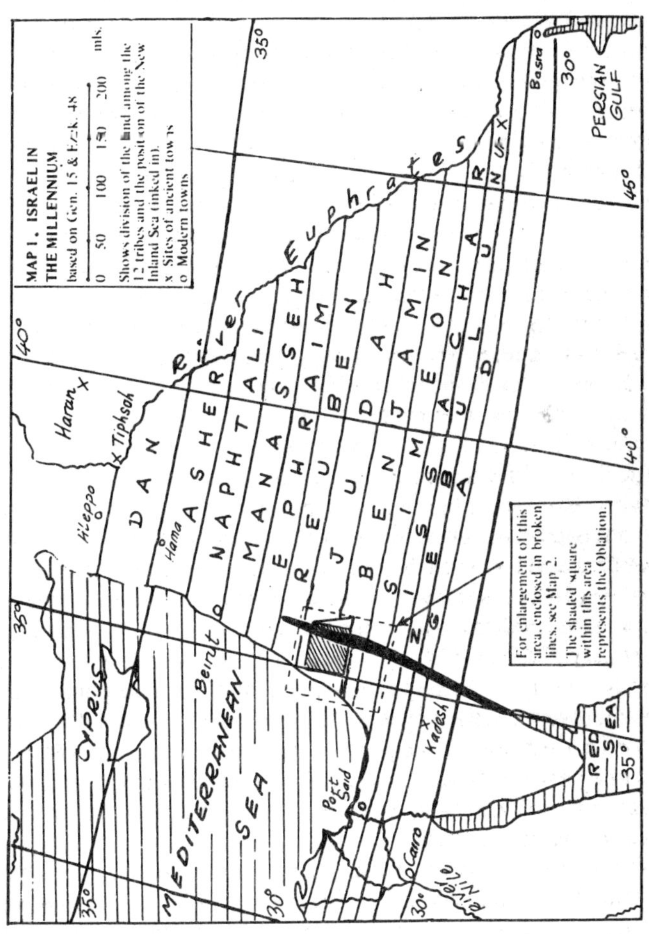

MAP 1. ISRAEL IN THE MILLENNIUM
based on Gen. 15 & Ezek. 48
0 50 100 150 200 mls.
Shows division of the land among the 12 tribes and the position of the New Inland Sea (inked in).
x Sites of ancient towns
o Modern towns
CYPRUS
MEDITERRANEAN SEA
Hileppo
Haran
Tiphsah
Hama
Beirut
Port Said
Cairo
River Nile
Kadesh
River Euphrates
Basra
PERSIAN GULF
RED SEA
UR
DAN
ASHER
NAPHTALI
MANASSEH
EPHRAIM
REUBEN
JUDAH
BENJAMIN
SIMEON
ISSACHAR
ZEBULUN
GAD
35°
40°
45°
30°
For enlargement of this area, enclosed in broken lines, see Map 2.
The shaded square within this area represents the Oblation.

tribe, the widths of the strips have been correspondingly decreased, from Dan in the north to Gad in the south. The southern border of Gad will be of course the southern border of the nation, too, and is stated (v.28) to pass by Kadesh (or Kadesh-barnea — now identified with the modern Ain Kadis) and extend westward to 'the river toward the geat sea'. The 'great sea' is of course the Mediterranean Sea and 'the river' denoted *the river of Egypt.* This italicised phrase is used in Scripture either for the Nile or for the brook, now called the Wadi el-Arish, 100 miles (160 km.) or more east of the Nile — according to which of the two original Hebrew words for river is used.

In specifying the extent of Solomon's dominions, the word meaning the Wadi was used (1 *Kings 8*:65) to mark their S.W. limit, whereas in God's original promise to Abraham the word for the Nile was used. Thus, according to the promise we have taken the *Nile* (the most westerly branch of its delta) as being the S.W. border of the new Israel, although, strangely enough, the 'river' in the passage (*Ezekiel 48*) we are studying, and which applies to her future land, is the Wadi. The reason for this may be that it was not God's purpose to reveal to Ezekiel the full extent of the promised land. In his vision, indeed, it is within much narrower limits that in the promise to Abraham — not only, as just indicated, in the position of its S.W. boundary, but also with regard to its eastern border. Thus there is no mention at all of the Euphrates; only the Jordan is specified in this connection, and even Solomon's empire reached to 70 miles (112 km.) east of that river. Of course, it must be noted that Ezekiel's prophecy was written at a time when the Jews were in captivity and it would have been extremely unwise, from a human point of view, to mention the Euphrates, a river in the territory of their Babylonian captors! Another possible reason why this river is not alluded to by the prophet is that it may no longer exist when the prophecy is fulfilled, because of the cataclysmic changes produced by the great earthquake of the seventh plague; or even before this, in the sixth plague, by which the Euphrates is 'dried up' (*Revelation 16*:12), taking the verb literally. Whether the river as such will exist or not when the new Israel is formed we believe that the land will extend to the position of the present Euphrates, in fulfilment of the original promise to Abraham and in accordance with his expectations, and we have so drawn Map 1.

The Oblation. The Oblation (or offering) in the millennial kingdom will comprise a square of land (and water) 'offered' to the Lord by His elect people of Israel (*Ezekiel 48*:20). Its general position is shown in Map 1 but we shall need to refer to the enlargement (Map 2) for its detailed study. In the centre of the oblation is Israel's new temple with its inner and outer courts (described later) and its spacious enclosure, almost one square mile — each of its four sides measured 500 reeds (*Ezekiel 42*:16—20). A reed is stated to be 6 cubits long: assuming twenty inches to the cubit, the measuring reed would thus be ten feet in length (just over 3 m.). The oblation itself is a vast square of territory, each side of 25,000 reeds (*Ezekiel 48*:20) or a fraction over 47 miles (76 km.).

The central section of the oblation (containing the temple) is allocated to the priests. It is rather surprising that such a large area, equal to the north section given to the Levites — should be allocated to such a relatively small body of men compared with a whole tribe like the Levites. It may be, however, that the extra land — over and above what the priests require for themselves and their families — will be utilised by those coming from all over the world for instruction in the law of God, as previously intimated.

In the smaller, southern section of the oblation lies the *new city*, named 'The Lord is there' (*Ezekiel 48*:35). In the original Hebrew it is called Jehovah-Shammah, but in the Millennium this name may well be abbreviated or modified. The city, a 8½ mile (14 km.) square, will thus be considerably larger than the present city of Jerusalem (ancient and modern), which it will replace. Its southern boundary will evidently lie some distance (a mile or so perhaps) north of the present city, which will have been at least partly destroyed (and engulfed?) by the seventh plague and by the cleavage of the mount of Olives, resulting in the influx of the Mediterranean Sea, at our Lord's coming to earth. The new city will be a world metropolis where, as its name imples, Christ will have His throne. Under Him the twelve resurrected disciples (Matthias replacing Judas Iscariot?) will 'sit upon twelve thrones, juding the twelve tribes of Israel (*Matthew 19*:28). A strip of land, ½-mile (800 m.) wide all round the city, will be for the 'suburbs' (*Ezekiel 48*:17), and the large area (19 × 9½ square miles — 30 × 15 sq. km.) to the west and east of the city will be to raise food for the city workers (v.18). Yet, according to our assumed position of the new Inland Sea (Map 2), most of the land to the east of the city will be covered with water, which would lessen its effectiveness for food raising.

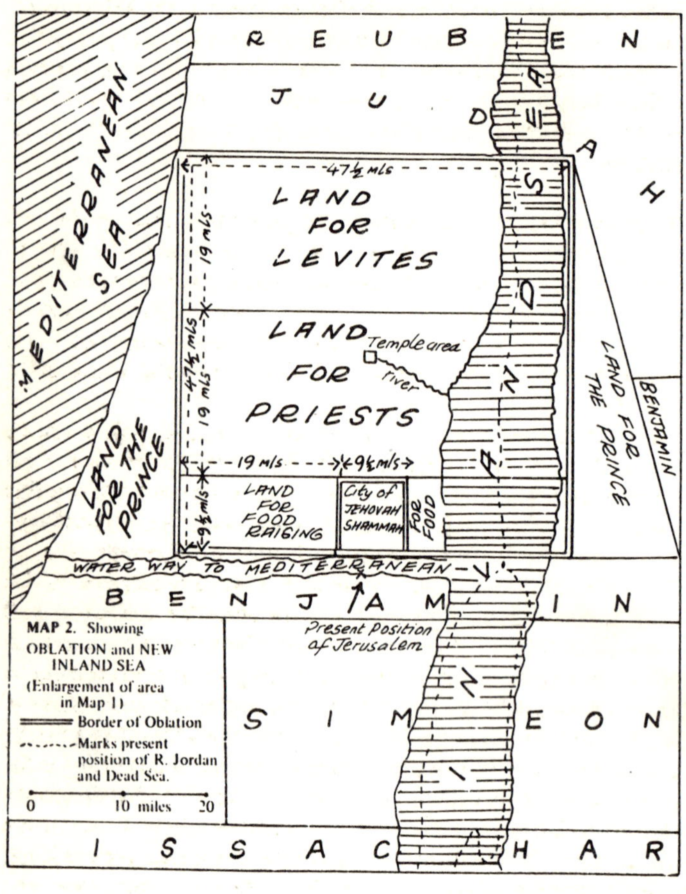

MAP 2. Showing OBLATION and NEW INLAND SEA (Enlargement of area in Map 1)

This suggests that the Inland Sea to the north of the present position of the Dead Sea may be narrower than we have assumed, its western shore being more easterly to leave more land to the east of the city. As we have already indicated, the topography of the present Jordan valley may be changed before the onset of the Millennium, due to displacement of land by the calamities occurring just before — which makes it impossible to predict with precision the position of the Inland Sea. Reverting to the new city, the water-way from the Mediterranean may allow ocean-going ships access to its outskirts.

The Prince. Outside the oblation, the portions of land on the east and west sides of it are allotted to 'the prince' (v.21). His western strip evidently reaches to the Mediterranean coast but there is no indication as to the extent of his territory on the eastern side. A reasonable assumption is that it will occupy the same area and have roughly the same shape as his western strip — as we have positioned it in Map 2.

Respecting the identity of the prince, at first sight it might be imagined that he will be Christ Himself, but the simple fact of the prince's relatively small allocation of land shows at once that this is not so, for Christ will be King of all the earth. Also, consideration of what is recorded of the prince's part in the temple services (*Ezekiel 45*:22), a principal role though it is, demonstrates that he is but human: he has to prepare a sin-offering for *himself* as well as for all the people. That he is a mortal being is proved, too, in the fact that he has sons, to whom he will give 'inheritance out of his own possession' (*Ezekiel 46*:18). An earlier reference (*Ezekiel 34*:23—24) to Israel in the Millennium mentions David as a prince and a shepherd — in a spiritual sense of course, ministering to the spiritual need of the people. It may well be therefore that the prince who is specially connected with the religious life of Israel in the Millennium will be able to trace his descent from the ancient king, perhaps through Mary, the earthly mother of Jesus (see His genealogy, *Luke 3*:23—31), and will also be named David.

The Temple and its Courts. The millennial temple in Israel is described in much detail (*Ezekiel 40—44*), which we have sought to embody in the accompanying Plan. Before commenting on this temple, the last of Israel's four temples, it may be of interest to list her previous three, thus:

1. Solomon's temple, completed 1012 B.C., destroyed (with the city itself) by fire in 587 B.C. by Nebuchadnezzar, on the 10th day of the 5th moon (*Jeremiah 52*:12).

2. Zerubbabel's temple: foundation laid in 520 B.C. on the *24th day of the 9th month* in the Jewish calendar (December 17th by our western calendar); rebuilt by Herod in 17 B.C.; destroyed (with the city) by the Romans under Titus in A.D. 70 — on the 10th day of the 5th month, exactly as with Solomon's temple!

3. The future temple: built after the translation of the Church by the present nation of Israel and possibly destroyed seven years later by the earthquake of the seventh plague.

The precise day and month of the founding of the second temple has been stressed above, because it was to be repeated remarkably in 1917 when Jerusalem (and later Palestine) was freed at long last from Moslem domination and the foundation laid for Israel to become a nation once more (see Appendix V). It is also singular that the destruction of this second temple was to occur on the same day of the same month as that of the first temple.

Returning to our brief consideration of the fourth temple to be built in the Millennium, we would call attention to the massive wall (10 feet — 3 m. — high and 10 feet thick) which surrounds both the outer and inner courts of the temple (*Ezekiel 40*:5; *41*:5). The length of the outer wall is not given directly but it can be calculated from the measurements that *are* given (*Ezekiel 40*), *viz* the distance between the northern outer and inner gates (100 cubits) and between the southern outer and inner gates (100 cubits); the length of the eastern inner court wall (100 cubits), and the lengths of the four gatehouses involved (4 × 50 cubits). Thus the total length of each of the four walls surrounding the outer court would be: (3 × 100) + 200 cubits = 500 cubits, or 278 yards (254 m.). As can be seen from the Plan (enlargement) the gatehouses contain guard-rooms so that the temple and its precincts can be adequately protected against possible intruders. The *east gate* is the most important because it is in direct line with the entrance to the inner court and to the temple itself. Also it is through this gate that 'the glory of the Lord comes into the house (temple)' — *Ezekiel 43*:4 — to consecrate it at its completion. The gate is therefore kept closed to all except the prince (*44*:1—3) who 'shall sit in it to eat bread before the Lord; he shall enter by the way of the porch of that gate, and shall go out by the way of the same'.

The Spring. A 'spring' issues from under 'the threshold of the house eastward: for the forefront of the house stood toward the east' (*Ezekiel 47*:1 etc.), doubtless to supply fresh water for the temple personnel. The spring then flows through the temple courts in the direction suggested in the Plan: presumably openings would have to be made in the inner and outer walls for the water to pass through them. It starts as a stream, reaching ankle-depth in about a third of a mile, and becomes an impassable river in less than a mile and a half. A mile or more of this course would traverse the ground of the outer enclosure (1 mile — 1.61 km. — square) of the temple and its courts. The river continues downwards — the temple is built on a high mountain (*40*:2) — till it reaches the sea (the new Inland Sea?), a distance of about ten miles in all. On both banks of the river, at least over its course through the outer enclosure, 'shall grow trees for meat, whose leaf shall not fade, neither shall the fruit be consumed: it shall bring forth new fruit according to his months, because their waters issued out of the sanctuary: and the fruit thereof shall be for meat, and the leaf thereof for medicine' (*47*:12). It is not easy to see how this passage can be taken otherwise than literally, in a context (*Ezekiel 40—48*) abounding with material details, and we must therefore conclude that, in the Millennium, there will be in the region of Israel's temple, trees of a type hitherto unknown.

The Temple Offerings and the Feasts. In the ancient Tabernacle ritual, the priests who offered the sacrifices were frequently unworthy, with the notable exception of Zadok who remained faithful in the midst of the apostasy (1 *Kings 1*:7—8). In the millennial temple, only the 'sanctified' descendants of Zadok (*Ezekiel 48*:11) will be allowed, under the prince, to exercise the priest's office in offering sacrifices. Indeed, it seems strange that animal sacrifices should have to be offered at all after Christ has given Himself as the one sacrifice for sin. In this present era of grace, if any member of the Church should commit a sin he has only to *confess* it to God to be forgiven and cleansed (1 *John 1*:9). In the Millennium, although sinning will be the exception rather than the rule, Israel will once again be required to offer regular sacrifices, 'to make reconciliation for the house of Israel' (*Ezekiel 45*:17). There will be burnt

PLAN OF ISRAEL'S MILLENNIAL TEMPLE AND ITS COURTS

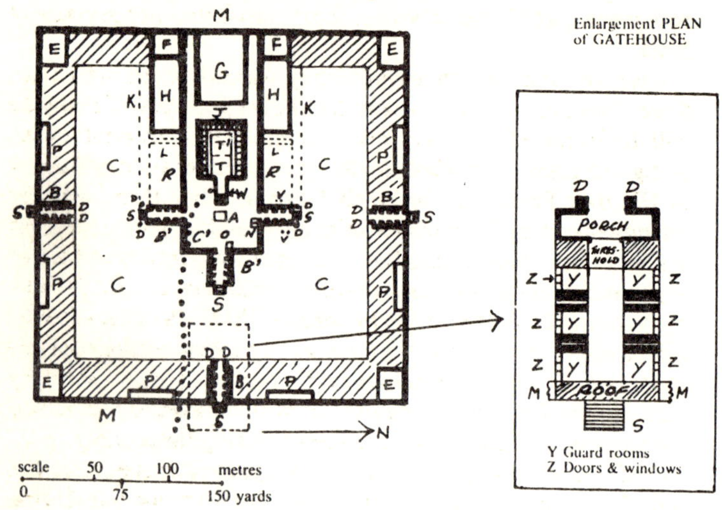

A	Altar, in front of temple porch
BBB	Three outer gatehouses
B′B′B′	Three inner gatehouses
C	Outer court
C′	Inner court
D	Columns in front of gatehouses
E	People's cooking places
F	Priests' cooking places
G	Building before 'the separate place' (*Ezekiel 41*:12, etc)
H	Priests' chambers
J	Space in 'separate place'
KK	Two walks
L	Screen walls
M	Wall of outer court
N	Chamber in inner court for priests and singers
O	Chamber for officiating priests
P	Sets (6) of 10 chambers, on the pavement (shaded area) all round outer court
R	Wall of inner court
S	Steps (seven to each outer gate, eight to the inner gate)
T	Temple (i.e. the holy place)
T′	Holy of Holies
	Round T and T′ on three sides are 3 storeys, each with 30 chambers
V	Places for killing sacrifices
W	Porch of temple

Approximate course of spring ....

offerings, sin offerings, peace offerings, drink offerings, trespass offerings and meat offerings — as in the tabernacle but frequently differing in detail. The offerings will be 'in the feasts, and in the new moons, and in the sabbaths, in all solemnities of the house of Israel'.

It is noteworthy that there will be only *two main feasts* in the year, those of the Passover and Tabernacles; the original Feast of Pentecost will be excluded. The Passover, in the Old Testament times, prefigured Christ's sacrificial death and was thus fulfilled at Calvary in His own Person as the Paschal Lamb. Since then, with the setting aside of the Jews and the bringing in of the Church, the Feast has been superseded by the Lord's Supper (the Breaking of Bread — commonly Holy Communion) which looks *back* to Christ's death in commemoration of it. In the Millennium the Feast of the Passover will be re-introduced, doubtless also as a continual reminder of that death and all that it has procured for humanity. It is especially fitting that the Feast of Tabernacles, originally celebrated as a harvest thanksgiving, should be observed again during the coming age, a time of fruitfulness (*spiritual*, as well as material) if ever there was one. This feast will be not only for Israel but for the Gentile nations who will be commanded (*Zechariah 14*:16—19) to 'go up year by year to worship the King, the Lord of hosts, and to keep the feast of tabernacles' — failure to do the former, at least, will bring 'no rain' and 'the plague' on the defaulting nation, notably Egypt. The Feast of Pentecost will not be observed by Israel, probably because it looked forward to the outpouring of the Holy Spirit — which was only *partially* fulfilled on Whitsunday, just after Christ's ascension, but will have its complete realisation for Israel, at least, in the Millennium. Clearly there will be no need for the shadow when the substance is present, so to speak.

THE IMMORTAL SAINTS

On earth during the Millennium will be a host of people with immortal bodies, similar to angels: the saints of the Church and of the pre-Church period (the Old Testament saints) translated together at the Rapture, and the saints of the post-Church period (the last seven years of the present age), resurrected at the Lord's return to earth. Pre-eminent among them will be the Bride (the erstwhile Church) indissolubly united to Him as the Lamb's wife and reigning with Him as Queen (*Psalm 45*:9). Also participating in His rule, as 'kings and priests', will be the pre-Church and the post-Church saints (see *Revelation 5*:10 and *20*:4—6).

The presence of these spiritual beings raises the question as to how they will have contact and communication with the world of people still 'in the flesh'. In the normal way, such beings — like angels — are invisible to the human eye, but in the Millennium presumably, they will have or be given the capacity to make themselves visible to humanity, either periodically or permanently. Whatever the answer is, it is plain that there will be a co-existence of mortal and immortal persons, unique in the history of mankind, perhaps serving as an introduction to the final (eternal) state of *all* spiritual existence subsequent to the Millennium.

Our present natural bodies are subject to severe and humiliating limitations; in respect of time, temperature, movement, health, dependence on the provision of food and drink, and subjection to the uncertain duration of life itself. The spiritual bodies of the saints are 'fashioned like unto his (Christ's) glorious body' (*Philippians 3*:21) and will not be subject to death, disease, hunger, thirst, cold or heat, physical laws (e.g. the law of gravity) or material obstacles (see *John 20*:26). The spiritual body will be infinitely more powerful than the natural body, and a true expression of the very self.

CHAPTER 13

THE LAST PHASE OF THE BATTLE AND AFTER

SATAN'S FINAL FLING

During the Millennium, with the Devil a prisoner in the abyss, the comparative infrequency of wrong-doing, although mainly the result of Christ's firm rule, will evidently be due to a considerable degree to the absence of Satan's evil influence. This becomes more obvious when he is released at the end of the thousand years and we see how effectively he renews his attack on humanity.

"When the thousand years are expired, Satan shall be loosed out of his prison, and shall go out to deceive the nations in the four quarters of the earth, Gog and Magog, to gather them together to battle: the number of whom is as the sand of the sea. And they went up on the breadth of the earth, and compassed the camp of the saints about, and the beloved city: and fire came down from God out of heaven, and devoured them" (*Revelation 20*:7—9).

We saw in an earlier reference (*Ezekiel 38* and *39*) that 'Gog and Magog' were the names given to represent Communist Russia (see under "The King of Fierce Countenance", p.39) characterised by their deceit and subversive propaganda, as inspired by Satan the arch-deceiver. Using similar tactics, on his release from the 'bottomless pit', the Devil (the antitype of Gog) will soon succeed in poisoning the minds of all the nations of the world (Magog?) against the 'saints'. These are, presumably, the 'sealed' ones of Israel and those of their descendants during the Millennium who have remained faithful to the Lord, and also the Gentile converts. (The immortal saints, those who reigned with Christ in the Millennium, will be of course immune from injury or death, and would not be the direct object of Satan's attack.) All the rest of humanity, a vast host, will be induced by Satan to attack the saints in their 'camp', probably in the area of the oblation in Israel, which would be spacious enough to accommodate them. Their resistance to this assault will prove unnecessary because, at the moment when the 'camp' and the 'beloved city' (Israel's capital) are surrounded by the attacker, God Himself intervenes and destroys their enemies by fire — a holocaust indeed, of which the Devil is the immediate cause. Again, but for the last time, he will have deluded man into thinking that he can rebel against God with impunity: the Deceiver and the deceived; Gog and Magog; the Devil and his dupes! Yet fundamentally they are to blame because, although perforce they submitted themselves to the Lord during the whole thousand years of His reign, they never, as individuals, yielded to Him their heart's allegiance.

Thus Satan fails in his effort to vanquish the Lord's people but succeeds in precipitating the doom of the rest of the world. For this success his satisfaction, if any, is short-lived:

"And the devil that deceived them was cast into the lake of fire, where the beast and the false prophet are, and shall be tormented day and night for ever and ever" (*Revelation 20*:10).

THE FINAL JUDGMENT

At this point of time, only the saints will be alive on the earth, *viz* the elect nation of Israel and the faithful among the other nations. These Gentile saints will include not only the 'sheep' (*Matthew 25*:33—34) — those who will have befriended Israel's elect and not submitted to the Beast during the last septennium of the present age, prior to the Millennium — but also all those who, as a result of Israel's teaching and example during the Millennium, will have been won for Christ. All these saints, of Israel and other nations, will evidently survive the Millennium because, at its close, as we shall see, only the *wicked dead* will be resurrected, to be judged at the 'great white throne' (*Revelation 20*:11—15). Before this event, however, the living saints much be changed into spiritual beings since there will then be no earthly dwelling-place for them: 'And I (John) saw a great white throne, and him that sat upon it, from whose face the earth and the heaven fled away; and there was found no place for them' (v.11).

The Destruction of the Universe. Before the Millennium, as already explained, there will be a *partial* disintegration of the universe. At the close of that period, before God administers the final judgment, there will be a *total* dissolution of all matter and also, it appears, a dissociation of the spiritual Heaven. Both the material and spiritual realms, since Satan's fall, have long been defiled. From that time his presence in Heaven has been tolerated by God, but he will shortly, we believe, be cast out — apparently at the commencement of the Great Tribulation (cf. vv.9 and 13—14 of *Revelation 12*). Since man's fall in Eden the earth has been defiled by his sin. The favourable conditions of the Millennium (under Christ's reign and with Satan expelled) finally will demonstrate that the human race, as a whole, is incorrigible and still succumbs to Satan's wiles. God's long forbearance will come to an end and He will destroy the old order of His creation, thus (2 *Peter 3*:7,12): 'But the heavens and the earth, which are now, by the same word are kept in store, reserved unto fire against the day of judgment and perdition of ungodly men' (v.7). The verse makes it plain that the fiery dissolution will be brought about by 'the same word', i.e. the word of God (v.5), which had called the worlds into existence — they were created and will be destroyed virtually at His command.

Later in the chapter the apostle explains that on two occasions (vv.10 and 12), apparently without any break between them, 'the elements shall melt with fervent heat'. The first occasion (v.10) is termed 'the day of the Lord' and therefore refers to the pre-millennial, partial disintegration of the universe, indicated above and fully described in Ch.11 (p.125). The second occasion is called '*the day of God*', a term which we have not met hitherto. The expression looks forward to a period of time under the control of God (the Father; see 1 *Corinthians 15*:24,28) as distinct from His Son, Who will then hand over all His present authority to His Father. It will be at a point of time when the Lord Jesus will have reigned and 'put all enemies under his feet' (v.25) — clearly after the Millennium and the last battle in which Satan is finally eliminated. At this point, God will set up His 'great white throne' and 'from whose face the earth and the heaven fled away: and there was found no place for them' (*Revelation 20*:11).

These considerations demonstrate that the 12th verse of 2 *Peter 3* has reference to the *complete* destruction of the universe by God at the close of the Millennium. The two events — the partial and total dissolutions of the universe — will, in fact, be separated by at least a thousand years: it seems that the first event serves as a warning for the second, the 'day of God'. Before that day, since man's creation, the **Son** of God will have been the conspicuous figure of the Holy Trinity: first as his Representative (the 'seed of the woman' — *Genesis 3*:15), then as his Redeemer and lastly as his King in the Millennium.

The Great White Throne. This throne of judgment, with God Almighty seated thereon, will be the centre of the final Assize, administered in the all spiritual realm, all material things having been dissolved and all the unbelieving dead resurrected (*Revelation 20*:12—15).

"And I (John) saw the dead, small and great, stand before God; and the books were opened: and another book was opened, which is the book of life: and the dead were judged out of those things which were written in the books, according to their works. And the sea gave up the dead which were in it; and death and hell delivered up the dead which were in them: and they were judged every man according to their works. and death and hell were cast into the lake of fire".

It will be recalled that the *first* (pre-millennial) resurrection will consist of the Old Testament saints (from the creation of man to Christ), the saints of the Church (from Christ to the Rapture, which will include the Old Testament saints) and the saints (mostly martyrs) of the post-Church period, raised seven years after the Rapture, at the end of the age and at the outset of the Millennium. All the rest of the dead, from the creation of man, will not be resurrected until the close of the Millennium (v.5). Their bodily remains, whether in the sea or on the earth, buried or cremated (vain hope that cremation will be the end!), will be reassembled in an immortal form and re-united with the soul from hell (Gr. Hades, the unseen world) where it has been existing since death in a state of torment. The scriptural passage (*Luke 16*:19—31) which describes this intermediate state is momentous and must be quoted in full — these are the words of the Lord:

"There was a certain rich man, which was clothed in purple and fine linen, and fared sumptuously every day: and there was a certain beggar named Lazarus, which was laid at his gate, full of sores, and desiring to be fed with the crumbs which fell from the rich man's table: moreover the dogs came and licked his sores. And it came to pass, that the beggar died, and was carried by the angels into Abraham's bosom: the rich man also died, and was buried; and in hell (Hades) he lift up his eyes, being in torments, and seeth Abraham afar off, and Lazarus in his bosom. And he cried and said, Father Abraham, have mercy on me, and send Lazarus, that he may dip the tip of his finger in water, and cool my tongue; for I am tormented in this flame. But Abraham said, Son, remember that thou in thy lifetime receivedst thy good things, and likewise Lazarus evil things: but now he is comforted, and thou art tormented. And beside all this, between us and you there is a great *gulf* fixed: so that they which would pass from hence to you cannot; neither can they pass to us, that would come from thence. Then he said, I pray thee therefore, father, that thou wouldest send him to my father's house: for I have five brethren; that he may testify unto them, lest they also come into this place of torment. And Abraham saith unto him, They have Moses and the prophets; let them hear them. And he said, Nay, father Abraham: but if one went unto them from the dead, they will repent. And he said unto him, If they hear not Moses and the prophets, neither will they be persuaded, though one rose from the dead''.

We have already referred to 'Abraham's bosom' (see p.78) or Paradise, the place of comfort to which the souls of all the dead saints are lodged until the resurrection. Although this heavenly abode is 'afar off' from Hades, with an impassable 'gulf' between, it is within sight and sound of it — of course, in these spiritual realms, all the terms can only be symbolic of the reality. Hades is a place of fiery torment in which the souls of those who have died in unbelief are incarcerated until their bodies are raised at the final judgment. Then the souls will be liberated from Hades, reunited to the bodies, and each whole personality, then immortal, will be judged at the great white throne 'according to their works' as recorded in 'the books'. Apparently, these books will contain a detailed account of all the deeds, words, and even thoughts (which are as culpable as deeds — see *Matthew 5*:22,28), perhaps 'played back', so to speak, in sound and sight to each individual, so that guilt will be self-evident. Thus every one is cast into the lake of fire — deserved in the first instance by the person's wicked works but finally because his name is 'not found written in the book of life'. This book is also called 'the Lamb's book of life' as it contains the names of all who have been justified, not by their own works but by the precious blood of Christ, the Lamb of God, which 'taketh away the sin of the world' (*John 1*:29). Unsaved reader, it is not your sin that will ultimately condemn you but your *unbelief*: in fact, 'he that believeth not is condemned *already* (*John 3*:18), and his final fate will be the lake of fire, the 'second death'.

The Lake of Fire. This is a place where 'the worm dieth not, and the fire is not quenched' (*Mark 9*:44), symbolic of the continuous gnawing of the conscience and the burning of self-judgment, which will constitute the everlasting torment of the people there. Unfailing memory will call up a vivid recollection of the sins committed in mortal life, and especially of the lost opportunities of being saved — a perpetual source of anguish which will cause 'wailing and gnashing of teeth' (*Matthew 13*:42). As in Hades, the presence of others in the same plight will be no consolation but rather an additional pang to the conscience, especially if they were relatives or friends (see *Luke 16*:27—30). Above all, Satan himself will constantly pervade this place of doom — prepared, in fact, for him and his angels (*Matthew 25*:41) — and he will certainly do nothing to mitigate the sufferings of the lost, who will then (too late!) bitterly realise how deluded they were on earth to give him their allegiance.

THE FINAL STATE OF THE BLESSED

The ultimate destiny of the saved ones from earth will be an everlasting life of bliss in the presence of God and Christ, and of satisfying service in a new environment.

The New Universe. The seer (John) describes the new order thus: 'And I saw a new heaven and a new earth, for the first heaven and the first earth were passed away; and there was no more sea' (*Revelation 21*:1). It is reasonably certain that the new creation will not be material, governed by physical laws, because it will be designed to suit a higher order of beings than that of humanity. The phrase 'no more sea' is doubtless symbolic, probably indicating that the 'nations' in this eternal abode will not be separated any more by such barriers as distance, race or language — a reversal of the punishment of Babel (*Genesis 11*:8—9), imposed because of man's sin.

The vision continues as follows (*Revelation 21*:3—5):

"And I heard a great voice out of the heaven saying, Behold, the tabernacle (dwelling place) of God is with men, and he will dwell with them, and they shall be his people, and God himself shall be with them, and be their God. And God shall wipe away all tears from their eyes; and there shall be no more death, neither sorrow nor crying, neither shall there be any more pain: for the former things are passed away. And he that sat upon the throne said,

Behold, I make all things new''.
Evidently there will no longer be a separate Heaven and earth but rather Heaven *on* earth (see under the heading that follows). The remainder of the passage (vv.4—5) speaks for itself concerning the eternal life and unalloyed joy of God's people in this place of bliss.

The New Jerusalem. 'And I John saw the holy city, new Jerusalem, coming down from God out of heaven, prepared as a bride adorned for her husband' (v.2). Apparently the 'city', outwardly, will be a manifestation of the Bride (the Lamb's Wife), as explained in the next sub-section; but in other respects (vv.12—27; also *Revelation 22*:1—5) it will virtually be Heaven itself. For example, it will be the dwelling place of 'the Lord God Almighty and the Lamb'; 'the throne of God and of the Lamb shall be in it'; the city had no need of the sun .... to shine in it: for the glory of God did lighten it, and the Lamb is the light therof'. Moreover, all sin is excluded from it: 'And there shall in no wise enter anything that defileth, neither whatsoever worketh abomination, or maketh a lie: but they which are written in the Lamb's book of life'.

In the Millennium, the world will be ruled by Christ from Israel's capital city, as we have seen. Similarly, in the eternal state, it may well be that the new Jerusalem will be the governmental centre — as it were, Heaven in the midst of the new earth. There, outside the city, as we shall show, 'the nations of them which are saved shall walk in the light of it' and will have the right of admission into it, through the 'gates' in the 'wall' of the city.

The Bride. Once, on earth, she was the Church; in the eternal state, she will appear, doubtless symbolically, as the city. Her place, as the Lamb's wife, will naturally be at the side of the Lord Jesus — He is consistently called the Lamb in this heavenly sphere, a perpetual reminder of His sacrifice on Calvary. As God and the Lamb are enthroned in the midst of Heaven, the Bride will be in the closest proximity to them on every side, in the three dimensions of the city depicted as a perfect cube — perhaps a symbol of the spiritual, whereas a square, of only two dimensions, might typify the purely material. The measures of the cube, 12,000 furlongs (1,500 miles — 2,414 km.) each side, cannot be taken literally (especially the height!): the numbers are probably symbolic of the spiritual vastness of Heaven. The faces of the cube are as a 'jasper stone, clear as crystal' (v.11), transmitting, as will the Bride, the light of the glory of God to those outside. No wonder that the whole city appeared to John, in his first view, as being the Bride herself! Her spiritual beauty will indeed, as a 'stone most precious', dazzle every eye.

The People of Israel. Surrounding the city, immediately outside, is 'a wall great and high', measuring 144 cubits (240 feet or 73 m.). It is not specified whether this figure is the height or the thickness of the wall; the fact that it is '*great* and high' would suggest that the number is a measure of both height and *thickness,* like the wall round the millennial temple. If so, it would intensify the symbolic application that the 'wall' will provide absolute security against unauthorised intruders — we need never fear that any such will enter Heaven! We might mention here that the measurements of both city and wall are multiples of *twelve,* which in Scripture is the number that signifies government or rule (see p.106). Certainly in Heaven there will be perfect rule which nothing and no one can disturb.

The wall has twelve gates, three on each of its four sides, inscribed with the names of the twelve tribes of Israel, and it has twelve foundations in which are the names of 'the twelve apostles of the Lamb'. Clearly these seeming material structures must be symbolic of spritual things or even persons, just as the 'city' is actually declared to be 'as a bride'. What then are their meanings to us? The names on the 'gates' and 'foundations' of the 'wall' may give us a clue: in both cases they are associated with the people of Israel — the twelve tribes and the twelve apostles, assuming the latter to be the twelve disciples. It is suggested that the wall, as a whole, represents the redeemed nation of Israel as she will be in Heaven, especially in so far as she may constitute a way of approach therein for the 'nations' outside, as already indicated. Of course there will be no question of shutting these saved nations out of the 'city' because 'the gates .... shall not be shut at all'; it is just that they will, as it were, take third place (being on a lower spiritual plane) in their nearness to God — the Bride coming first and the people of Israel second. That Israel, as such, will still be recognised in Heaven, is indicated by *Isaiah 66*:22. As the jasper wall with its jewelled foundations and pearly gates would adorn the city, already resplendent with its own jasper wall, so Israel might add lustre to the Bride and to Heaven itself, and indeed transmit some of its beauty to the nations outside 'who walk in the light of it'.

Also with Israel in the second 'circle' will be, it seems, the *angelic hosts* as represented by the twelve angels at the twelve gates of the city wall. As might be expected, they also take second place to the Bride. Presumably in addition to their usual duties they will collaborate with Israel and the apostles, perhaps to help them in their liaison with the nations.

The Nations and 'Kings of the Earth'. In the third 'circle' of Heaven, regarded as belonging rather to the earth itself — although Heaven, as explained, will be on earth too, but in the central position — will be 'the nations .... and the kings of the earth' who 'bring their glory and honour into it'. Presumably, the rank and file of the nations, although they 'walk in the light' of the celestial city, do not presume to enter therein but leave this privilege to their rulers. It seems that the nations as a whole — comprising, as already described, all the Gentiles saved after the translation of the Church — will need spiritual 'healing':

"And he (the angel) shewed me (John) a pure river of water of life, clear as crystal, proceeding out of the throne of God and of the Lamb. In the midst of the street of it (the city) and on either side of the river, was there the tree of life, which bare twelve manner of fruits, and yielded her fruit every month: and the leaves of the tree were for the healing of the nations" (*Revelation 22*:1—2).

The *tree of life,* from whose leaves they receive their 'healing', may represent a perpetual source of spiritual life in Heaven, available for the spiritual restoration of the nations on its border line but evidently not needed by those nearer to God. The 'tree' draws its own life from the *river of water of life,* proceeding directly from 'the throne of God and of the Lamb'. It is noticeable in this heavenly scene that three times the two persons of the Godhead are coupled together, the Son being called *the Lamb.* The other two occasions are in connection with the heavenly temple and light:

"And I saw no temple therein; for the Lord God Almighty and the Lamb are the temple of it. And the city had no need of the sun, neither of the moon, to shine in it; for the glory of God did lighten it, and the Lamb is the light thereof" (*Revelation 21*:22—23).

Apparently, in the future Heaven on earth, the Father wishes to be closely associated with His Son — in *the throne, the temple and the light,* perhaps in appreciation of Christ's sacrificial death as the Lamb of Calvary.

Before leaving the consideration of the nations, we shall look at perhaps another reference to them, by the Lord Jesus Himself, at the approach of His second coming (*Revelation 22*:14):

"Blessed are they that do his commandments, that they may have right to the tree of life, and may enter in through the gates into the city".

The fact that such people have to earn their right to Heaven by obedience rather than by faith would suggest that they will indeed be those saved after the day of grace (the Church period), in this instance the Gentile believers who will form the 'nations who are saved' in the outer region of Heaven — Israel, as suggested, would have a nearer place to God.

APPENDIX I

THE BIBLE: THE AUTHORISED VERSION AND OTHER VERSIONS

The more one reads this wonderful book the more one is convinced that it is what it claims to be (e.g. 2 *Timothy 3*:16) i.e. the inspired Word of God, Who committed the writing of it to 'holy men of God' (2 *Peter 1*:20), from Moses to the apostle John. Of its two parts, the Old and New Testaments, the former begins with an account of the creation of the universe and of man, and the latter part opens with the first coming of Christ to the world. In a sense He divides the Book, just as He has in fact divided man's era (B.C. and A.D.) as the central figure of it. Christ is indeed the main theme of the Bible from cover to cover (*John 5*:39): the Old Testament points forward to Him in prophecy and type; the New Testament first describes His Person and work as seen by eye-witnesses (the four Gospels), then explains the full significance of His work (especially His death and resurrection) as it concerns mankind (the Epistles), and finally foretells of His second coming and of events associated with it (the Revelation).

As God inspired the original writing of the Book — the Old Testament in Hebrew and the New Testament in Greek —, so, obviously, He overruled the translation into the various languages of the world, ensuring that it would be faithful to the original text. As regards our own mother tongue, after a few tentative versions had been made, the English Bible was finally given to us in a form which has come to be known as the *Authorised Version* (A.V.) because it was authorised by James I who, perhaps significantly, regarded himself as king by *divine* right. One might almost say that it was authorised by God Himself, Who must certainly have led this king to produce a version which was to remain unchallenged for nearly three centuries. The question today is whether the numerous subsequent versions, those of 1881 to date, have been equally inspired. Of course, the Revised Version of 1881 never seriously challenged the A.V., being used mainly for reference by Bible students. In fact it was not until the Revised Standard Version (R.S.V.) was published in 1952 that the A.V. began to be superseded by the R.S.V., which became increasingly used in public reading in churches and chapels throughout the country.

The alleged aim of the R.S.V. and of subsequent versions has been primarily to make the Bible more relevant to the English-speaking world. Men have come to look upon *themselves* as being responsible for making the Bible understood and applicable to our times. This attitude virtually assumes the prerogative of the Holy Spirit and has resulted in a tampering with the essential contents of the inspired Book, as we shall show in due course. It was He Who inspired holy men to write it in the original tongues, and who can doubt, after reading the translators' preface to the Authorised Version, that they were all men in full sympathy with the spiritual contents of God's Word and had a reverent regard for it. This attitude is reflected in the version itself which shows that the translators were careful to set down in English only the legitimate rendering of the original Hebrew and Greek words — even when, frequently, it involved the production of phrases which were probably obscure to them as indeed they still are to most of us today, but they can yield their true meaning to the spiritual mind which diligently and prayerfully seeks it. Designedly, the deeper truths of Scripture do not lie on the surface, as it were, but have to be dug for like gold and are similarly rewarding. Any effort, as in the modern versions, to make these obscure phrases understandable by manipulation of the text will only give a perverted meaning and is in fact an infringement of the strict command: 'Ye shall not add unto the word which I command you, neither shall ye diminish aught from it (*Deuteronomy 4*:2).

Of course, in translating a foreign language, certain words have to be inserted in order to make sense; in the A.V., but not in modern versions, these are always put in italics to show that they were not expressed in the original language. These considerations are sufficient in themselves to demonstrate that the modern versions are indeed the work of man independent of the Holy Spirit, and that, on the contrary, the translators of the A.V. showed by their special care in translating the inspired original writings, that they were similarly inspired to translate them. It is a pity that the title of the A.V. is being modified today to 'King James' Version' or 'Authorised King James' Version', which detracts from the essential divine authority of the A.V. and exalts a man, albeit a king.

Let us examine in some detail *the R.S.V.* as being the first of the modern versions seriously to challenge the Authorised Version. It was 'authorised' in the U.S.A. by the National Council of Churches of Christ, which for years had been dominated by modernistic leaders:

Dr. H.E. Fosdick, an outstanding spokesman for this Council, said: "Of course, I do not believe in the Virgin Birth, or in that old-fashioned doctrine of the Atonement; and I do not know any intelligent minister who does".

*Dr. H.S. Coffin wrote on pages 118—121 of "The Meaning of the Cross": "Certain .... hymns still perpetuate the theory that God pardons sinners because Christ purchased that pardon .... There is no cleansing blood which can wipe out the record of what has been .... The Cross of Christ is not a means of procuring forgiveness".

Dr. G.A. Buttrick: "Literal infallibility of Scripture is a fortress impossible to defend .... Probably few people who claim to believe 'every word of the Bible' really mean it. That avowal held to its last logic would risk a trip to the insane asylum" (from page 162 of "Christian Fact and Modern Doubt").

These are some of the men who were responsible for the production of the R.S.V.; could we expect it, in any sense, to be a divinely inspired version?

What about the *translators?* The names of some of the more notable are as follows: Professors C.T. Craig, E.J. Goodyear, F.C. Grant, H.F. Cadbury, Millar Burrows. It is unnecessary to describe the views of these men individually. Their publications show that they were all modernistic in one form or another: a disbelief in the deity (pre-existence) of Christ, in His virgin-birth, His propitiatory atonement, His present high-priestly intercession, His personal return, and in the inspiration of the Bible. That such views would lead to an unreliable translation might be expected and a brief look at it will provide evidence for this. Especially does the version

*For sources of information about the people listed above, see p.170, bottom of page.

belittle the Person of Christ, albeit in a subtle way, as follows.

In the Gospels of the R.S.V. the Lord Jesus is consistently addressed as 'You', both before and after His resurrection, and even after His ascension when He appeared to Saul on the road to Damascus, as described in Acts. Evidently the translators did not believe in the deity of Christ because, in the introduction, they stated that 'Thou' ('Thee' etc.) was used only when the Deity was addressed; in all other instances 'You' was used. Thus, in *Psalm 45*:6, they put 'Your divine throne' in the place of the A.V. 'Thy throne, O God', degrading the positive noun ('Elohim' = Almighty God) to the less definite adjective 'divine'. Also, in *Matthew 27*:54; the R.S.V. has "truly this was a son of God" for A.V. "Truly this was the Son of God", again denying Christ's deity. This denial becomes more striking in v.40 of the same chapter in which the R.S.V. in this instance copies the A.V. and puts 'the Son of God', because here the phrase is used in mockery and unbelief. Another form of denying Christ's deity is met with in *Proverbs 8*:22. The R.S.V. reads, "The Lord *created* me in the beginning of His work", alleging that the Person alluded to was only a creature; whereas the A.V. has "The Lord *possessed* me in the beginning of his way". which certainly translates the verb 'qanah'. The R.S.V. 'created' is a most unusual rendering of the Hebrew word; in fact it is never so translated in the A.V., which gives some seventeen alternative renderings for the word among the eighty five reference to it. The normal Hebrew word for 'create' is 'bara', so it looks as if the English word has been put in by design to belittle the Son of God, the Person undoubtedly referred to as 'Wisdom' in the passage (vv.12—36). On these grounds alone, the R.S.V. cannot be accepted as the uncorrupted Word of God in the English tongue.

The R.S.V. gave the signal for a spate of other English versions to be thrust upon the long-suffering public during the years that have followed. They are no more to be relied upon than the R.S.V. and show, in general, less care in strictly translating the original text. The multiplicity of these modern versions causes *confusion* and for this reason only they are to be distrusted, for 'God is not the author of confusion, but of peace, as in all the churches of the saints' (1 *Corinthians 14*:33). Such confusion is surely a sign that we are approaching the end of the age and the kingdom of the Beast; Babylon (= confusion). If God did indeed inspire the writers of the A.V. it would seem that, in thc modern versions in this closing (Laodicean) age, He purposely withdrew His spiritual guidance from the translators and permitted them, in their self-dependence, to produce the Bibles that luke-warm Christendom wanted. By the time the Beast appears, the Bible may well be radically revised, if indeed there will be one at all!

From all these considerations, the scriptural quotations used throughout this book have been taken from the *Authorised Version* as our sole standard of reference. It is essentially accurate. Although a large number of new manuscripts have been discovered since the A.V. (1611), the majority are in close agreement with those on which the AV is based. Most modern versions leave out or alter many verses to make them agree with the 4th century Vatican and Sinai manuscripts, which are regarded as more accurate because older than those from which the A.V. is derived. Yet these later MSS may well be copies of much older and more accurate MSS than those of the Vatican and Sinai, which would have been available to the A.V. translators and passed over by them as inferior to their own.

One striking omission, among numerous others, in modern versions, *Mark 16*:9—20, follows the Vatican and Sinai copies, which, in many respects are defective and untrustworthy. The great majority of the later manuscripts, including the Codex Alexandrinus and Codex C, contain these verses, concerning Christ's resurrection and ascension to God's right hand in Heaven — a proof of the Lord's Deity, which those translators who reject this truth would seek to exclude when there happened to be a suitable manuscript available to support them!

The majority of Christians are completely unaware of these fundamental defects in a modern version of the Bible, which they are induced to have in preference to the A.V., simply because it is more up-to-date, more understandable and at least as accurate. If the first two epithets are largely true, the third is certainly false, as we have shown; and do you, Christian friend, still wish to use a Bible that belittles the Person of your Lord and Saviour? Far better be willing to forego its relatively small advantages and go back to the trustworthy A.V. which honours your Lord. True its words and phrases are old-fashioned but that dignifies it and distinguishes it from secular literature, and with a little effort they can readily be understood. A large number of these phrases are still in current use, strangely enough, even in the secular press, because in fact they are much more colourful and impressive than modern phraseology, and widely known to the general public. *One* Bible, the A.V., is quite sufficient for those who, although perhaps do not wish to possess a copy and have no real interest in it, quite frequently quote its phrases. Indeed it is the religious world, influenced by unspiritual church leaders, which must take the blame for all these modern versions, which the average Englishman has no time for, even if he is aware of them. A multi-version Bible is to be deplored, not only for the above reasons but also because it is against God's principle of unity: 'There is one body and one Spirit, even as ye are called in one hope of your calling; one Lord, one faith, one baptism; one God and Father of all' (*Ephesians 4*:4—6); one might add 'one Bible'.

We stated that the presence of old-fashioned words and phrases distinguishes the Authorised Version of the Bible from contemporary non-sacred literature. In a similar way, the use of 'Thou' ('Thee, etc.) in addressing God provides a means of distinguishing Him from His creature, man — especially in these days of easy familiarity when titles are ignored. Deplorably, during the last few decades (starting about the time, significantly, when the R.S.V. appeared), it has been increasingly the practice to address God by the irrevent 'You' ('Your', etc.) thus contravening His command "Hallowed by Thy Name" and also perhaps the older injunction (*Proverbs 22*:28) 'Remove not the ancient landmark, which thy fathers have set'.

* On page 168 the information given about the men responsible for the R.S.V. has been obtained from the following booklets. Publishers, where stated, are named; only one booklet (a magazine) has a date, the others were published, I imagine, soon after the publication of the R.S.V. (1952).

1. "The Revised Standard Version" by Pastor Perry F. Lockwood — reprinted from "The Gospel Standard", a monthly magazine of The Peoples Gospel Hour, Halifax, N.S., Canada.
2. "The Revised Standard Version of the New Testament" by R.C. Foster (Professor of Greek), Cincinnati Bible Seminary, Cincinnati, Ohio.
3. The Magazine "Faith and Freedom", April 1955; published by "The Council Sponsoring I.C.C.C. Interests in S.A.", 66, Pirie Street, Adelaide, South Africa.

The above booklets, and others concerned with various versions of the Bible, were obtained from The Trinitarian Bible Society, London.

APPENDIX II

EVOLUTION DISPROVED

In the scientific sense, evolution is the theory that the higher forms of life gradually, over long ages, develop out of lower forms. In its widest scope it means that Man, the most highly organised being, sprang from the most primitive living thing, such as the one-cell microbe. Yet in the 6,000 years of man's history, there has been no sign whatever of any basic change in any kind of plant or animal: the rose is still the rose, the dove remains a dove, the ass continues to be an ass — and man, though physically the same, has spiritually and morally degenerated. The evolutionist argues that six millennia constitute far too short a period for any such change to occur. Before we examine this assertion, let us briefly consider the basic structure of living things.

From microbe to man they are all composed of one or more microscopic cells. Each cell is filled with fluid (the cytoplasm) in which floats a rounded body, the nucleus, which is the centre of its life. Within the nucleus are the chromosomes, rod-like bodies, which are constant in number for any given species of organism (living thing). Arranged on the chromosomes are the genes, responsible for passing on specific characteristics from parent to offspring, each gene representing a unit of character. Thus any change of character in an organism must be induced by a change in the nature or number (or both) of its genes. If a gradual change did occur, it might not be apparent for a large number of generations, a very slight change possibly occurring at each successive generation (e.g. one cell becomes two, two cells become four, etc.). Thus, the greater the number of generations of any particular organism, the greater the possibility of a detectable change in it, the time factor being a secondary consideration. Certainly, in the case of man, the 200 generations produced from our first parents during the last 6,000 years or so have led to no genetic change in him. We cannot go back in *time* further than this period to test the theory of evolution, at least with regard to man, or indeed to animals or plants in general. Yet it can be tested conclusively if we take in our test an organism at the lowest level of the life-scale, a one-cell microbe.

Fortunately there is a readily available substance, known to every one, YEAST, which is made up of such one-cell organisms and which has a special property that characterises it, as we shall show presently. The immeidate point is that, within the last 6,000 years, during which man has produced some 200 generations, one cell of yeast could have produced 50 million generations, assuming an average generation-time of one hour. Of course, under natural conditions, yeast would rarely grow at this optimal rate but might, nevertheless, be expected to produce in a few thousand years a sufficiently large number of generations to permit the development, if evolution were true, of fundamental changes, doubtless facilitated by frequent sporulation (the formation of spores, sexual cells, within the yeast cell). The crucial question is, has yeast basically altered in character during such a period? As already indicated, yeast has a special property associated with it that enables us to answer this question irrefutably. The property is its ability to ferment sugar, yielding alcohol and carbon dioxide. Yeast is used in the bakeries for bread-making; the carbon dioxide evolved causes the dough to rise. It is also used in the distilleries for the production of potable spirit (whisky, etc.); in the wine factories for wines, and in the breweries for beer. There is an abundant evidence that yeast has been used for thousands of years for baking and brewing (etc.), for example, by the ancient civilisations of China and Egypt. It is an established fact, therefore, that yeast, ever since it has been known, has had the capacity of fermenting sugar to produce alcohol and carbon dioxide, according to the following equation:

$$C_6H_{12}O_6 \text{ (grape sugar)} = 2\ CO_2 \text{ (carbon dioxide)}$$
$$+\ 2\ C_2H_5OH \text{ (alcohol)}$$

This equation is much more complex than it would appear, since it involves a sequence of intermediate chemical changes, brought about by a number of enzymes present in the yeast, under the control of at least as many genes. This property has remained unchanged through hundreds of thousands of yeast generations during the history of man; whereas, if evolution were a fact, one might expect a large number of genetic changes with such a rapidly multiplying organism for such a period. If only one gene necessary for the fermentation were eliminated or basically altered during this period, the essential chain of reactions would be broken and the property lost. There is no evidence for *one* such change; yeast has retained its fundamental character. Instinctively obeying the law of its Creator that it must keep to its 'kind' (*Genesis 1*:24—25), it has remained true to type.

If all living things are capable of basic change — for the better, as the evolutionist asserts — one of the most primitive forms of life should most readily reveal any such change, *provided that* the micro-organism tested has a characteristic property which enables the change to be detected. We have demonstrated that a living substance, yeast, well-known for thousands of years by mankind in various parts of the world, during which time it must have multiplied to at least 100,000 generations, has undergone no genetic change, as proved by its constant capacity to ferment sugar. Yeast is ideal for such a test because it is capable of very fast growth, doubling itself every hour, whereas higher forms of life are much slower. Mankind, at the highest level of life, doubles his population about every thirty years, and would therefore require three million years to produce the number of generations which yeast could easily grow through in the 6,000 years of man's history.

It may be added that if the simplest living thing, like yeast, can be shown to be incapable of change in a specific property it has, more complex forms of life, such as fish, birds and animals, would certainly not be expected to be capable of fundamental change, for example from such forms to man.

Although, unfortunately, evolution is still taught in schools as if it were a fact, it is generally becoming a more and more discarded theory, unsupported by the evidence. The present article is offered as a simple but decisive disproof of it.

APPENDIX III

BIBLE CHRONOLOGY

Apart from the Bible there is no chronological history of mankind earlier than the seventh century B.C., in which Rome was founded and the first vague historical records of other existing nations (Greece, China, etc.) appeared. In fact it is only when we come to the Egyptian astronomer Ptolemy of the second century A.D. that we find anything which could serve as a basis for a system of chronology. The Bible is most valuable because, if for no other reason, it provides precise chronological information from the very creation of man to the first year of Nebuchadnezzar, king of Babylon. Since secular chronology, through the researches of Ptolemy, was traced back to that ancient monarch and the year of his accession accurately fixed as 604 B.C., we can now compile a complete chronology which will enable us to fix, with some degree of accuracy, the year of man's creation. The tables which follow, based on 'The Wonders of Bible Chronology' by Philip Mauro (1922), demonstrate how this can be done.

The figures in the first column of Table 1 are derived from the chronological data of Scripture and show the age of mankind at any row of the table — the 'A.H.' at the head of the column stands for Anno Hominis (in the year of man). The figures in the second column give the corresponding dates B.C. (Before Christ) — obviously, these dates could not be known until the date (year) of man's creation had been determined from the final figure in the A.H. column of Table 4. To anticipate, therefore, this figure will be found to be 3521 years, the age of mankind at the accession of Nebuchadnezzar in 605 B.C., adopting the Jewish method of reckoning regnal years (see "The Coming Prince" by Sir Robert Anderson, p.232). Adding these two figures together gives *4126 B.C.* as the year of Adam's creation, the first figure in the BC column of Table 1.

The period covered in Table 2, 430 years, is referred to thus:

"Now the sojournings of the children of Israel who dwelt in Egypt, was four hundred and thirty years. And it came to pass at the end of the four hundred and thirty years, even the selfsame day it came to pass, that all the hosts of the Lord went out from the land of Egypt" (*Exodus 12*:40—41).

TABLE I

From the Creation of Man to the Birth of Abram

	A.H.	B.C.
Adam created	0	4126
Adam's age at the birth of Seth	130	3996
Add Seth's age at the birth of Enos	235	3891
Add Enos's age at the birth of Canaan	325	3801
Add Canaan's age at the birth of Mahaleel	395	3731
Add Mahaleel's age at the birth of Jared	460	3666
Add Jared's age at the birth of Enoch	622	3504
Add Enoch's age at the birth of Methuselah	687	3439
Add Methuselah's age at the birth of Lamech	874	3252
Add Lamech's age at the birth of Noah	1056	3070
Add Noah's age at the start of the Flood	1656	2470
Add 37 years to the birth of Salah	1693	2433
Add Salah's age at the birth of Eber	1723	2403
Add Eber's age at the birth of Peleg	1757	2369
Add Peleg's age at the birth of Reu	1787	2339
Add Reu's age at the birth of Serug	1819	2307
Add Serug's age at the birth of Nahor	1849	2277
Add Nahor's age at the birth of Terah	1878	2248
Add Terah's age at the birth of Abram	2008	2118

TABLE 2

From the Call of Abram to the Exodus

	A.H.	B.C.
Abram, aged 75, sets out for Canaan	2083	2043
Sodom and Gomorrah destroyed	2107	2019
Birth of Isaac	2108	2018
Birth of Esau and Jacob	2168	1958
Death of Abraham	2183	1943
Birth of Joseph	2259	1867
Death of Joseph	2369	1757
Birth of Moses	2433	1693
Birth of Caleb	2474	1652
Exodus of the Israelites from Egypt	2513	1613

The 'sojournings of the children of Israel' began when their progenitor, Abraham, started on his journey from Haran to Canaan, in response to God's call: 'By faith Abraham, when he was called to go out .... sojourned in the land of promise' (*Hebrews 11*:8—9).

The period is further described (*Galatians 3*:16—17): "Now to Abraham and his seed were the promises made .... And this I say that the covenant, that was confirmed before of God in Christ, the law, which was four hundred and thirty years after, cannot disannul".

The call and the promise (or covenant) to Abraham are recorded in *Genesis 12*:1—3: "Now the Lord had said to Abram, Get thee out of thy country, and from thy kindred, and from thy father's house, unto a land that I will show thee: and I will make of thee a great nation, and I will bless thee, and make thy name great; and thou shalt be a blessing: and I will bless them that bless thee, and curse him that curseth thee: and in thee shall all the families of the earth be blessed"; and in v.4 we have Abraham's obedience to the call: "So Abram departed, as the Lord had spoken to him; and Lot went with him: and Abram was seventy and five years old when he departed out of Haran".

It is immaterial whether we take as our starting-point the giving of the promise (prior to the departure from Haran) or the commencement of the 'sojourning' in the promised land — from either point it is 430 years to the year of the Exodus. Only by a matter of months does the period from the 'promise' to 'the law' (two months after the day of the Exodus) exceed that from the 'sojourning' to the very day of the Exodus (15th Nisan), new-year's day, 'the selfsame day' of the entry into the promised land.

From Table 3 it can be calculated that from the Exodus to the 4th year of Solomon's reign was a period of 594 (554 + 40) years; but according to 1 *Kings* 6:1 the period occupied only 480 years: 'And it came to pass in the four hundred and eightieth year after the children of Israel were come out of the land of Egypt, in the fourth year of Solomon's reign ....'. At first sight there seems to be a large discrepancy here, and some chronologists, as Jackson, Hales and Clinton, have rejected the verse as a manifest contradiction of the more detailed scriptural chronology of the period (as in Table 3). Martin Anstey, however, in his "The Romance of Bible Chronology" (1913), reports his striking discovery that the

TABLE 3

From Entrance into Canaan to Solomon's 4th Year

	A.H.	B.C.
Israel enters Canaan 40 years after Exodus	2553	1573
Add 6 years to division of land by Joshua	2559	1567
Add 14 years to the oppression by Cushan	2573	1553
Add 450 years for the period of the Judges	3023	1103
Add 40 years for Saul's reign	3063	1063
Add 40 years for David's reign	3103	1023
Add 4 years to the 4th year of Solomon	3107	1019

difference of 114 (594 less 480) years is *exactly the measure* of the six servitudes and the one usurpation in the time of the Judges. In God's overall reckoning of the period, as given in 1 *Kings* 6:1, He deliberately omits this period during which His people, because of their idolatry, were cut off from His rule (through His appointed overseers, the Judges) and given into the hands of the various heathen kings.

Table 4 which follows, takes us up to the 1st year of Nebuchadnezzar's reign when, as already intimated, sacred chronology ceases and secular chronology commences.

In Table 4, no figures have been given for the reigns of the various kings of Israel (the 10-tribed kingdom) and few for those of the kings of Judah (two tribes) who followed Solomon. This is because the thorough researchs of Dr. Anstey (loc. cit.) have already obtained for us, as accurately as possible, the chronology of these reigns — enabling us to ascertain the total period covered in the table, which is all that is necessary for our purpose. A few events of interest, however, have been included. It will be noticed that two kings of Judah, Hezekiah and Jehoiakim, are mentioned. The former was a notably good king and the dates of two important events in his reign have been included in the table: the fall of the ten-tribed kingdom in his 6th year, and the destruction of Sennacherib's army (referred to earlier) in his 14th year. With regard to the other king of Judah, Jehoiakim, it was in his 3rd year that Jerusalem was captured by Nebuchadnezzar (*Daniel 1*:1) reigning as co-regent of Babylon with his father, the aged Nabopolassar.

TABLE 4

From Solomon's 4th Year to Nebuchadnezzar's 1st Year

	A.H.	B.C.
The 4th year of Solomon's reign	3107	1019
Fall of Israel's 10-tribed kingdom	3406	720
Sennacherib's army destroyed	3414	712
Death of Hezekiah after 29 years' reign	3429	697
Jerusalem captured by Nebuchadnezzar	3520	606
4th year of Jehoiakim and the 1st year of Nebuchadnezzar	3521	605

The last date of Table 4 — which ends detailed scriptural chronology and marks the beginning of profane chronology — is referrred to (*Jeremiah 25*:1) very aptly as being *both* the 4th year of Jehoiakim and the 1st year of Nebuchadnezzar, the former a king of God's people and the latter a heathen emperor. It is as if God is telling us that when His own nation is put aside in favour of Gentile domination, He ceases to inform us (through His Word) about chronology, which henceforward must be obtained through the effort of man. Certainly from this point onwards, precise chronological records must have been kept by the empires that followed the fall of Israel, because such were evidently utilised in the so-called canon of Ptolemy, to whom reference has already been made. His proper name was Claudius Ptolemais, and we are indebted to him for chronological lists of ancient Babylonian and Persian kings up to Alexander the Great (336 B.C.), from whose time we are in no doubt as to the chronology of mankind up to the present day. Table 4 then, concludes Bible chronology at the point 3,521 years from the creation of man. The age of mankind at the present year (1987) would thus be: 3521 + 605 minus 1 (B.C. 1 to A.D. 1 = 1 year) + 1987 = 6,112 years.

THE END OF THE AGE

When the Lord Jesus Christ comes with His saints to reign over this world, the present age will come to an end and His millennial kingdom will commence. By God's reckoning, one day is as a thousand years and a thousand years as one day (2 *Peter 3*:8), so He could regard the Millennium as one day — perhaps *the* Sabbath Day, as it will be a period of righteousness and peace. By analogy, the six days of creation, preceding the seventh day of rest, might typify the 6,000 years of this age, preceding the Millennium. Yet, according to the above chronological study, the age has already exceeded this period by 112 years. The explanation may be that, by God's reckoning, the period of 114 years, divinely omitted in the overall period from the Exodus to Solomon's 4th year, is also left out of the period from the creation of man to the Millennium. If so, the present year (1987) would be 6112 less 114, i.e. 5998 years from man's creation, and there would still be two years to run before the 6th 'day' expires — in the year A.D. 1989 (see Appendix V).

APPENDIX IV

NUMERIC VALUES OF ROMAN, GREEK AND HEBREW LETTERS. THE MARK OF THE BEAST

The expression of numbers by figures is comparatively modern; the ancients used the alphabet not only for their letters but also for their numbers. The Romans used only six letters of their alphabet for this dual purpose: D for 500, C for 100, L for 50, X for 10, V for 5, and I for 1. The letter M, now used to denote 1,000 was not used as such by the Romans; they adopted the symbol CIↃ (later joined together as M) for this number. The Hebrews and Greeks used *every* letter to express a number, as follows:

HEBREW		
Aleph	א	1
Beth	ב	2
Gimel	ג	3
Daleth	ד	4
Hei	ה	5
Vav	ו	6
Zain	ז	7
Cheth	ח	8
Teth	ט	9
Yod	י	10
Chaph	כ	20
Lamed	ל	30
Mem	מ	40
Nun	נ	50
Samech	ס	60
Ayin	ע	70
Phe	פ	80
Tsaddi	צ	90
Kooph	ק	100
Resh	ר	200
Scheen	ש	300
Tav	ת	400

GREEK		
Alpha	α	1
Beta	β	2
Gamma	γ	3
Delta	δ	4
Epsilon	ϵ	5
Zeta	ζ	7
Eta	η	8
Theta	θ	9
Iota	ι	10
Kappa	κ	20
Lambda	λ	30
Mu	μ	40
Nu	ν	50
Xi	ξ	60
Omicron	ο	70
Pi	π	80
Rho	ρ	100
Sigma	σ	200
Tau	τ	300
Upsilon	υ	400
Phi	φ	500
Chi	χ	600
Psi	ψ	700
Omega	ω	800

The Greeks had no letter for 6 so they used a number-symbol (Stigma), represented thus, ϛ .

Since every Greek and Hebrew letter had a numeric value it followed, naturally, that all their words had a numerical equivalent, obtained by adding up the numbers represented by the letters of the word — this total number of any word is termed its gematria (pl. gematriot). In the ordinary use of words, their gematriot were just chance values and carried no significance; but the original Hebrew and Greek words of the Bible frequently have gematriot which convey spiritual truths (see 'Spiritual Arithmetic' by R.T Haish, 1926) — as might be expected from a divinely inspired Book. The spiritual significance of a gematria in the Bible depends upon its particular numeric value. For example, the name *Jesus* in the Greek as the gematria 888, thus:

I	E	S	O	U	S	
10	8	200	70	400	200	=888

To find the significance of this triple form of 8, we must search Scripture (with the aid of a commentary) for the places where the simple number occurs and consider the circumstances associated with it. Usually, as already mentioned, the first scriptural reference to the number gives the clue to its hidden meaning. In the present instance, the first allusion to the number, although it is not specifically mentioned, was in the time of the Flood in which *eight* people (Noah and his family) were saved to begin a *new life* on earth. The number therefore could denote resurrection and this is confirmed by the fact that Christ rose from the dead on Sunday, which is virtually the eighth day — Saturday, the Jewish sabbath, being the 7th day of the week. The repeated number in the above gematria indicates an intensified significance of the digit and it is obvious that the Lord's resurrection was outstanding. If He had not risen from the dead His death for us would have been in vain (1 *Corinthians 15*:17) and there could be no eternal life for any one — in fact, He *is* the Resurrection and the Life (*John 11*:25).

We are now in a position to elucidate the *number of the Beast*, the mystic 666, the 'number of a man' (*Revelation 13*:18). In the original Greek his number, or mark, is represented as χξ (600 + 60 + 6), which itself suggests that it has a secret meaning — everywhere else in Scripture, both in Greek and Hebrew, numbers are given in words, not (as here) in letters (or signs) having the particular numeric value. What then is the hidden meaning of the Beast's mark? That we are encouraged to seek for the answer to this question is clear from the verse itself; in full it runs thus:

"Here is wisdom. Let him that hath understanding count the number of the beast; for it is the number of a man; and his number is Six hundred and threescore and six".

Hence we learn that the number six, in its triple form, is associated with a *man*. In fact, Bible references to the number, both in its simple and compound form, consistently demonstrate that it speaks of Man. Thus, from the first reference we learn that man was created on the sixth day. However, the number relates to man, not only in his innocency at the beginning, but also to him after his fall in his self-will and rebellion against God. For example, the giant who defied God, stood 6 cubits and a span in height, and his spear's head weighed 600 shekels of iron. The use of the higher number based on six has the effect of increasing its significance, as does the addition (of a span) to it, and certainly Goliath, in his exceptional physique and as an enemy of God's people, stood out among men. Similarly, Nebuchadnezzar's golden image (*Daniel 3*:1), set up probably to represent himself, for all to worship — was 60 cubits high and 6 cubits broad, the numbers again relating to a man, in this instance as he seeks to deify himself.

The Beast's number, a triple form of six, represents man in his most powerful and evil condition, combining the features of Goliath and Nebuchadnezzar on a greater scale — truly a superman, who will be a world conqueror and the direct object of its worship. His triple number also occurs as a gematria in certain significant secular names connected with Rome and her church. Thus it first appears in the Hebrew of the name Nero Caesar, the cruel Roman emperor who was noted for his persecution of the Christians in the first century of this era, clearly a forerunner of the Beast who will 'make war with the saints and .... overcome them' (*Revelation 13*:6):

N	(E)	R	O	N	K	(E)	S	(A)	R	
50	—	200	6	50	100	—	60	—	200	= 666

There are no letter vowels in Hebrew except Vav (o or u) and Yod (i).

The number (666) also appears in the Latin form of the popes' title, "Vicar of the Son of God", as follows';

V	I	C	A	R	I	V	S	F	I	L	I	I	D	E	I	
5	1	100	—	—	1	5	—	—	1	50	1	1	500	—	1	= 666

Such blasphemous pretensions will also characterise the Beast.

So, upon this religious system and its heads in particular is stamped the mark of the Beast who will, for a period, be strongly associated with Rome religiously, as he will (like Nero) be with Rome politically. This association is confirmed in our final example of the gematria of 666 in the Greek word for Latin:

L	A	T	E	I	N	O	S	
30	1	300	5	10	50	70	200	= 666

APPENDIX V

THE NEAR RETURN OF CHRIST

The *exact* time of the Lord's second coming is purposely not disclosed in Scripture because we are always to be in expectation of it and in readiness for it:

"Then shall they see the Son of man coming in the clouds with great power and glory .... But of *that day and that hour* knoweth no man, no, not the angels in heaven, neither the Son, but the Father. Take ye heed, watch and pray: for ye know not when the time is" (*Mark 13*:26, 32—33).

It must be noticed that our Lord did not say no one (except His Father) would know the *year* (for example) of His coming but He specified 'the day and hour'. This phrase, as it stands, would mean the actual date — a certain hour of a certain day — of His return, and it would not do for mankind, at least, to know it. Yet it is widely taught that we should not attempt to put forward with any degree of precision even the approximate time of Christ's coming, although scriptural evidence be adduced to justify it. Such teaching is said to be scriptural but, in fact, it is reading into our Lord's words (cited above) more than He actually stated.

It might be argued that other passages of Scripture support the teaching: let us examine a few of them. Firstly from the chapter from which we have already quoted, v.35: 'Watch ye therefore: for ye know not when the master of the house cometh, at even or at midnight, or at the cockcrowing, or in the morning'. This verse says nothing to contradict the 'day and the hour' of Christ's earlier assertion; indeed it would rather narrow down the time of His coming. Further (*Acts 1*:7): 'And he said unto them, It is not for you to know the times or the seasons, which the Father hath put in his own power'. This was the Lord's reply to the apostles' query (v.6), 'Lord, wilt thou at this time restore again the kingdom to Israel'. They had previously (v.4) been commanded to wait for 'the promise of the Father', referring to the outpouring of the Holy Spirit at Pentecost. Yet they evidently thought the promise might also include the restoration of their kingdom. The Lord knew, of course, that that would not be in their time but in their far future; so, perhaps, in order not to discourage them, He told them that it was not for *them* to know the times or seasons. We are not to conclude that what was inexpedient for the earlier disciples to know in their day, would also not be desirable for us who live so much nearer to Christ's coming and to His subsequent kingdom — which they, mistakenly, thought would be confined to Israel. In fact, concerning His coming, the 'times and seasons' preceding it will definitely be known (2 *Thessalonians* 2:3):

"Let no man deceive you by any means: for that day shall not come, except there come a falling away first, and that man of sin be revealed, the son of peridition".

The 'day' referred to is the 'day of Christ' (v.2), better known in Scripture as the 'day of the Lord', when Christ will return to judge the world and then set up His millennial kingdom. His coming referred to here is to be distinguished from that of v.1 'the coming of our Lord Jesus Christ and .... our gathering together unto him' (the Rapture, as it is termed), which we believe will precede His public coming (v.2) by seven years. This is the only scriptural passage, as far as we are aware, in which are linked together the two phases of Christ's second coming: the Rapture and the Return (to earth). The *Rapture* relates to His coming into the clouds to translate ('catch up') to Heaven with Him the saints (the living changed and the dead raised) of the Church and pre-Church eras. The *Return* consists of His coming from Heaven, with His saints, to judge the world and to reign for a thousand years. During the seven years between these two events, there will be, as indicated above, 'times and seasons' and indeed signs, to those that look for them, of the Return (the 'day of Christ' v.2). The first intimation they will have will be the appearance of the Beast (the 'man of sin', v.3) at the outset of the period; but a more definite sign will be apparent later, half-way through the period, when he will sit in the Jews' temple, claiming to be God (v.4). Thus, although it is not for us to know the 'day and hour' of Christ's coming, we are certainly told to look for signs of the times to enable us to ascertain, possibly within a year or so, the approximate time of the Lord's return.

THE SIGN OF THE FIG TREE

As our Lord sat on the mount of Olives, the disciples asked Him, (*Matthew 24*:3): '.... What shall be the sign of thy coming, and of the end of the world (age)'. In His reply, He dealt first with the latter part of their question, concerning the end of the age. He made it clear that there was to be an end-*period,* the *beginning* of which being marked by certain unmistakable events (vv.7—8), notably the outbreak, for the first time (cf. v.6), of a world war. This proves that the beginning of the end occurred within the period 1914—1918 of World War I. Truly, as our Lord termed it, was it the beginning of sorrows. The Greek word for 'sorrows' literally means 'birth-throes', suggesting that the end-period would not only be a time of intense suffering for humanity but also that it would culminate in the birth of a new age, Christ's millennial kingdom. Undisputably, as He foretold, a period of unprecedented trouble did begin with the first world war. Among other disastrous happenings (famines, pestilences and earthquakes of unusual frequency) during the period was World War II (1939—1945). This war, as we know, was characterised by its affecting the civil populations to a greater extent than in World War I, and saw the use of far more destructive weapons. Such weapons have since become so deadly as to make a third world-war conflict inevitably the last.

The above end-period, described by Christ, is evidently identical with 'the time of the end' (*Daniel 8*:17, etc.), which has been shown by our previous study of Daniel's prophecies to commence in the year 1917. This brings us to the first part of the disciples' question to our Lord, concerning the *sign* of His coming; for His more complete answer we have to leave Matthew's gospel and consult Luke's. Christ refers to this end-period thus (*Luke 21*:25—26): 'And there shall be .... upon the earth distress of nations .... men's hearts failing them for fear, and for looking after those things which are coming on the earth'. Then He goes on to make the striking observation that the time when 'these things begin to come to pass' (v.28) would be marked by a special event which, however, He described in a symbolic form as a special sign for us (vv.29—33):

"Behold the *fig tree and all the trees;* when they now shoot forth, ye see and know of your own selves that summer is high at hand. So likewise ye, when ye see these come to pass, know ye that the kingdom of God, (i.e. the Millennium) is nigh at hand. Verily I say unto you, *This generation shall not pass away,* till all be fulfilled. Heaven and earth shall pass away: but my word shall not pass away".

Our Lord is here assuring us, with all possible emphasis (v.33), that He is giving us a definite indication of the time when the end will come; telling us, in effect, that it will be barely a generation after the occurrence of a certain event, symbolised by His 'parable' of the fig tree. We know, of course, the fig tree in Scripture is a type of Israel as a nation; but we are bidden in the passage (v.29): 'Behold the fig tree and *all the trees*'. The parallel accounts in the gospels of Matthew and Mark give only, 'Learn a parable of the fig tree'. Why is Luke more specific, inviting us to 'Behold', and adding 'all the trees'? He is perhaps trying to tell us to look for a scripture in which other trees are mentioned along with the fig tree, preferably a passage relating to the time of the end.

Such a scripture is *Haggai* 2:18—19: "Consider now from this day and upward, from *the four and twentieth day of the ninth month,* even from the day that the foundation of the Lord's temple was laid, consider it. Is the seed yet in the barn? yea, as yet the vine, and the fig tree, and the pomegranate, and the olive tree, hath not brought forth: from *this day* will I bless you".

The passage evidently refers to the end of the age, when the Lord will come to 'shake the heavens, and the earth .... and all nations, and the desire of all nations (i.e. the Messiah, Christ) shall come' (vv.6—7). All the trees mentioned here, as fully explained earlier, typify the nation of Israel in one aspect or another, and the fact that they are all mentioned together would indicate the importance of the prophecy to her. The 24th day of the 9th month, by the Jewish calendar, was originally the day when the foundation of their second temple was laid in 520 B.C. Yet one might expect that the ultimate fulfilment of the prophecy, having regard to the context, would be the *start* of Israel's final blessing in the Millennium. Now it is a remarkable fact that on that very day in 1917, December 9th (the 24th day of the 9th month, in the Jews' calendar), when General Allenby commanding the British forces entered Jerusalem to liberate Israel from her age-long subjugation by foreign powers, the foundation, as it were, was laid for her to become a nation again. We have already demonstrated that the beginning of the end-period was in the year 1917. Now, we can say with more precision that it began on December 9th, 1917. The Lord has been pleased to reveal to us, through His ancient prophet, the exact day from which we can start counting the years of 'this generation', which will not pass away entirely till He returns to earth at the end-point of the age.

This Generation. Some superficial expositors, perhaps among those who do not wish particularly to enquire into the time of Christ's coming and may think it wrong to do so, hold that 'this generation' was that present during His life on earth. Certainly it could not have consisted of the actual people who lived then, because they have long since passed away and all the things predicted of the end-time are still unfulfilled! It may be argued that when the Lord said 'this generation', He meant 'this *type* of generation' — the 'wicked generation' then living, who sought for a sign from Him but no sign was given except 'the sign of the prophet Jonas' (e.g. *Matthew 16*:4) — which, it is said, would persist until the end of the age. It is true that our generation is certainly no less wicked than that of His time, but it should be realised that, in the text we have been studying (*Luke 21*:29—33), the Lord is talking *to His disciples* to give them — and us who are looking for Him — the sign asked for, so that we, if not they, may be encouraged to expect His near return (v.28). Whereas, addressing the evil generation of His own time, He refused at first to give them any sign but later gave them the sign of Jonah, specially for that particular generation which would witness Christ's three days in the grave. Apart from these considerations, His talk about the fig tree would have no real meaning for us if 'this generation' did not signify, as the context proves, that of the end-period.

THE END OF THE AGE AND THE RAPTURE

We have shown that the end-period *began* on December 9th, 1917. In order to ascertain the approximate time of the end itself, as the Lord evidently wished us to do, we must determine the number of years in a Biblical generation. A common meaning of the word is the average time interval between the births of successive generations, about 30 years. For example, the number of generations from the creation of Adam to the present time (say 6,000 years) would be some 200. Of course, the people living in any one generation would continue to live on after the birth of the next generation. What we wish to know for our purpose is this *total* time for any generation: in other words, the average age of man. According to the Bible, his allotted span is 70 years (*Psalm 90*:10). Taking this figure for the period of 'this generation', the age would end in December, 1987. Yet many people born in December 1917 are likely to live longer than 70 years, and it is possible that our Lord might have had at least some of these in mind. If so, the end of the age might be some years later than 1987.

It should be mentioned that another starting-point of 'this generation', although not supported by Scripture — as is the year 1917 — could be the year 1948 (May) when Israel became a recognised State. It is certainly remarkable that a 'generation' from that date — if the word is interpreted in its narrower scriptural meaning as 40 years (*Numbers 32*:13; *Psalm 95*:10) — would bring us to 1988, which indeed is very close to the previous postulated end-point (1987+) and midway between the latter and that, 1989, obtained from our study of Bible chronology.

The convergence of the above three dates, obtained by three different methods, strongly suggests that they approximate to the true figure. Yet even the latest (1989) of the three dates is only two years ahead of the present year (1987), which period is much too short to accommodate the future events predicted by Scripture to occupy at least seven years — see the following 'List of Coming Events', A-D. We know, of course as affirmed by the Lord Himself, that the 'days' of the Tribulation will 'be shortened' (*Matthew 24*:21—22) but clearly not to the required extent. We know also that although God (the Father) has apparently appointed the 'day and the hour' of the end of the age, He may well defer it, being 'longsuffering to usward, not willing that any should perish' (2 *Peter 3*:9): in particular He would defer the Rapture, and indeed, from our studies, He seems to have done that already. However, that event may now occur at any time, so believers, 'look up .... for your redemption draweth nigh' (*Luke 21*:28).

LIST OF COMING EVENTS

A. The Translation to Heaven (the 'rapture') of the saints — i.e. believers of the B.C. (Old Testament) and A.D. (New Testament) eras.

B. The 'Day' of Jesus Christ in Heaven — a period of 7 years.

1. The judgment seat of Christ — for the translated saints, all accountable to Him for their deeds done on earth.
2. The marriage supper of the Lamb, at the close of the 7-year period. The N.T. saints (His Church) form His *Bride;* the O.T. saints become the *wedding guests.*

C. Satan's Sway on Earth — a period of 7 years, concurrent with the Day of Jesus Christ.

The First 3½ Years

1. The formation of the 10-kingdom union of Europe.
2. The rise of the 'Beast' — the Roman 'prince'. His mark, '666'.
3. The rise of the false prophet in Israel — the antichrist.
4. The 7-year pact between the Beast and Israel.
5. The building of Israel's 3rd temple and the restoration of her temple sacrifices.
6. The formation of the apostate world church (the 'great whore'), dominated by Roman Catholicism under the Beast.

All the above events will occur early in this first 3½-year period. At its close the Beast has the apostate church destroyed, assumes world power and commends all to worship him. His kingdom, in character, will be a revival of Babylon but will be based on Rome goegraphically.

The Final 3½ Years — the Great Tribulation

1. The 'sealing' of Israel's 'elect', to preserve them from injury and death during this time of affliction.

2. The Beast breaks his 7-year pact with Israel and abolishes her temple offerings.

3. The Beast himself occupies the temple as God ('the abomination of desolation').

4. An image of the Beast is set up (probably in Israel) by the false prophet and its worship enforced.

5. The false prophet orders all to be branded with the Beast's mark ('666') — no one will be able to buy or sell without it.

6. The coming of God's two witnesses (Moses and Elijah re-embodied?).

7. The 'everlasting gospel' preached to the world by an angel. It constitutes the promise of eternal blessing to the faithful and a solemn warning to worshippers of the Beast.

8. The seven trumpet-plague judgments — antitype of the plagues of Egypt?

9. The battle of Armageddon — initiated by the invasion of Israel during the sixth plague, almost at the end of the period.

Again all the above events, except the last (No.9), occur (or open) almost at the start of this final 3½-year period. As the period closes, the 'great and terrible day of the Lord' opens.

D. The Day of the Lord. This is probably a short period in which events follow one another in rapid succession. It is heralded by signs in the sun and moon, the falling of the stars and the 'shaking' of the heavens. The earth itself is shaken by the greatest-ever earthquake.

   1. The appearance of Christ, the Lamb, in Heaven — an awe-inspiring sight to earth dwellers, especially those engaged in the culmination of the battle of Armageddon, occurring at this point.

   2. The Lord's descent towards earth, accompanied by His saints, to judge the world. Probably just prior to his reaching

the earth He intercedes in the battle, destroys all the armies gathered round Jerusalem and consigns the Beast and the false prophet to the 'lake of fire'.

3. The judgment of Israel's unfaithful; her elect 'remnant' are of course exempt — 'the one shall be taken (in judgment) and the other left (for blessing)'.
4. Satan bound — for 1,000 years.
5. The resurrection of the post-church saints, those who have been martyred during the last 7 years of the age.
6. The cleavage of the mount of Olives, resulting in the opening up of a waterway from the Dead Sea to the Mediterranean Sea.
7. The occupation of the new Israel by the elect remnant.
8. The judgment of the Gentile nations.

E. The Millennial Reign of Christ.

F. The Release of Satan and the Final Battle.

G. The Final Judgment of the Wicked Dead and the 'Great White Throne'.

H. The New Heavens and the New Earth — the New Jerusalem. Heaven *upon* Earth.

INDEX OF SUBJECTS AND AUTHORS

INDEX OF BIBLE REFERENCES